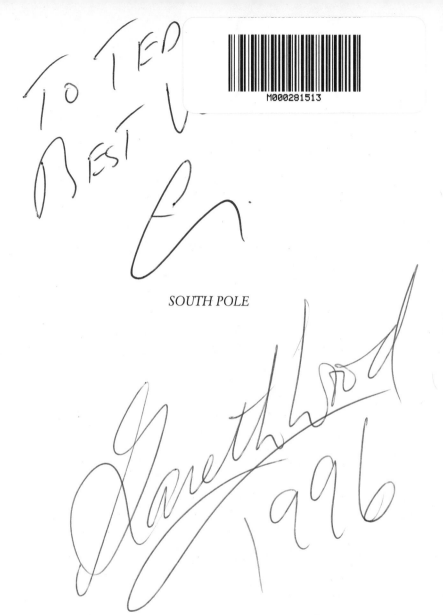

To Ted

Best ...

SOUTH POLE

Gareth Wood
1996

GARETH WOOD ASSOCIATES
A Matishak Group Inc. Associate
320A 4th Ave. Campbell River, B.C.
Canada   Tel/Fax (250) 287-2269
email: owenwood@cr.island.net

In memory of Giles Kershaw who
died at the age of 41, in the
Antarctic, on March 6, 1990

SOUTH POLE

900 Miles on Foot

by

Gareth Wood
with
Eric Jamieson

HORSDAL & SCHUBART

Horsdal & Schubart Publishers Ltd.
Victoria, B.C., Canada

Maps by Brian Stauffer, Prince George, B.C.
Cover photograph by Gareth Wood. Back-cover insert photograph of Gareth Wood at Cape Evans courtesy of Roger Mear.

Excerpts from "The Waste Land" and "Little Gidding" in *Collected Poems 1909-1962,* by T.S. Eliot, appear by permission of the publishers, Faber and Faber Ltd., London. Excerpt from "Little Gidding" in *Four Quartets*, copyright 1943 by T.S. Eliot and renewed 1971 by Esme Valerie Eliot, reprinted by permission of Harcourt Brace & Company. Excerpt from "The Waste Land" in *Collected Poems 1909-1962* by T.S. Eliot, copyright 1936 by Harcourt Brace & Company, copyright © 1964, 1963 by T.S. Eliot, reprinted by permission of the publisher. Every effort has been made to trace the owners of other quoted material.

Horsdal & Schubart Publishers Ltd. thank The Canada Council for giving financial support to our publishing program.

This book is set in Classical Garamond.

Printed and bound in Canada by Printcrafters Inc., Winnipeg, Manitoba.

Canadian Cataloguing in Publication Data

Wood, Gareth, 1951-
South Pole

Includes bibliographical references.
ISBN 0-920663-48-6

1. Wood, Gareth, 1951- 2. Antarctica — Discovery and exploration. 3. South Pole. I. Jamieson, Eric, 1949- II. Title.
G875.W66A3 1996   919.8'904   C96-910419-7

FOREWORD

by Pat Morrow

F EW ADVENTURERS CAN adequately convey in words the monu-
mental changes they go through during and after an
expedition. And some say the passage of time dulls the memory. I
know that in my case this is so. I'm afraid I'm suffering from "old
climber's" disease.

Not so Gareth Wood. Ten years before this book was written he
set foot in Antarctica, and began to record in his journal the daily
events that would lead to this richly distilled account of an adventure accessible to only a handful of explorers in all of history.

If one tries to trace the journeys of Marco Polo across Asia by
reading the account he wrote seven or eight years after the fact, one
soon tires of all the discrepancies and vagueness. In Gareth's lucid
mind, and with the help of his own and his colleagues' meticulous
notes, events leading up to and following his arrival at the South
Pole become crystal clear.

Partly through the wisdom of hindsight, and the cognitive powers
gained through hard-won experience on that icy continent, Gareth
is able to share with us some of the psychological lessons he learned
about discovery of "self." To keep it all in perspective, he humbly
alludes to the colossal geographical discoveries of his predecessors
Scott, Shackleton and Amundsen.

My own involvement with the frozen continent began just the
year before Gareth arrived, in my bid to climb the highest peak on
all seven continents. Unlike Gareth and his mates, I had planned to

reach my objective by using "unfair" means. Our team would fly by ski-equipped airplane to the base of 4897-metre Vinson Massif, in the Ellsworth Range. However, like the "Footsteps of Scott" expedition, ours was dogged by a combination of bad luck, equipment damage, and active resistance by the pseudo-scientific "old boys' club" that rules the continent. On our first night in Antarctica a violent wind storm nearly destroyed our plane, forcing us to retreat for another year.

The aircraft we used to reach our mountain the following year, under the banner of Adventure Network International and piloted by our partner Giles Kershaw, was also pressed into service for the "Footsteps" expedition. That's how I came to know Gareth. We met shortly after his arrival back in Canada.

Having spent the previous two years immersed in a deprivation tank of sorts, Gareth was, as he himself admits, a bit of a basket case on his return. At the time, I felt he should have been rejoicing about his return from a great adventure, but he seemed preoccupied with minor administrative details that should have been left behind on the ice.

I lost touch with him for a few years, after that first meeting, but began to take notice as he started to piece his life back together. This book goes a long way toward explaining the powerful grip Antarctica still had on Gareth when he returned. And it offers inspiration to others who, like Gareth, have undergone severe personal hardship on their quest to reach their own "South Pole."

CONTENTS

INTRODUCTION

WE HAD BEEN travelling for a month across the Ross Ice Shelf, 400 miles of untracked frozen sea broken only occasionally by a few yawning crevasses. It was December 4, 1985, and I was in the lead position. I stopped and quickly took another bearing, then fixed my sight on a small hummock of wind-crusted snow far to the south. I concentrated fiercely on not losing sight of the hummock among a myriad of similar ripples and blowing ground drift. I had moved in its direction for only a few minutes before succumbing to my painful feet. I stopped to adjust my boot. Roger, who was right behind me, accused me of losing too much time with my constant stops, and stormed past, assuming the lead.

Half an hour later, with only 15 minutes left of our first, three-hour leg, I lofted my poles skyward in a large X to signal that I must stop. I was exhausted and my feet were now so painful that I could not continue. Roger and Robert were furious at the loss of time and once inside the tent accused me of being soft and behaving weakly.

Roger was understandably angry, having expected that I would take more of the navigational duties from him. Robert, immersed in his own private agony, found me a convenient target. What my problem was I was not entirely sure at that point, but it was clear that my companions were less than sympathetic. Roger wrote in his diary on January 8, "We have seen too much too deep of each other. ... " And now the rigours of the journey were adding another stressful dimension to our lives.

As a team, our strength lay in our single-minded purpose and the diversity of our skills, but our relationships were severely strained, teetering on the brink of ruin. Nowhere had I read about how other expeditions had dealt with similar dissension, but I knew that historically, it was inappropriate to talk, and certainly to write, about them. Although there had been more than a hint of what was to follow while we were preparing for the journey in London, we were so engrossed with logistics that we ignored the human element, hoping that it would sort itself out. After our return from the Antarctic, the British explorer Ranulph Fiennes wrote of one of his Antarctic journeys during which his relationship with his partner deteriorated to a feeling of *mutual hate* due to the stresses associated with planning and implementing an expedition and the inevitable close living arrangements. I was relieved to find that we weren't alone in our feelings.

Perhaps it was the magnitude of the expedition, which conventional wisdom suggested was impossible, that had us all on edge. When we first began to plan the trek to the South Pole, an 883-mile walk across a frozen wasteland, we knew that we would stretch the limits of our endurance, and we also knew that the risk, without radios, dogs, support parties, food caches, air support or outside contact of any kind, might be greater than our collective wills. Camaraderie wore very thin as we endured endless bitter nights in our tiny tent at the bottom of the world. Most space-flight physicians believe that isolation is the main source of emotional stress, and it has been documented that when small groups of people are set apart, hostility and anxiety become very real problems. That we completed the journey together, despite our differences, says more about who we really are than our animosities would suggest. It has taken many years, but the three of us have now come to understand the real meaning of teamwork and we are better friends and better people for the experience. As my polar companion Robert Swan said many times afterwards, "No one said it would be easy."

This account deals with some of the human aspects of the trek. It was a journey in which we learned more about ourselves and what it takes to work together than about the physical challenges of the Antarctic. I would also like to think of it as a record of one man's travels; his struggle, his survival, and yes, his growth. That man is me. After ten years of reflection, I wanted to draw some meaning, other than the physical, from what we had experienced and finally accomplished together.

Gareth Wood

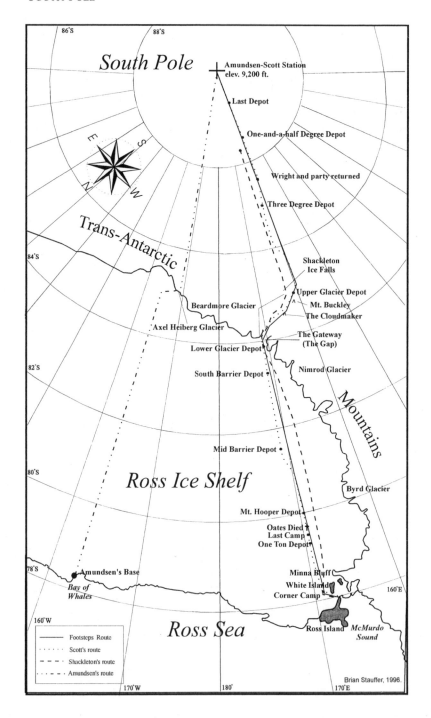

South Pole

Amundsen-Scott Station
elev. 9,200 ft.

Last Depot

One-and-a-half Degree Depot

Wright and party returned

Three Degree Depot

Trans-Antarctic

Shackleton
Ice Falls

Upper Glacier Depot
Mt. Buckley
The Cloudmaker

Beardmore Glacier

Axel Heiberg Glacier

The Gateway
(The Gap)

Lower Glacier Depot

South Barrier Depot

Nimrod Glacier

Mountains

Mid Barrier Depot

Ross Ice Shelf

Byrd Glacier

Mt. Hooper Depot

Oates Died
Last Camp
One Ton Depot

Amundsen's Base

Bay of
Whales

Minna Bluff

White Island
Corner Camp

160°E

Ross Island

McMurdo
Sound

160°W

Ross Sea

170°W

180°

170°E

Footsteps Route
.... Scott's route
– – – – Shackleton's route
–·–·– Amundsen's route

86°S   88°S   84°S   82°S   80°S   78°S

Brian Stauffer, 1996.

X

Antarctica

0   500   1000 Kilometers
0   500   1000 Nautical Miles

• Research station.

South Atlantic Ocean

Drake Passage

Sanae (S.A.)•

Dakshin Gangotri (India)

Weddell Sea

Teniente Marsh (Chile)

General Belgrano (Argentina)

Halley (U.K.)

Syowa (Jap.)

Teniente Carvajal (Chile)

Ronne Ice Shelf

Mawson (Aust.)

Indian Ocean

Zhangshan (China)

Bellingshausen Sea

^ Vinson Massif (16,067 ft.)

▸Amundsen-Scott (US)
South Pole

Mirnyy (Russia)

Amundsen Sea

Trans-Antarctic Mountains

• Vostok (Russia)

Casey (Aust.)

South Pacific Ocean

Ross Ice Shelf
Scott (NZ)

Ross Sea

Ross Island

Dumont d'Urville (Fr.)

^ Mount Minto

South Magnetic Pole +

Brian Stauffer, 1996.

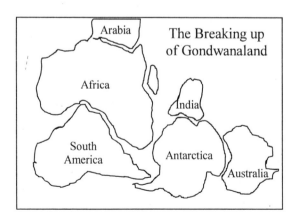

Arabia

The Breaking up of Gondwanaland

Africa

India

South America

Antarctica

Australia

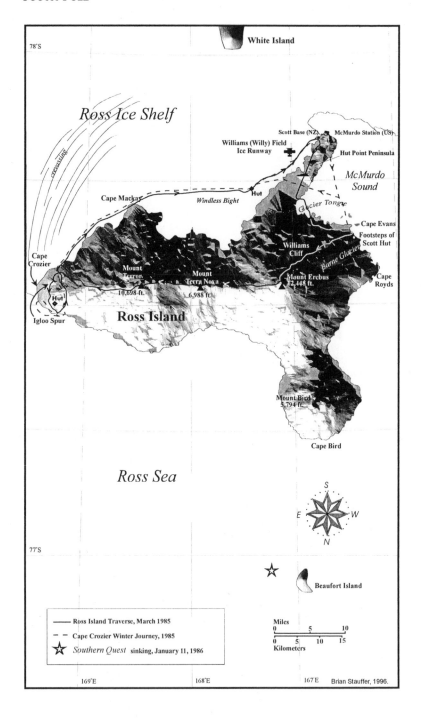

White Island

78°S

Ross Ice Shelf

CREVASSES

Scott Base (NZ)   McMurdo Station (US)

Williams (Willy) Field
Ice Runway

Hut Point Peninsula

*McMurdo
Sound*

Cape Mackay   *Windless Bight*   Hut

Glacier Tongue

Cape Evans

Footsteps of
Scott Hut

Williams
Cliff

Barne Glacier

Cape
Crozier

Mount
Terror
10,698 ft.

Mount
Terra Nova
6,988 ft.

Mount Erebus
12,448 ft.

Cape
Royds

Hut

Ross Island

Igloo Spur

Mount Bird
5,794 ft.

Ross Sea

Cape Bird

S

E   W

N

77°S

☆

Beaufort Island

———— Ross Island Traverse, March 1985

– – – – Cape Crozier Winter Journey, 1985

☆   *Southern Quest* sinking, January 11, 1986

Miles
0   5   10
0   5   10   15
Kilometers

169°E   168°E   167°E   Brian Stauffer, 1996.

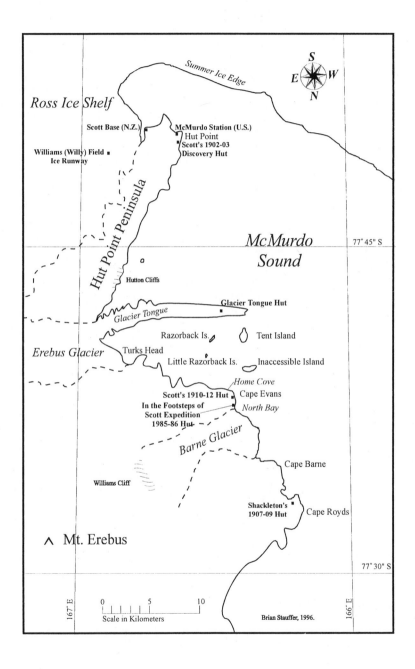

We shall not cease from exploration
And the end of all our exploring
Will be to arrive where we started
And know the place for the first time.

T.S. Eliot

CHAPTER ONE

THE LAST GREAT PRIZE

"How'd you like to come to the Antarctic?" Roger asked, without shifting his gaze from the road.

We were in his Austin 1100, chugging toward the climbing shop in the nearby town of Bethesda, Wales. The windshield wipers were struggling to cope with the driving rain, and I remember that we had just passed Tryfan, one of the classic Welsh climbs. With a roll-up cigarette dangling from the corner of his mouth, Roger was leaning forward, concentrating on the bleak landscape ahead.

"Are you serious?" I replied, gaping in disbelief.

"Yes," Roger chuckled, enjoying catching me off guard. "As far as I'm concerned you're in. I'll talk to Robert."

Growing up in Victoria, British Columbia, had not prepared me for anything quite so adventurous. Emigrating from England as a child, I was 19 when I first returned to explore my roots. I had taken a holiday from my job as a printing-press operator in Victoria. Two years later I joined a three-month expedition organized by a British adventure travel company to cross the Sahara Desert by Land Rover. The next few years were punctuated by journeys to southern Mexico, Belize and Guatemala to explore the Mayan ruins, and to Australia in 1976 to circle that continent on my Moto Guzzi motorcycle. In 1978 I enrolled in an Outward Bound course and was introduced to the challenges of the outdoors, and I soon left the security of the printing industry to pursue a career teaching climbing and canoeing.

A series of coincidences brought me to Britain when an expedition to retrace Robert Falcon Scott's Antarctic journey was being organized. I was instructing at Plas-y-Brenin, the National Mountaineering Centre in North Wales, where I met Roger Mear. Small in build, with a degree in fine arts, he was one of Britain's leading mountaineers, and was known in climbing circles as a "hard man." Over the next two years we became friends and I often spent my days off struggling to follow him up the local rock and ice climbs. I knew that he was working on a South Pole expedition, but it was not until July 1983 that he asked me if I would like to review some of the project's logistics. I was immediately enthusiastic. From the local library I borrowed every book I could find on Scott and polar exploration, including Scott's diaries and *The Worst Journey in the World* written by one of his companions, Apsley Cherry-Garrard. I dreamt that I too might take part in such an expedition.

The romance of exploration had captured my imagination as a youth and within the sheltered confines of my eager mind I think I had always lived with the excitement of adventure. I recalled being entranced by the adventures of Scott, Roald Amundsen and Ernest Shackleton, the three key South Pole explorers who, between 1900 and 1912, played out a drama that now caught my attention again.

Roger had already spent a year in the Antarctic with the British Antarctic Survey (BAS) as a field guide. There, he had met Robert Swan, who conceived the expedition. Robert was employed as a general assistant, and had gone to the Antarctic to learn as much as he could about the continent. I had met Robert earlier when he dropped in to see Roger at Plas-y-Brenin on his way to Iceland where he was to take part in a training expedition to cross the Vatnajokull Ice Cap. Robert had no experience in polar travel or mountaineering, but seemed serious about his training. He impressed me as very British. He had a charismatic personality and one was immediately swept up in his nationalistic fervour and apparent need to carry the Union Jack to the ends of the earth. Over a wrinkled business shirt and desperately thin tie he wore a light pullover cinched at the waist with a wide belt, accentuating his broad shoulders and powerful build. His hair was slicked back aggressively and he bore the rugged set of a man of action. The most striking feature about him though was his deep, blue eyes.

Robert was a visionary, motivated by a dream. It was while studying history at Durham University and seeing the 1948 film classic, "Scott of the Antarctic," starring John Mills, that he developed a plan to retrace Scott's 1911-1912 trek to the South Pole.

From Scott's base at Cape Evans, on the Antarctic coast, Robert planned to use dog teams and manhauled sledges, as Scott had done, to pull food and supplies forward and lay depots along the route to the Pole. Again, like Scott, Robert would manhaul sledges through the depots, across the Ross Ice Shelf — 400 miles of frozen sea — 124 miles up the Beardmore Glacier and approximately 355 miles across the Polar Plateau to the Pole. He would then return by the same route, replenishing his supplies from the previously laid depots.

The trek, a total of about 1,758 miles, would be a modern attempt to duplicate Scott's dramatic journey, as if Robert's success might somehow atone for Scott's tragic defeat. Later, Roger and I would question Robert's increasing obsession with his dream and wonder if he was planning to repeat that journey to the death if he thought it necessary. Scott's death had branded him a hero, over-shadowing the Norwegian Amundsen's glorious achievement of attaining the Pole first. Had Scott not died, would his name be as prominent as it is today?

Roger had no such allegiance to history, but the concept piqued his interest. His detachment and pragmatism nicely balanced Robert's romantic ideals. As an alpinist he wondered whether it would be possible to apply modern, lightweight, alpine-style moun-taineering techniques to polar travel. His proposal was for two men, Robert and himself, to manhaul their food and equipment on light sledges one way without dog teams, pre-laid depots, motorized vehicles or air support. Although his plan was to cover only half of Scott's journey, the unsupported nature of the trek would make it just as challenging.

Conventional wisdom in 1984 suggested that an unsupported journey of that length, about 880 miles, was impossible. But Roger believed that his suggestion was no different than proposing a new route up one of the world's great mountains. Robert, although disap-pointed at having to modify his dream of duplicating Scott's journey exactly, agreed to Roger's plan. With that compromise he began to gather about him the people needed to give the expedition life.

One of the first and decidedly the most important was Sir Peter Scott, the elderly naturalist son of Britain's fallen hero. A man of considerable influence, he agreed to become the first of the expedi-tion's patrons. Its name was changed at his request from "The Scott Antarctic Expedition" to "In the Footsteps of Scott Antarctic Expedition."

I soon began to realize the vast size of the project. Roger, with Robert's blessing, had invited me aboard to assist with planning and organization — it was later that he would ask me to join the Pole team. Not only was I asked to figure out and organize everything that was required to build a base in the Antarctic, but Roger wanted me to assist in the evaluation of all elements of safety and risk management. Roger wrote of me at the time, "Behind his tall, gracious and polite exterior was hidden a tenacious grit, and he brought a systematic attention to detail that we sorely lacked."[1] He later added, "I wanted his caution and practicality to balance Robert. ... "[2]

I look back on that with humour now, as I was to learn very quickly that it was these same qualities that the others were to find so irritating, and I am sure they contributed to the stress and conflict that seemed to grow daily between us during the planning stages of the expedition. Several months after we arrived in the Antarctic, our base doctor, Mike Stroud, put it bluntly in his diary, "Gareth could be irritating. He was meticulous in the extreme. It was a trait that had already annoyed Roger. ... "

Although I was thrilled to be involved, I also considered the plan ambitious. It was audacious to suggest that anyone could ever fill another man's shoes, especially one so ennobled, as Scott, by time and tragedy. As well, the continent can be terrifying. If the Antarctic deigned to let us survive I knew that it would be only partly due to our ability. It was a land of unpredictable extremes and we would always have to be on guard. It was this very inhospitality, I believe, that was the impetus for early conquest of the continent. How better to loft one's status than meeting and surpassing an awesome physical challenge, how better to demonstrate the might of human endeavour.

While historically many people believed science was a thinly veiled cover for exploration, others considered Antarctic research only a means to legitimize territory. Some would still ask if the end justified the means, but polar exploration, most notably the race to the Pole, has generated its own rewards.

Among the first scientific expeditions was one led by Carsten Egeberg Borchgrevink, a Norwegian who, under the British flag explored Cape Adare on Ross Island in 1899 and took the first hesitant steps on the Ross Ice Shelf. More importantly, his expedition, which was the first to winter over, proved that men could indeed survive in the cruel Antarctic.

While Borchgrevink was conducting rudimentary science in the Antarctic, another expedition was gathering steam in England. Sir

Clements Markham, the effervescent president of the Royal Geographical Society, an organization well known for its exploits and influence, was the energy behind the drive to place Britain at the South Pole first. Although Markham was rebuffed by the Admiralty, he eventually persuaded the Prince of Wales to become the patron and Parliament to give a £45,000 grant. With funds at hand the expedition evolved from fancy to fact.

On June 5, 1899, a 31-year-old naval lieutenant, Robert Falcon Scott, already known to Markham, applied to lead the expedition. A year later he was made commander of the National Antarctic Expedition to lead a scientific team to the unexplored continent.

On August 6, 1901, the ship *Discovery*, built for the expedition, left the Isle of Wight bound for Antarctica. The ship's hull was 26 inches thick and her bow was protected by steel plate as a defence against the ravages of pack-ice she expected to encounter. On board were Scott, three other naval officers, 20 hand-picked men, scientists and merchant seamen. Many of them would play pivotal roles in Scott's later and final expedition. Among the higher ranks was a merchant officer, Ernest Shackleton, who would figure prominently in his own later expedition.

Scott, Dr. Edward Wilson and Shackleton left Hut Point in McMurdo Sound for the Pole with sledges and dogs on November 2, 1902, and within days hunger gnawed mercilessly, the pain of snow-blindness crippled them and the dogs died one by one. Scurvy eventually forced them to admit defeat on December 30 after they had reached latitude 82° 16' south, the farthest south that any man had ever achieved. Shackleton's scurvy was so bad that his gums were swollen, he was coughing blood and he could barely stand. On February 3, 1903, two crew members of the *Discovery* met the exhausted trio trudging toward the ship dragging their sledge, the ailing Shackleton barely upright on his skis. They were quickly assisted to safety aboard the ice-bound ship which then spent another year locked in the ice before it could return home.

Although his first attempt on the Pole had failed, Scott was better prepared for his next and final assault. In the meantime, however, Ernest Shackleton made his own attempt. On February 11, 1907, he announced to the Royal Geographical Society in London that he would lead an expedition to the Antarctic. Scott's supporters cried foul, as Scott was planning a second expedition and many felt that he had first right. Shackleton refused to step aside but a compromise was eventually reached by which he agreed to Scott's prior claim to the already-established base in McMurdo Sound. On August 7, 1907, his ship, the *Nimrod*, set sail from England for the Antarctic, reaching pack-ice in mid-January, 1908. After being turned away from his planned destination by heavy ice, Shackleton was forced, against his word with Scott, to settle at Cape Royds in McMurdo Sound.

From that base, Shackleton, with three of his crew, Adams, Wild and Marshall, made a start for the Pole on October 29, 1908, having laid his depots soon after arrival. Suffering starvation, exhaustion and extreme cold, he not only pioneered an efficient route to the Pole, but came within 97 nautical miles of the goal, establishing a new farthest south position. As he and his men struggled back through incredible hardship, Shackleton, hungry and spent, felt a presence by his side that would later be immortalized by T.S. Eliot in "The Waste Land":

> Who is the third who walks always beside you?
> When I count, there are only you and I together
> But when I look ahead up the white road
> There is always another one walking beside you
> Gliding wrapt in a brown mantle, hooded
> I do not know whether a man or a woman
> — But who is that on the other side of you?

Returning to London in June 1909, only partly victorious, Shackleton had nevertheless paved the way for Scott. Even as King Edward VII dipped the sword of knighthood over Shackleton's broad shoulders, Scott's preparations for a second attempt were under way. Although Scott was relieved that Shackleton would not be contesting his bid, he was aware that other expeditions were being planned. Many countries were competing to place their flag at the South Pole, one of the great prizes of the early part of the century.

Across the North Sea, a confident Norwegian, Roald Amundsen, already a veteran of the Arctic, had planned to be first to reach the North Pole, but when his goal was summarily snatched from beneath his nose by the American naval officer Robert Peary, who claimed that victory on April 6, 1909, Amundsen's attention turned toward the south. If he could not win the North Pole he was determined to be first to the South Pole. Amundsen was aware that Scott was in the final stages of organizing another attempt, so not wishing to cause Scott to hurry his efforts, he kept his change of plans to himself, disclosing them to his officers only on the evening of their departure. Amundsen would not reveal the news to Scott and the world until he knew that he was beyond contact.

Scott received the telegram from Amundsen without comment in Melbourne, Australia, although the news caused him some anxiety. On January 4, 1911, he landed his contingent of 65 men — with the dogs, three motor sledges and Manchurian ponies that would form the basis of his transport system — on Ross Island next to a spit of land he christened Cape Evans. Exactly ten days later, Amundsen's ship, *Fram*, carrying Amundsen's party of 19 men and a large number of dogs, eased into the Bay of Whales on the eastern edge of the Ross Ice Shelf. There he established his base, Framheim. Amundsen had a slight advantage; he was already 60 nautical miles nearer the Pole.

It was inevitable that the two parties would meet. Amundsen expected that Scott's eastern party, led by Lieutenant Victor Campbell, would eventually discover them in the Bay of Whales and was therefore not surprised when the Englishmen appeared on February 4. It was Campbell who was nonplussed. Speculation had been that Amundsen was based on the other side of the Antarctic.

Regardless, there was little time to fret over the progress of the other party. Winter was almost upon them and depot laying was an immediate priority. That, Amundsen did with alacrity, laying three depots at 80°, 81° and 82° south latitude. The first two were reached with relative ease, the sledges skimming over the surface behind his eager dogs, but to reach the last the dogs needed whipping on. Scott, meanwhile, was trudging ponderously through deep drift behind his ill-suited ponies. In the end, Amundsen's last depot was 150 nautical miles farther than Scott's, at which point he was 480 nautical miles from the Pole. In total, he succeeded in transporting three tons of supplies to Scott's one ton, which was at 79° 28' 30". Scott had originally intended his one-ton depot to be at 80°: the difference would prove fatal.

After one false start, Amundsen departed for the Pole on October 20 with four sledges, 52 dogs and five men; on November 3, he was just short of his depot at 82°. On that same day, Scott was only leaving Hut Point, days behind his two motor sledges chugging across the Ross Ice Shelf where only dogs and ponies had gone before. These machines were constant trouble from the outset, and the last one broke down after only 51 miles.

Amundsen was wise to the advantages and use of dogs as both a mode of transport and a ready source of dog food, and was gaining time and distance from Scott daily. On December 8 he reached Shackleton's farthest south position of 88° 23', a point Scott would not reach until January 9, thus stretching an initial 14-day lead to a month. On December 15, 1911, running before his dogs at the insistence of his companions, he heard his men simultaneously cry "Halt!" The sledgewheels indicated that the South Pole was his! Scott, meanwhile, was still manhauling up the Beardmore Glacier, approximately 400 miles from the Pole. The remaining ponies, exhausted, were shot and the dogs turned around at the bottom of the Beardmore.

After Amundsen planted his country's flag, a duty he shared with all four of his companions, he erected a reserve tent within which he placed a message to King Haakon of Norway and a covering letter to Scott, asking him to forward it (as a safeguard against Amundsen's failure to return and broadcast his achievement to the world). Then, after careful navigational observations, where he "boxed" the Pole to ensure it was not missed, he and his companions turned their sledges toward Framheim.

Scott did not get to Amundsen's tent until January 18, the day after he reached the Pole. A feeling of great despondency swept over him and his companions, already weakened by the brutal work and a meagre diet. It had all been for naught. Scott's anguish was reflected in his prophetic words, "Great God! this is an awful place and terrible enough for us to have laboured to it without the reward of priority."[3]

Eight days later, Amundsen, as vigorous as ever, arrived back at Framheim. Meanwhile, Scott, labouring in harness, was plodding back across the great Plateau, bargaining against fate for his life. As each day passed, the party's plight became more desperate.

First it was Evans who perished on the Beardmore, then Oates purposely stumbled from the tent to disappear into the white void, his frozen feet barely supporting his wasted body. A few days later, Scott, Wilson and Bowers died together in their tent only 11 miles from their "One Ton Depot." As Scott so aptly wrote, "These rough notes and our dead bodies must tell the tale, ... "[4] Indeed they would.

It was the sharp eye of Toronto-born Charles Wright, the expedition physicist and one of a number of Canadians to distinguish themselves in the Antarctic, that discovered the outline of Scott's snow-shrouded tent eight months later. Apsley Cherry-Garrard would describe that moment in *The Worst Journey in the World*: "We with the dogs had seen Wright turn away from the course by himself and the mule party swerve right-handed ahead of us. He had seen what he thought was a cairn, and then something looking black by its side. A vague kind of wonder gradually gave way to real alarm. We came up to them all halted. Wright came across to us. 'It is the tent.' I do not know how he knew."[5]

My dreaming and reading about the Antarctic were soon replaced by more practical matters as Roger drew me deeper into the expedition's affairs. Little did I know they would consume much of the next five years of my life.

Returning to London in January, after a two-week skiing vacation in France, I called Roger from the bus station. He gave me directions to B1 Riverside, Metropolitan Wharf, where "The Footsteps of Scott Expedition" was headquartered in an old warehouse. Upon arrival, I found it gloomy, and worse, empty. Light glowed dully through a grimy window at the river end of the room, weakly illuminating a few sticks of furniture and a small stack of supplies that the fledgling expedition had managed to squeeze from a few hesitant sponsors. The project, by necessity, was growing from a simple plan with modest requirements to a complex organization whose needs were close to overwhelming, and politics had played a major role.

Antarctica has never been populated, but technology has now made it possible for humans to live there year-round in relative comfort. The U.S. even operates a research station at the South Pole. During the summer, about 8,000 people live in scientific stations, mainly along the coasts, though the population drops to about 1,000 in the winter. It was the International Geophysical Year, in 1957-1958, when 12 nations mounted a scientific assault on the continent, that laid the groundwork for the 1959 Antarctic Treaty and the spirit of cooperation that has existed to this day. The treaty temporarily froze existing territorial claims, banned military activity, promoted the continent as a non-nuclear zone, and fostered shared scientific work.

The continent, however, remained embroiled in controversy and high-stakes political posturing. The treaty did not deal definitively with the issue of territorial claims, and many nations were scrambling to get their foot in the door should the Antarctic ever be sliced up. Other nations sought to ban any future exploitation; still others saw it as a common heritage for all mankind and were promoting a World Park concept. What was at stake was a possibly enormous storehouse of mineral wealth. Scientific evidence points to deposits of many valuable minerals, including oil, and the largest coalfield in the world. The Footsteps expedition arrived at a time when the treaty signatories were wrangling with high emotions, political manoeuvring and conflicting agendas prior to the 1991 treaty review. A few years after our expedition, the 1991 *Protocol on Environmental Protection* would be agreed to, placing a moratorium on any kind of oil or mineral extraction in the Antarctic for 50 years. It was against this backdrop that Roger and Robert attempted to secure a plane.

Originally, they had anticipated flying from the American base of Antarctic operations in New Zealand to the U.S. research station in McMurdo Sound. From there they would take three months to manhaul sledges along Scott's route to the U.S. research station at the South Pole. They would return by air first to McMurdo and then to New Zealand, utilizing the American Hercules air support that served these two bases. A visit to Dr. Edward Todd, head of the National Science Foundation's (NSF) Polar Division in Washington, D.C., however, soon quashed that plan. He informed them that it was Antarctic Treaty and U.S. government policy not to assist private expeditions.

As there were no available private aircraft capable of operating in the Antarctic, flying was out of the question. The only other avenue was by ship, but marine access was limited to a small window of time in late January when the sea-ice was open. This meant that the expedition would have to arrive about nine months in advance of the November trek, and would necessitate the purchase of a ship, the construction of a base and the purchase of equipment and food for at least a year.

The job seemed so immense that I was unsure where to begin, but this challenge was the reason I had agreed to join and I started by writing letters and making lists of our base and equipment requirements. After completing my last instructing obligations with Plas-y-Brenin, I moved to London in the first week of March. While I mulled over radios, base dimensions, fuel requirements and generators, Robert and Roger returned to Washington to appeal again to Dr. Todd for assistance. They still needed air transport from the U.S. Amundsen-Scott Station at the South Pole back to the base that we expected to establish in McMurdo Sound. Now they could assure him that they would have their own marine transport although at that point we had yet to purchase a ship. Dr. Todd not only reiterated U.S. government policy but overstepped the bounds of diplomacy by advising them that he considered their ambitious plan foolhardy. This second rejection merely steeled their resolve to become totally independent of the Americans.

Todd later wrote, in a letter to Roger, about the proposed location of our base, "Useful space on Ross Island is a scarce commodity allotted between the U.S. and New Zealand program needs through a land use review panel. I would like to discourage, but am not in a position to prohibit, your establishment of a camp or facility on Ross Island."

The trip to Washington did nothing to solve the problem of how to get Robert and Roger back from the South Pole. As there was no way but to fly, the polar team would have to organize their own flight. The man chosen for that task was a veteran polar pilot, Giles Kershaw, who was familiar with the Antarctic, having flown for the British Antarctic Survey as early as 1974. His contacts were extensive — he knew all the aircraft in the world that could do what we required. His first choice was a privately operated Tri-turbo DC3 which would be under charter in the Antarctic when we were there. If that machine was not available, a smaller Twin Otter would be suitable but had the disadvantage of requiring pre-laid fuel depots. Whatever aircraft Giles eventually chose, we had complete trust in his judgment that it would be appropriate.

Now that our transport arrangements were sketched in theory, the next step was to purchase a ship. A friend of Robert's, Peter Malcolm, who had the most marine experience among the lot of us, was charged with that responsibility. On the recommendation of Ken Cameron, a marine engineer with Ranulph Fiennes' 1979-1982 Transglobe Expedition, Peter began to look at trawlers, the time- and storm-tested fishing vessels of the North Sea. His determined efforts eventually bore fruit with the discovery of a bright red trawler in the Scottish port of Fraserburgh. The vessel was in such good condition he had to ask twice if it was the correct ship. The *Cleanseas I*, as she was called, had definite potential; £500,000 had been spent on her two years earlier to convert her to an oil-pollution-control vessel. Her brasswork glinted and her paint was fresh. She would need a refit to remove an oil-skimming arm and to modify her six forward holds, which had been converted to hold recovered oil, but otherwise she was perfect.

The night he found her, Peter ate fish and chips in the spotless galley with the vessel's engineer, Jimmy, who lived and worked aboard her, and then capped his inspection off with a night in the captain's quarters. It was February, and as he lay in his bunk he could hear a Force 10 gale raging. The ship was moored outside the breakwater and the might of the North Sea bore down hard upon her. She took it in stride. It was a pivotal moment. Peter knew then that the ship would give the expedition the credibility we needed to raise the balance of the sponsorship and, more importantly, take us safely to the Antarctic.

Although the £65,000 asking price was well beyond the expedition's meagre budget, Peter, an incurable optimist, was determined. He had just been bequeathed £20,000 from his uncle's estate and could use it as a down payment. He and Robert, who arrived on the overnight train from London to meet Andrew Salvesen, the owner, and Peter King, the managing director of Salvesen Offshore Services Ltd., hoped for sponsorship at best but were prepared to negotiate either a reduced price or time to pay. Salvesen, who owned one of the largest fishing fleets in Britain, informed them immediately that he was not interested in sponsorship but would concede to delayed payment providing they put up a 20% down payment. The price, he said, would be left to Peter King.

Robert returned to London while Peter Malcolm remained to haggle with Peter King. The two quickly became friends and the price was dropped to £50,000, with four months to pay. As well, upon receipt of the £10,000 down payment, Salvesen agreed to insure her until the debt was fully paid, and even offered the use of a crew.

After their agreement, Peter returned to London to arrange a berth for the ship and to see Lloyd's about upgrading her hull to Ice Class III standards. The expedition was offered free moorage in front of the Tower Hotel at Irongate Wharf, in the shadow of Tower Bridge near where Scott's first ship, the *Discovery*, had been

The SOUTHERN QUEST and Tower Bridge. (PHOTO BY GARETH WOOD)

12

docked many years before. The Tower Hotel had generously provided us with two rooms for a couple of months in exchange for our conducting some of our promotions on site. On March 26, the *Cleanseas I,* skippered by one of Salvesen's captains, set sail from Fraserburgh bound for London, and three days later she arrived at her berth. Stretched from forward to aft masts was a gigantic white banner proclaiming "IN THE FOOTSTEPS OF SCOTT ANTARCTIC EXPEDITION 1984-85."

In order to get to the wharf the ship had to turn in mid-river — it could not travel under Tower Bridge — and, compensating for the fast-running tide, slip neatly alongside. The moment of arrival was pregnant with anticipation. The captain, not used to such a small ship, especially one where all messages to the engine room had to be sent by ship's telegraph, misjudged the time required to reverse her engine. To the astonishment of waiting reporters and guests, the vessel's hull loomed ever larger until John Tolson, the first mate, screamed at them from the bow to " ... get the hell out of the way!" The bow rammed the dock with a solid smack, scattering broken bricks after the fleeing crowd. I reached for one of the nearby glasses of complimentary wine and downed it with a gulp. The ship then drifted back toward Tower Bridge, snapping the stern mast off on a lower bridge strut before regaining way and pulling into place as if nothing had gone wrong. I felt like crawling under a rock. Robert broke the tension by climbing into the rubble, turning to the crowd, and proclaiming, straight faced, that the mishap was clear evidence of the ship's ice-breaking capability. I downed two more glasses of wine in quick succession and then, following Robert's lead, mingled with the crowd as if nothing had happened.

That evening the crew was dismissed and the ship left in Peter Malcolm's care. A telephone was installed and the captain's cabin became a second headquarters. There, Peter, very committed now that he had risked his own capital, struggled to find sponsors to complete the ship's purchase and cover her refit.

At the end of June, the *Cleanseas I* sailed north to Readhead's cooperative dry dock in South Shields, downstream from Newcastle, to be upgraded to Lloyd's specifications. A coal strike was in progress and the dry docks were jammed with colliery vessels. It would be weeks before she could undergo the required transformation to make her safe for Antarctic duty.

Meanwhile, we were working diligently in London, building momentum toward a goal that was now in sight. As contributions rolled in we found ourselves in a dilemma. Our second-storey warehouse had no vehicle access and we had no equipment to load a vessel from the second storey. So, in early July, just after the ship departed for Readhead's, we approached the Port of London Authority about more suitable quarters and were offered an abandoned, ground-level warehouse at West India Dock. It was perfect. We could deliver supplies by vehicle and load a ship directly in front. Although its size (2,000 square feet) and high ceiling made it appear immense, we eventually filled it and another shed before we were through. At one point I organized the erection of our prefabricated base hut inside the warehouse to prime and paint its walls with a special fibreglass mixture and to ensure that it actually went together. Coincidentally, our new headquarters was close to Scott's own departure point, and the very energies that fuelled his legendary preparations soon began to infect our own.

Because of our warehouse's less than desirable location and our concern for the security of our equipment and supplies, I elected to make it my home. We scrounged a ragged chesterfield, a stove and fridge and a propane heater, had a telephone installed and made a desk from a plank and two packing crates. The only drawback, besides the rats and dirt, was that there was no bathroom inside. Outside, there was a facility for the whole complex which was dirty and often used by strangers. For showers, I made the circuit of London friends in the evenings, being careful to vary the host so as not to wear out my welcome.

CHAPTER TWO

PREPARATIONS

THE PRESSURE OF trying to pull the expedition together by November began to take its toll on all of us. Each of us had different ideas on how the project should evolve and we frequently found ourselves at odds. Robert walked into the warehouse on one occasion and announced to Roger and me that we were needed the following day. The three of us were to be filmed by television news rappelling down the side of a London warehouse. Under the guise of "polar training," Robert explained that this was a great opportunity to generate some publicity. Roger and I refused to participate, believing that our professionalism and credibility were at stake and that Robert was just grandstanding. Turning on the news that evening, I had second thoughts. It was a good news spot, Robert performed well and I realized that most of Britain must have then become aware of our expedition. Perhaps Robert was right.

Robert and Roger were especially having a rough time. Officially they were co-leaders of the expedition and Robert's habit of frequently referring to us as "my men," when dealing with the press, was becoming quite irritating. At one particular meeting, with Robert in attendance, Roger put me on the spot.

"Do you respect Robert?" he asked.

I shot him a "for god's sake" look before carefully responding.

"I respect what Robert has done for the expedition," I said.

"No, that's not answering my question," he said sharply. "I asked, do you respect Robert?"

I repeated my answer, refusing to be drawn into Roger's private battle. Later that evening Roger accused me of fence sitting and failing to say what I really felt. My comments didn't help build any bridges with Robert either.

The very strengths that each of us brought to the expedition — Robert's dynamism and vision, Roger's initiative and strong desire to succeed, and my planning and organizational abilities — attributes we thought should have made us an effective and dynamic team, now seemed to divide us. As a result of this ongoing struggle Roger threatened to leave the expedition more than once, and a few days before we were to travel to Switzerland to test our equipment on the Concordia Glacier in the Swiss Alps he quit in disgust. It took all of my efforts and those of others to persuade him to return. His skills were essential.

"Look," Roger said to me after an exasperating evening discussion with Robert, "this expedition's much bigger than any of us ever anticipated and it's obvious now that Robert isn't going to be trained in time. He's not even planning to come to Concordia. He says he doesn't have time. I need skilled support on the journey to the Pole. So, how do you feel about coming along as third man?"

"You know I'd like that more than anything," I replied without hesitation, "but what about Robert. Will he agree?"

"Leave Robert to me," he said firmly. "He's got no bloody choice."

The following morning, while we were loading our borrowed van with equipment we were to test on the glacier, Robert came out to say goodbye. As I shook his hand he looked at me contemptuously and said, "So you got your way." It was obvious he was annoyed by this unexpected turn of events. In spite of our differences I empathized with Robert, understanding that his concept of "two to the Pole" had come unglued. Still, I was thrilled, knowing that the experience would be a significant event in my life. At the same time I was cautioned to keep it to myself — all the expedition publicity had been designed around two to the Pole; a third might confuse the issue and disturb the public's trust. And then Roger issued a final caveat.

"You know," he said, "the final choice of who'll walk, and this includes Robert and myself, won't be made until we're ready to go. There might be insurmountable problems between us, or I might break a leg. You never know."

Despite our differences, we were a healthy organization. The five winterers had been chosen; in addition to Roger, Robert and me, they were Dr. Michael Stroud, our base physician, and John Tolson,

The five winterers. L. to r.: Gareth Wood, Mike Stroud, Robert Swan, Roger Mear, John Tolson. (FOOTSTEPS OF SCOTT COLLECTION)

professional seaman and cameraman who would produce our documentary film. Both Roger and Robert had met Mike aboard the *Bransfield* while they were in the employ of the British Antarctic Survey. John, affectionately known as "Mad Jack" for his social escapades in Greek restaurants, had a wealth of Antarctic experience from duty aboard BAS ships.

On the Concordia Glacier Roger and I established camp and proceeded to test our equipment. The weather was far too warm for our polar gear — we baked in our goose-down clothing and our fibreglass sledge was virtually impossible to pull through the sticky summer snow. That we were pulling only 240 pounds, 60 pounds less than Roger had estimated we would require for the Pole, was discouraging. We both wondered, not for the first time, whether the expedition was physically feasible, although we knew that conditions in the Antarctic would be vastly different.

We spent the next few days continuing our tests and in camp we were visited by Bruno Klausbruckner, an Austrian climber who had contacted the expedition in London about transporting a team of climbers to the Antarctic. After learning our plans he told us about three men, one of whom lived in northern Italy, who had made an unsupported trek across northern Greenland, manhauling all their supplies on sledges. It suddenly seemed important to talk to this man, so later in the week we flew to Innsbruck, Austria, where we met Bruno; he drove us into the Dolomite region of northern Italy to the small town of Bozen. There we met the congenial leader of that extraordinary expedition, Dr. Robert Peroni, whose modesty marginalized his significant achievement.

His story is dramatic. He and two companions began their Greenland journey with only a few pounds more than we were contemplating and when they found their sledges too difficult to haul, jettisoned precious food in favour of mobility. They had no safety equipment and before departure had agreed that should one of them become injured or ill he would not slow the others. This prospect filled Peroni and his men with unmitigated terror. In fact, it was fear that was their greatest challenge. The journey, he said, was not only an extreme test of their physical stamina but almost broke them mentally. Day after interminable day they plodded, lonely and silent, across the still, white plain that 88 days later led them to a small Eskimo village 838 miles from their beginning. They had only one day's food to spare.

There were lessons for us in his story, but more important, there were warnings — our success was suddenly not so certain. While we drove back to London, pondering the expedition's future, far to the north our ship was still being cut and pierced by welders' torches. Although it was already well past our planned departure date, the hull was not close to being ready and the propeller had still to be ice protected. Fortunately, the *Bransfield*, the BAS ship, was dry docked beside the *Cleanseas I*. Peter, after first obtaining blueprints of the *Bransfield*'s lower hull from her engineer, received permission to inspect her ice-deflection gear. The three massive fins that directed ice away from the propeller were copied in miniature for the *Cleanseas I*.

While the workers expanded the mess hall and installed six water-tight hatches on the forward holds, the remaining £40,000 was paid to Salvesen. Peter was expressing his joy that the vessel was now ours when Jerry Thompson, a Salvesen-paid engineer who had been assisting with the refit, slowly cautioned, "Oh dear, I think you may regret that."

"What do you mean!" Peter demanded.

"I think you'd better come with me," Jerry said, and Peter and the crew trooped anxiously behind him down the length of the exposed hull to the propeller.

"See that?" he said, pointing up toward a slight fracture in a cleaned area of the propeller boss. "That makes it useless. It needs replacing."

Peter was aghast. Although he was not concerned about the cost of replacing the propeller — the terms of purchase provided for such an eventuality — the ship had a pressing engagement in London with Princess Anne who had agreed to inspect her on August 28. Lloyd's refused to release the vessel from dry dock until the propeller was replaced, which could not possibly be done in time. Peter argued that it could be installed anywhere. Eventually, a compromise was reached by which Lloyd's agreed to let the ship proceed to London under escort.

Peter still had a problem. The ship had no captain. John Tolson knew of an ex-BAS captain, Graham Phippen, but doubted he would be interested after serving nine seasons in the Antarctic. Peter phoned him anyway. The answer was emphatically "NO," but Peter was persistent. Phippen had the qualifications and experience we required. Two weeks later Peter called again. After that, Phippen visited the London headquarters and then came up to Readhead's. The enthusiasm of the moment washed over him and he accepted the ship on the spot. His would be a difficult command, for most of the crew were not mariners. Phippen, fortunately, had the right temperament to handle such a motley assembly.

The crew worked diligently throughout the night to make the ship ready for departure. At 6 a.m. on August 25 she moved down the Tyne under tug escort. The *Southern Quest*, as she had been renamed by Robert's mother after Shackleton's last ship, *Quest*, steamed toward London at a steady nine knots. The propeller held and at the mouth of the Thames she accepted tug escort to guide her to her berth near Tower Bridge.

With only one evening to prepare for the royal inspection, the crew hustled to clean and tidy the ship. The next day, Princess Anne arrived, accompanied by Sir Vivian Fuchs, an Antarctic veteran, and Lord Shackleton, son of Ernest Shackleton, who after much persuasion had agreed to act as another of the expedition's patrons. Robert, who was to escort the Princess, appeared only moments before her, his normally dishevelled appearance barely altered by a somewhat wrinkled cotton suit hastily purchased at the local thrift shop.

Robert guided the stylishly dressed Princess past the gawking crew, which included me, up the creaking gangplank and onto the ship. The inspection came off nicely, and the Princess appeared excited by our efforts. Her appearance did more than just mirror the Royal Assent granted historic expeditions; it gave us credibility in the eyes of the British public. I marvelled at how Robert had pulled it off.

A few days later the ship was escorted up the river to a floating dry dock at West India Dock directly across from our warehouse. Blackwall Engineering Ltd. was to replace the propeller at Salvesen's expense. While it was being fitted, which took two weeks, a half-inch slack was discovered in the rudder pintle. It, too, required refitting and delayed the ship a further two days. We were becoming anxious. November 10 was deemed to be the last day we could possibly depart and still catch the open ice window, though we learned that we could have left much later.

After the repairs were complete, the ship returned to our warehouse where we prepared to load her. This had to be done in a systematic manner so that the items required in the Antarctic would appear in the right order. While organizing this we were hit with a staggering blow. When the ship was in Readhead's, the British Ship Research Association had conducted a computer analysis of the hull, allowing for the cargo she would carry and the ice that would build up on her superstructure once she was in the Antarctic. The result was that her G/Z curve, the curve between the ship's angle of heel and her righting moment, dipped dangerously. In short, her hull needed greater buoyancy and could be in danger of capsizing in rough seas. Although we were not compelled to comply with ministry regulations as long as the *Southern Quest* was registered as a pleasure craft, we had no wish to discover the consequences of ignoring this warning.

The estimated £70,000 cost threatened to break us, but in the spirit of the expedition we rallied to the cause. Otherwise, we would have had to delay the expedition a year. By then the momentum would have been lost — none of us could have sustained the furious pace at which we had worked for the past year.

To increase the hull's buoyancy, welders began to enclose the port and starboard alleyways. The job would take two weeks, bringing us to November 3, dangerously close to our cutoff date. With time short, we began to load the forward holds while the refit was in progress. Michael Seeney, ship's carpenter, constructed cupboards and shelves to contain the flood of equipment and supplies flowing aboard. Two days before our actual departure, dozens of volunteers helped us move a mountain of gear from the warehouse to the ship.

On the last evening, Robert caught the welders packing up their gear early. Robert argued furiously, pleading with them not to abandon us in our hour of need. Finally they agreed to complete the job, persuaded, in part, by Robert's offer of large, steaming mugs of tea liberally laced with rum. Several more doses of the convincing mixture were required before the night was through. With the job done, the tension of a long year evaporated.

Early on November 3, a crowd of people, most of whom had assisted with the final frantic preparations, waved in unison as the bright red trawler gained way down West India Dock on the first leg of her 14,000-mile voyage south.

The five winterers were not aboard. We were to fly to New Zealand late the following January to meet the ship in Lyttelton, near Christchurch, on the east coast of New Zealand's South Island. We still had to load a container of last-minute items for shipment to New Zealand aboard a fast freighter.

As the ship departed, most of the crowd jumped into their cars and raced around to the other side of the West India Dock to watch the ship move toward the lock which would take her out into the main flow of the Thames. There we gathered, together with a small contingent of British press, for the final sendoff. As the ship entered the lock, rather quickly, a stern line was thrown off to check her forward momentum. Unfortunately, no one, including me, standing nearby, had been briefed to collect it. Tim Malloy, a seaman friend of Peter's, recognizing the problem, leapt for it just as the ship looked as if it might crash through the lock gates. Fumbling with the line, he eventually secured it but as it drew taut he was jerked straight into the lock with a coil of rope about his neck. Fortunately, he had the good sense to throw it off and was rescued unharmed. We all sighed with relief as the ship, its forward momentun checked, found reverse and pulled alongside to wait for the lock to fill. The final few minutes were tense. The crew were anxious to be away but at the same time lamented their separation from family and friends.

The *Southern Quest*'s first stop was Cardiff, Wales, where she loaded 16 tons of coal for our hut stove. Scott had also taken on coal at Cardiff, and had been so appreciative of the city's hospitality that he had promised it would become the *Terra Nova*'s home port.

Several days later, in the cold and wet of a miserable November 10, the voyage began in earnest. A small group of bystanders was silent witness to the ship's unpublicized departure. The previous day, two Harrier jets had performed a flypast, but they had no way of knowing that delays had set departure back 24 hours. The next stop was Las Palmas in the Canary Islands and from there the *Southern Quest* steamed toward Cape Town, South Africa, before making directly for Lyttelton. There we would load the container of equipment that had arrived aboard the fast freighter ahead of the *Southern Quest*. I also had a long list of last-minute items for the base that I had not had time to acquire in London, including bamboo poles, orange flagging, coal sacks, rubbish bags, nails and various bits of hardware and tools. Surprisingly, I managed to tick off every single item of my 60-item list before the ship sailed.

Lyttelton's history is closely linked to that of the Antarctic. To the same quay and, perhaps, according to Apsley Cherry-Garrard, to the same shed, have come many Antarctic adventurers. Scott's *Discovery* and *Terra Nova* expeditions, and Shackleton's *Nimrod* expedition, all spent time there repairing ships and reprovisioning for voyages south. Meeting the *Southern Quest* was Christchurch resident Bill Burton, Scott's stoker on the *Terra Nova* and the last of that great era. At 96, his memory of Scott was still strong.

While there, Roger and I confirmed with the New Zealand post office authorities that we could use the public post office at Scott Base, New Zealand's Antarctic scientific research station at McMurdo Sound. From there we could send telexes and radio phone anywhere in the world, and occasionally send and receive mail. Roger and I also took the opportunity to meet Bob Thompson, director of New Zealand's Department of Scientific and Industrial Research's (DSIR) Antarctic Division. Although Robert had met Thompson several times, I had only communicated with him by letter early in our preparations the year before. I had written to inform him of our intentions and ask that we be permitted access to their Scott Base radio frequencies for general communication with their base personnel and for relaying messages back to our contacts in New Zealand.

His reply made it very clear that access to radio frequencies would be regarded as assistance which was contrary to their government policy of refusing support to private expeditions and tour operations. Shortly before our departure from London, Thompson was quoted in the London *Daily Telegraph* as calling our expedition "bloody stupid" and, "In this day and age, for anybody to suggest walking to the Pole is idiotic, because there is nothing to it. ... The exploratory days are over. You have planes to get there in two hours."

Roger and I had come to formally tell him of our intentions and now assure him of our independence. At the end of the interview, however, we were disappointed, realizing that his opinion of the expedition was unchanged. Fortunately, the disdain expressed by Thompson was not shared by all DSIR employees, some of whom, in direct defiance to posted orders, later risked their jobs just to visit us.

On January 27, the *Southern Quest* departed under tug escort from the *Lyttelton*, the same vessel that had guided the *Terra Nova* from the harbour years before. Roger, Robert, Robert's girlfriend, Rebecca, who had come with us from England and who would accompany the ship to the Antarctic, and I were not aboard. We still had some items to obtain and would meet the ship in Port Chalmers approximately 200 miles south. Robert and Rebecca left on their own the following afternoon and Roger and I followed in a rented van the next day, arriving to find the ship in its usual state of chaos. Ship parts were required, we were still waiting for a load of equipment, including sleeping bags, and the Sperry autopilot was malfunctioning — Captain Graham, as I was to call him, soon discovered that it had not been switched on.

On January 30 we left Port Chalmers to the raucous cheer of a boisterous knot of locals, praying that the ice window to McMurdo Sound, where we would establish our base, would be open. As the ship motored slowly from the harbour I took a last look at the verdant hills crowding the town, knowing that it would be at least a year before I would see such a scene again.

For two whole days our little ship bucked her way south through a wind-whipped maelstrom, repeatedly wallowing in dark troughs and struggling back up under green seas that broke and cascaded upon the foredeck. Spray was flung over the bridge and rained down amidships. To venture out was to risk an immediate soaking.

Outside, unperturbed by the weather and seemingly curious about this ugly red intruder, rode a noble albatross, its coal-black wings and cotton-white body rock steady in the strong breeze. When the weather allowed an infrequent foray on deck, I saw two dolphins riding our bow wave, guiding us south. On February 4 the first iceberg was sighted. It was, for all of a few foggy seconds, an intellectual curiosity, a vanguard for an army of ice that was soon to follow. A great flat slab, chalk white on top, it lay inert while the sea crashed against it.

The *Southern Quest* was now covered in ice, which festooned lines and rails with icicles and clothed everything with a heavy white coat. As we ghosted through the thick fog, keeping a wary eye cocked for icebergs, I could feel the cold begin to creep in around us. Captain James Cook, who was the first to circumnavigate the continent, although he never did see it, wrote in his log on January 28, 1775, "It is however true that the greatest part of this Southern Continent (supposeing there is one) must lay within the Polar Circle where the Sea is so pestered with ice, that the land is thereby inacessible. The risk one runs in exploreing a coast in these unknown and Icy Seas, is so very great, that I can be bold to say, that no man will ever venture

23

farther than I have done and that the lands which may lie to the South will never be explored. Thick fogs, Snow storms, Intense Cold and every other thing that can render Navigation dangerous one has to encounter and these difficulties are greatly heightned by the enexpressable horrid aspect of the Country, a Country doomed by Nature never once to feel the warmth of the Suns rays, but to lie for ever buried under everlasting snow and ice."[1]

It comes as a surprise to many visitors that there are no polar bears or native peoples here. Antarctica is our least known continent and I was amazed to learn that it is as large as the United States and Mexico combined. It is surrounded by frozen sea and its size swells by as much as a third in the winter. Mountains rise to over 16,000 feet and Antarctica boasts the highest average elevation (7,500 feet) of any continent, due to its ice cap, in some places almost three miles deep. The continent harbours approximately 90% of the world's ice and in that ice an astounding 70% of the world's supply of fresh water.

Antarctica has a healthy representation of marine mammals and birds, but the continent itself, besides a few insects and primitive plants, is devoid of life. It has not always been so, however, for fossils of plants and animals have been discovered which suggest that the continent once supported a temperate climate. Antarctica is believed to have been part of a gigantic supercontinent known as Gondwanaland that broke apart 200,000,000 years ago to form the present continents.

It was not until 1820 that the continent was formally sighted by the Russian naval captain, Thaddeus von Bellingshausen. At almost the same time, the British naval captain, Edward Bransfield, sighted the Antarctic Peninsula and a year later American sealers reported sighting the Southern Continent as well. It was many decades, however, before the continent was populated and then only on its outer islands where whaling stations gave temporary dominion.

It was close to the U.S. coastal station, McMurdo, that the *Southern Quest* was now heading. On the ninth day the sea was relatively calm and clear of ice and on the dogwatch of February 8 I caught my first glimpse of Ross Island. It glistened like a jewel in the crown of the Southern Continent. Mount Erebus was shrouded in heavy, dark cloud and to one side I could barely make out the diminutive Mount Bird. I was apprehensive about our chances of approaching Cape Evans unimpeded, the last report suggesting that ice would be a problem. Fortunately our passage was uninterrupted.

As we glided toward our anchorage in North Bay later that day, the surface millpond calm, both crew and winterers crowded the foredeck, anxious for a glimpse of Scott's weathered grey hut, contrasting sharply with the coal-black beach. This remote beach is to be our home for the next year, I thought. As if to welcome us, gull-like brown skuas wheeled far above in the summer-bright sky and on the beach a seal humped its way toward the water, disappearing with a splash.

The SOUTHERN QUEST in North Bay, showing the Barne Glacier, with Scott's hut in the foreground. (PHOTO BY GARETH WOOD)

CHAPTER THREE

A VISIT WITH SCOTT

SEVENTY-FOUR YEARS earlier, Scott had chosen this location because it was not easily cut off from the Ross Ice Shelf, its deep bay remaining frozen until late in the season. When I stepped ashore for the first time, wading the last few feet from the inflatable to the black sand and cinder ash beach, I paused in wonder, my attention riveted on Scott's hut. A strong sense surrounded this weathered building. Robert described it as reverence. For him it was a veneration beyond mere respect — to know the history was to be awed but to be actually near the hut was to be close to the glory itself.

In front of the hut, a fluke still partially buried in the weathered beach, was one of two rust-caked anchors from Shackleton's Ross Sea party's *Aurora*, which on the night of May 6, 1915, was blown out to sea in a howling gale. Carried north at the whim of the pack-ice for ten months, she travelled 1,100 miles before being freed. We were the first to settle at the Cape since that event. Although it was tempting for the winterers to take the time to explore Scott's hut, we had literally tons of supplies and equipment to unload and limited time in which to do it. Captain Graham, nervous that weather and ice conditions might change, endangering the ship and perhaps even locking her in the ice, kept up the pressure to unload.

The whole of that first day, February 9, was spent dragging three 400-yard mooring lines ashore to make the ship fast so that unloading could begin in earnest the next day. In our hearts and minds we knew that three lines would be inadequate if the weather and ice conspired against us. The *Aurora* had been tethered to seven lines and two anchors. The following morning, after eating several of Bernie the cook's breakfasts, we set to work. Mike Seeney had constructed an ingenious pontoon float in New Zealand. Made out of timber and empty 45-gallon drums, it was powered by a 45-hp outboard. The *Spirit of Incompetence*, as he christened her, was as useful as she was unique. Now we did not have to rely upon the inflatable boats, which were good only for light work.

Our first morning was a brutal introduction to a climate we had heretofore only read about. From the calm of the previous day the weather deteriorated to wind and driving snow. We occasionally lost sight of the *Southern Quest* as she rode out the storm unperturbed. Roger and Mike, with some difficulty, erected a box tent onshore and it was to this that we retreated when the cold, wind and snow became unbearable.

The ship's windlass was broken so all supplies and equipment had to be moved by hand. Roger and I directed operations on shore, while Graham Phippen and Ken Marshall, the first mate, directed offloading. Here, Robert demonstrated his great strength and energy, heaving 50-pound sacks of coal up, over his head and on to the next man. His endurance seemed unlimited and he worked steadily at this all day. Since our arrival, however, I had noticed a dramatic change in Robert's behaviour. He was no longer calling the shots. It then occurred to me that even though his brute strength might not in itself be enough to get us to the Pole, another attribute — his extraordinary ability to sell a dream — was what had got us this far.

By February 12 we had finished transporting the coal from ship to shore. Over 600 bags had been hoisted from the hold, 50 to a pontoon load, and then carried 75 yards up the beach to a prearranged location near where the hut would be constructed. It was a gruelling day and I was exhausted. My back and arms were so sore that I had difficulty picking up a knife and fork and I nearly fell asleep at the table. We did not have to contend with blowing snow, but the day was intensely cold. Despite several pair of gloves, balaclavas, etc., my hands and feet felt frozen as soon as work stopped. Everything was encased in ice, including the pontoon and the three mooring lines. The bay was threatening to freeze as well.

The next morning the weather deteriorated to Force 8 to 9 with temperatures of -11°C in shelter and an estimated -35°C with windchill. Captain Graham decided it was too dangerous to launch the boats. Instead, I spent the day collecting odd bits of equipment from around the ship and the deck crew emptied the holds of the remaining drums of fuel. They were placed on deck ready for unloading the next day.

By February 14, most of the equipment had been brought ashore, the generator requiring two good hours just to winch it by hand from the hold. We now had the complete hut in pieces on the beach and, with the winterers in agreement, a level spot was chosen 200 yards north of Scott's hut where the base beams of the 16- by 24-foot structure were laid out. Although we recognized that our choice was exposed — we had been monitoring the action of wind and snow since our arrival — there was no other place as good. The following day I supervised the erection of the walls. It was then that Mike Stroud voiced an objection to the direction the windows were facing.

Annoyed that this should be noticed now, my immediate response was to cut Mike short and explain that there was nothing we could do; the panels making up the hut walls had to be erected in a specific order. He was determined that we should dismantle the hut and turn it right around if necessary. Frustrated, I could not think of any good argument against his request and prepared to dismantle the hut. Mike Seeney eventually saved the day by figuring out a way to modify the panels, so that we could move just a window panel to the view side of the hut. It saved an immense amount of time and, to my embarrass-

Unloading 60 tons of stores and equipment. (FOOTSTEPS OF SCOTT COLLECTION)

The Footsteps hut with the sea beginning to freeze. (PHOTO BY GARETH WOOD)

ment, proved to be a relatively simple task. Mike was right — it would have been a shame to live on the edge of paradise and not have a view of McMurdo Sound and the western mountains. Roger, Mike Seeney and I then finished erecting the lower walls and installing the upper floor. We now had a weatherproof box and in this hollow shell we sheltered, exhausted, for our first night ashore. It was 2:00 a.m.

The crew of the *Southern Quest* were to depart in a few days, but before leaving they wanted to see inside Scott's hut. It was kept locked by the New Zealand authorities, but Robert persuaded Peter Malcolm to open it. Peter's father, who was once a senior officer in the Ugandan police, had shown Peter how to pick a lock, but cautioned him to use this knowledge only in an emergency. Robert spent considerable time convincing Peter that as the crew had travelled 70 days to see the hut this was just such an emergency. Peter reluctantly complied but no one was allowed to watch. Aware of the embarrassment we might cause our patrons should we damage anything, and remembering that we did not have official permission to enter this historic dwelling, Captain Graham carefully supervised small parties of two or three individuals as they toured the hut. He ensured that nothing was moved or removed, not even a nail. Later, when the Kiwis asked us how we had got into Scott's hut, Robert told them that the lock was unclasped. We imagined that someone got roasted at Scott Base, but we couldn't tell the real story.

29

The following day the ship prepared to leave for Hut Point, 17 miles farther south and close to the U.S. and New Zealand research stations. Mike and I were left behind to continue work on the hut. Four days later the *Southern Quest* returned, everyone excited by the visit. I recorded in my diary that night, "Think people at McMurdo and Scott Base quite happy to see us and gave odd help etc. in spite of official line from Washington, D.C. and Christchurch. ... "

Now that the *Southern Quest*'s mission was over, the crew was anxious to leave. After a spectacularly rowdy meal aboard ship, we were ferried ashore, and all of us watched her steam north just as Scott's men must have watched the *Terra Nova* so many years before. It was our last solid link with the outside world, but it was not a sad departure for me: rather a kind of relief that the real task could now begin. All the effort to get this far suddenly seemed very remote.

Our little base quickly became a hive of activity. On February 24, the day after the ship's departure, I wrote in my diary, "Roger built shelves north corner of hut and set up meteorological equipment. John and I finished hole in ceiling and finished chimney. Stove started and went like a charm." Our first hot meal, however, was less than palatable. Roger was the first to voice an objection.

"God! This porridge tastes like burnt wood," he grimaced, jerking the spoon from his mouth.

Robert, the cook, refused to look up from his place at the table and continued to eat his portion in stony silence. He was oblivious to the complaint, quantity, not quality, being his specialty. Robert was a "big picture" man. He would leave the details to the rest of us. One of those was as fundamental as life itself — water.

Surmising that there would be an abundance of fresh-water ice in the Antarctic, we had taken water for granted. When we found no such accessible ice deposits during the unloading of the ship, Roger took the first initiative by motoring to the nearby Barne Glacier ice cliffs in one of the inflatables and towing a large calved chunk 200 yards to the beach in front of the hut. Melted in our water tanks, it lasted the rest of February. When it was gone, and before winter winds heaped water in the form of great hog-backed drifts of snow at our doorstep, we were forced to don hip waders to comb the surf for loose chunks of glacial ice.

Outside, the temperature began to drop, almost as if on cue with the ship's departure, and wisps of fog curling from the sea often obscured the Barne Glacier ice cliffs. Inside, we were warm, content and too busy most days to consider what was happening outside.

There was still an incredible amount of work to be done, including assembling the generator and, the most frustrating of all, erecting radio antennas. Working outside in -15° to -20°C was not a problem, even when windchill made it far colder, but the wind itself played havoc with the antenna masts, blowing them over almost as fast as they were erected.

Most of the hut's ground floor, a total of 380 square feet, was soon converted into a kitchen and living area. On one side of this 16- by 16-foot room reposed the little Esse, the coal-fired stove, which provided heat as well as a cooking surface and oven. Immediately beside it was a sink and food-preparation area and farther along were two clean, 45-gallon steel drums for melting snow. Access to these drums was gained from the outside through an ingenious hatch constructed by Roger in the hut's wall. Beside them, and wrapping around the corner of the hut, were shelves of food, the result of our weekly "shopping" trips to the food dump outside. A plywood table and five chairs occupied the centre of the room.

In the opposite corner were our radios, and running along that side of the room was a long bench supporting a computer, our video equipment and Dr. Mike's tiny medical laboratory. The remaining area was partitioned into four small rooms, each four feet by six feet — a pantry, darkroom, mudroom and chemical toilet which required emptying into the sea every few days. (Dexterity and strength were important attributes for carrying the nearly full honey bucket over mounds of rafted sea-ice to open water for disposal.)

Behind the toilet wall was an uninsulated porch with a workshop, coal bunker and storage for our sledges and climbing gear. Throughout the winter its floor was often dusted with snow, which both sifted in under the outside door and was stamped from our boots before we entered the living portion of the hut. The gear hanging from its walls was usually covered with rime.

Access to the upstairs sleeping quarters was via a ladder located between the radio bench and the food-storage shelves at the opposite end of the hut. Each of us was assigned a small cubicle, which we sought to individualize as Scott's men had done theirs. Robert's had a desk and shelves crammed with Antarctic books and homey paraphernalia. One had to enter by crawling on hands and knees under the desk and if he was working at it his chair would block both the passageway and the entrance to Mike's den across the hall. John's and Roger's were the most ornate, with sheepskin rugs on the floor and patterned bed linen. In contrast, mine was austere with no more than a few rough shelves for clothing and

31

books. Each cubicle, although far from private, was a sanctuary, if only in our minds. Each was a place where we could retreat with our own private thoughts and dreams, a place to cool anger when the passions of five men living in cramped quarters became too emotional, and to mull over the chunk of time the expedition was demanding from our lives.

I had been too busy with the hut and equipment to explore. When I finally ventured forth the Cape revealed itself to me slowly. It was the barren, hilly terminus of a low peninsula extending about a mile and a half into North Bay. It was neatly framed to landward by a long moraine of sand, angular lava and various-sized erratics discarded by the Barne Glacier in its path to the sea. From the top of this rise, known as the Ramp, an amazing vista unfolded. A scattering of dark islands was visible to the south, the larger ones known as Tent, Inaccessible and Big Razorback.

Directly opposite the islands a high bluff known as Turks Head protruded into Erebus Bay. And south of that point was the Erebus Glacier Tongue, stretching eight miles into McMurdo Sound. To the north, separating Cape Evans from Cape Royds, flowed the imposing Barne Glacier, named for Lieutenant Michael Barne of Scott's 1901-1904 *Discovery* Expedition; its icy ramparts blocked North Bay's northern extremity.

The Footsteps hut and Scott's (right) with Mount Erebus behind. (PHOTO BY GARETH WOOD)

Behind the hut the terrain was a wasteland of black cinder and large chunks of lava tilted and scattered like headstones in an abandoned graveyard. Around and between were stark white deposits of fine crystalline snow that blew and settled in every nook and cranny.

Also behind, but to the east of the hut, was the frozen surface of Skua Lake. There, in season, skuas gathered to breed. Directly south was Wind Vane Hill, atop which was a cross erected by Shackleton's Ross Sea party in memory of Hayward and Mackintosh who were lost in May 1915, while crossing temporary sea-ice between Hut Point and Cape Evans. From this vantage point I saw Hut Point Peninsula to the south, on the other side of which lay the American station, McMurdo, and New Zealand's Scott Base. As well, I could not help but notice Scott's weathered hut on the beach below. Although I had not yet taken the time to visit the hut, I felt I must if I were to preserve any sense of the excitement that had gripped me upon first sighting it from the ship.

I walked slowly about the hut's 25- by 50-foot perimeter. Here and there were stacked some whole but mostly shattered boxes of unused provisions scarred by time and weather. In faded black letters I could barely make out the words "Cap. Scott" and "BAE Shore Party" and on others the manufacturers' labels were just visible. Peering into one open box filled with biscuits, I was amazed at their state of preservation. After 74 years in the open they still looked fresh enough to eat. Glass jars of table salt spilled from another, their pale yellow labels still bright under the leaden sky.

A stack of rusted tins, long emptied of their liquid contents, looked so much like a garbage dump that it was hard to separate what had been discarded from what had just not been used. Beside the hut and sheltered from the rasp of the wind sat an empty box marked "New Zealand Kakaramea Creamery Butter," its label as fresh as the day it had been stamped, and against the stables were stacked wind-eroded bales of compressed hay brought by Scott for the ponies. Against the hay leaned a pair of weathered wooden skis, dull grey like the hut.

In 1947, when Admiral Richard Byrd, the American pilot who was the first to fly over both Poles, arrived at Cape Evans, he had been amazed at the state of preservation of the hut and its contents. Met by the still-standing but frozen carcass of a husky, he recorded that the provisions were still fit to eat and a box of matches lighted easily. Although we found no huskies standing, the mummified remains of a few dogs are still there, one still tethered to the hut with leather collar and chain — a mute defender of a long-forgotten faith.

Leaving the stables I walked along the beach past the rickety latrine and the two rust-caked *Aurora* anchors and turned into the hut's entrance. Like Robert, I was seized with an urge to announce my presence, such was the sense of life within. Stepping across the threshold was like travelling back in time, into a simple world where a man's muscle counted for something. The silence that greeted me from the recesses of that dark and lonely room was as loud as the din of activity that must have reverberated within its walls 70-odd years ago. Only my respectful footfall and the wind's whisper broke the quiet.

On my immediate left was the acetylene gas plant that provided light, and directly ahead was a small table around which the men of the mess deck must have gathered in the evening to play cards and chat. On my right was the galley. The massive cook stove was heaped with rusted pots and pans, and lining the shelves around it were boxes and bottles of the most amazing collection of condiments and preserves. Among them were bottles of Heinz Tomato Ketchup and Lea & Perrins Worcestershire Sauce, cans of Colman's Mustard and Bird's Baking Powder, and boxes of Tate cube sugar and Fry's Pure Concentrated Cocoa. In a corner of the galley was the bunk upon which Thomas Clissold, the cook, slept and above his bunk a motley assortment of cups hung from shelves stacked with a similarly mismatched assembly of plates.

Scott's 1910-1912 hut in 1985. (PHOTO BY GARETH WOOD)

34

Straight down the hut from the galley was what Scott called the wardroom. Then, a row of wooden provision boxes had separated the seamen from the officers. It is now one long room, symbolically mixing in death what Scott had actively discouraged in life. Just beyond the galley on both sides of the hut were the bunks of the men. Behind the galley was the geologists' corner inhabited by Frank Debenham, Griffith Taylor and Tryggve Gran, the Norwegian ski expert. (Taylor, known as "Griff," ended a distinguished academic career as a professor of geography at the University of Toronto.)

On the other side of the room were the "Tenements" where five of the men slept. The diminutive but tenacious H. R. "Birdie" Bowers slept in the top left bunk and Apsley Cherry-Garrard was below him. In the middle stood the bunk of the soldier L.E.G. "Titus" Oates, now draped with the harness of the dogs and ponies, and beside it were the bunks of Cecil Meares on top and the surgeon, Edward Atkinson, below.

Separated from the Tenements by a wall was Scott's cubicle, now stripped of the personal effects that had made it his last home. Bits of clothing hung from its walls, and on a table separating his sleeping quarters from Wilson's lay a stuffed penguin and a British newspaper, *The Weekly Press*. The clothing probably belonged to Shackleton's 1914-1917 Ross Sea party, whose two-year forced stay at the Cape, when the *Aurora* was blown to sea in a gale, had disrupted the hut and turned everything greasy black from their prolonged use of seal blubber for fuel.

Wilson's bare bunk across from Scott's provided little insight into this gentle man whose delicate watercolours celebrated the very environment that became his undoing. He was arguably a better leader than Scott, often communicating with the lower ranks to maintain morale, oblivious to class, listening with a caring ear to the men's complaints. Above his bunk the shelves were stocked like a mini-pharmacy with multi-hued bottles of tinctures and tonics, the tools of his short-lived trade.

Beside Wilson's bunk at the end of the hut was a crude door through which Herbert Ponting, Scott's photographer, would disappear into his darkroom. Broken glass plates lay on the floor, the benches heaped in disarray. On the other side of the darkroom was the scientific laboratory of the Canadian physicist, Charles Wright. In the middle of the room opposite the Tenements was a long table about which the men of the wardroom gathered each evening. A warming stove sat at one end and just behind it at one time there had been a pianola on which Cherry-Garrard and Debenham entertained the men.

As I moved toward the door with my flashlight, the shadows scuttling back toward their haunts in the corners, I could not help but turn, feeling that someone was watching me. I held my breath waiting for a declaration — none came. Closing the door gently, I walked reflectively back to our hut, warm and vibrant with activity.

Entering, I interrupted a lively discussion of our impending excursion up Mount Erebus, an active volcano, at 12,448 feet. Roger, who had been driving us for days to prepare for our climb, was ready to leave and was angry that no one else was. When I supported the argument for another day's delay, he snapped at me.

"Look Gareth," he said, "you're down here to prepare for the Pole. There's more to this expedition than radio masts and generators."

Roger was right, but I found it difficult to balance my obligations to sponsors with my preparations for the Pole. Because of my preoccupation, my relationship with Roger deteriorated the closer we moved toward the winter we were all dreading. Annoyed at having been rejected by the group, he wrote in his journal, "I hope that the events of today and this evening will repair my motivation and strength in order that I will be able to forgive past hurts and ridiculous self induced burden of hurt pride and self pity."

Two days later, on March 10, with a favourable weather report from Scott Base, we found ourselves lined up outside the hut posing for photographs, ready to climb. We struck off in a northeasterly direction toward Williams Cliff, our first day's goal, ten miles up the wind-swept slope of Mount Erebus. Our skis slipped and shied on solid blue ice and where small pockets of snow had gathered in low spots protected from the full force of the wind, we encountered wind-scoured snow slab with sastrugi. It was my first real introduction to these wind ripples, much like wave patterns on a sandy shore. Sometimes they were 12 inches high, and our ski tips constantly snagged them which on more than one occasion catapulted me into a cursing heap. I envied Mike and Roger their skiing ability.

Roger moved strongly up the slope on skis. Mike, right behind him, kept up for the most part, and I was next with Robert and John following slowly on crampons. Looking back I could see Robert's lopsided pack towering above his bowed head as he laboured up the steep slope. He would never have admitted it, but he was having a tough time. He was not as exhausted as John, however, who was clearly out of his element.

At 7:30 p.m. Roger reached Williams Cliff and found a sheltered spot on a snowy ledge close against a fall of rock where he pitched his small Limpet tent. All of us eventually arrived to join him. After a meal of soup, noodles, hot chocolate, biscuits, butter and tea, Robert and John retired to the tent at Roger's invitation while the rest of us bivouacked in our bags under the stars.

I slept soundly, waking at 7:30 to prepare breakfast from my bag. At 9:30 we departed for the snow bowl on a ridge above the Three Sisters, three small volcanic cones issuing from the side of the main slope above Williams Cliff. Roger maintained his position in the lead for the whole day, Mike was second and I fluctuated between third and last as I dropped back occasionally to check on John who was having difficulty with the altitude and energy required for the uphill work. Toward the end of the day I left John and pushed on up past Mike to meet Roger at the bowl. He was cold, having been there for some time.

"I don't think John's capable of doing this trip," I said hesitantly, unsure of Roger's reaction.

"I've noticed," Roger replied.

"I've been checking on him all day," I said. "I don't think he's going much farther. Maybe we should turn back."

"Yes, as much as I hate to quit, we're just not ready," Roger said as he disappeared down the slope to help John with his pack.

That night both Robert and I slept in a small bivy tent while Mike, John and Roger occupied the Limpet. Although Roger had found the same tent crowded with three on Mount McKinley, his companions then were bigger men than either Mike or John. As we zipped the tent flap closed, the wind, at 5,500 feet, began to pick up. In Roger's tent, a moment of hilarity at John's expense broke the sombre mood.

"So, John, have you ever done anything like this before?" Roger asked amusedly from deep within his bag.

John, somewhat distressed by the wind which was almost lifting the little tent from the side of the steep slope, answered calmly nevertheless, "My parents took me camping in Cornwall once."

Recognizing the absurdity, all three immediately burst into laughter.

By morning the wind had increased to Force 5 with zero visibility. On the descent we quickly became disoriented in the cloud and swirling snow and after several discussions about the correct direction Roger took charge. Breaking out his compass he had us rope up before leading off in a completely different direction. Our awkward feet found every rock, slick patch of ice and sastrugi as we stumbled blindly down the slope. When visibility finally improved we found ourselves near Williams Cliff. We were surprised at how far out we had been and realized the danger of navigating without a compass in white-out conditions. Roger and Mike then put on their skis and promptly set off down the glacier. Robert, John and I decided to follow slowly on crampons. The surface of solid blue ice was heavily crevassed, but covering all the gaps were obvious lids of fragile snow, or so I thought.

Almost immediately, John screamed ahead to me, "Gareth! Stop! Robert's down a crevasse."

Dropping my pack I raced back to find John assisting Robert out of a two-foot-wide fissure. Thereafter Robert and John followed closely behind me as I picked my way carefully over the fractured surface. At 9:00 p.m. we arrived back in the warm hut — Roger and Mike had beaten us by an hour and a half.

Later that evening we assessed our first excursion. It was a small but important victory, one that we hoped to repeat in a few days' time when Roger, Mike and I — Robert and John elected to remain at the hut — would attempt to ski over the three summits of Ross Island: Mount Erebus, Mount Terra Nova and Mount Terror.

While we prepared, a gale raged outside. Snow drifted over our food depots as we had predicted and the wind created a sizeable wind scoop on the hut's windward side. By 10:00 each evening the sky was coal black, every day consuming a few more minutes of precious daylight. Within a few weeks we would be totally dependent upon artificial light.

It seemed that I had hardly cleaned up from our Erebus trip when Roger indicated that he was ready to depart. Any delay angered him, which in turn angered me, and did little to add harmony to our confined community. On March 15 I spilled all to my diary, "Am finding increasingly difficult every day to tolerate Roger — I hope it doesn't show."

Roger, on the same date, recorded in his diary, "I spent the whole day in low spirits initiated by two little conflicts with Woody, whom I find at times so difficult to talk with and grossly without imagination."

On March 17, to ease the tension in the hut, Robert cooked a special meal to commemorate Captain Oates' death. Robert was a devoted student of Antarctic history and was forever regaling us with tidbits and tales of historic expeditions. Although I was enthralled, I was at the same time concerned about his preoccupation with the past and his apparent reluctance to deal with the present. Particularly worrying was his decision not to accompany Roger, Mike and me on our next journey. He had much to learn before the polar journey.

Three days later we reached the summit plateau of Mount Erebus where a row of icy fumaroles rose vertically to several feet above my head, steam puffing from their vented tops. We moved between them and toward the active crater. The altitude was draining, causing us to stop every few yards to restore oxygen to our heaving lungs. Reaching the summit, we peered down from the ice-rimmed edge, but could see nothing of the lava-hot crater lost in the murk.

From this altitude the view was spectacular. Far beyond I could clearly make out White Island and Minna Bluff set in the white expanse of the Ross Ice Shelf. The frozen sea's vastness was intimidating and I was immediately apprehensive about sledging across it on our way to the Pole.

Twelve days later we arrived home after having covered 130 miles. We had succeeded in traversing the three summits and then descended to Cape Crozier before returning along the southern coastline to Cape Evans. It was a significant journey, and while I had suffered from badly blistered feet, I felt exhilarated and very satisfied with our accomplishment. Scott Base had recorded -35°C at sea level, and estimated the temperature on the summit of Mount Erebus to be -50°C. Mike's fingertips had already begun to turn black from frostbite while Roger, ever the "hard man," looked after himself and seemed to take the whole journey in stride.

Gareth and Mike at the crater on the summit of Mount Erebus. (COURTESY OF ROGER MEAR)

Our travels also took us back and forth to both McMurdo Station and Scott Base where we struck up many friendships. Those employees who were permitted to travel visited us in return. The frenzied activity at these bases was in direct contrast to the modest pace of our little operation and we were awed by it. Despite our size, however, the challenges we faced were many and frequent. But the greatest had yet to test us — the long polar night.

It was now dark at six each evening, but a little after five the most amazing sunsets emblazoned the northern horizon. North Bay was now almost totally fast with ice which caught and drew the sun's reflection right up to the door of the hut. For the next few days we worked cheerfully together and at dinner on April 7, Roger remarked, "Isn't it nice that we all get along so well."

His comment was greeted with awkward silence. Later that night, while I was in bed, I overheard Roger and Mike talking downstairs.

"I found it remarkable that there was no comment to my observation that we all get along so well," Roger said.

Mike answered gently, "Perhaps they didn't hear."

"We don't have much fun here, do we?" Roger said, ignoring Mike's response. "I certainly hope it changes this winter."

On June 22 we celebrated midwinter day which was our secular Christmas. The day began with Robert and John bringing the rest of us breakfast in bed, and finished with the meal to end all meals. Our

Mike preparing dinner on the Esse stove. (PHOTO BY GARETH WOOD)

40

The celebratory midwinter dinner, on June 22. (PHOTO BY GARETH WOOD)

living area was draped with the flags of our sponsors, balloons and crepe paper, much as Scott's hut had been decorated for his midwinter celebration. Mike prepared a pork roll, roast potatoes, peas and beans, followed by brandy butter, mince pies and Christmas pudding, and washed down with an assortment of alcoholic beverages. We hoisted our glasses to each other in a rare display of friendship. After dinner we watched a video of the play, "Terra Nova," dramatizing Scott's last epic journey. It was ironic to be watching it on the very spot where it had happened.

CHAPTER FOUR

WORST JOURNEY

A s THE POLAR dark drifted over us, displacing our light-born habits and blurring all sense of time until mornings, after-noons and evenings became one interminable night, our thoughts turned toward one of the most arduous treks in the history of Antarctic exploration, the winter journey to Cape Crozier in 1911 by Dr. Bill Wilson, H.R. "Birdie" Bowers and Apsley Cherry-Garrard. Here was a journey that even in the stygian black and crystal frost of winter begged to be repeated. That we would be the first party to make this epic winter trip since the three men made their horrific "Worst Journey" added even more fuel to our resolve.

The trek, which we had planned in London, would not only be a repeat of what Cherry-Garrard called "the weirdest bird's-nesting expedition that has ever been or ever will be,"[1] but would also serve as a reliable long-term trial of our equipment, especially our sledges, which we had yet to field test for any extended period. Roger was the driving force behind our organizing for the journey and although I was anxious to participate I was again slow to commit myself due to a number of unfinished chores. Roger grew impatient with me while Mike was ready and eager.

Not all of us would take part. John, pleading that he was a photog-rapher, not a mountaineer, and that he really didn't feel up to sledging such a distance, bowed out only days before our departure. This was not as surprising as Robert's insistence that he would remain as well; he said he was saving himself for the Pole. How would he

Bowers, Wilson and Cherry-Garrard leaving on the winter journey to Cape Crozier. (Courtesy of the Royal Geographical Society)

react to the stress of the polar journey with no prior experience, and how would we work together, I wondered. Especially since failure then might spell disaster for us all. I did not like it one bit, but kept my concerns to myself, not wanting to jeopardize my position on the polar team. Ironically, our little party matched, man for man, the historic "bird's-nesting" expedition of decades earlier. I was happy with the historic parallel, but fervently hoped that this would be the only facet of that hellish expedition we would duplicate.

The object of the original Crozier winter journey was to obtain Emperor penguin eggs for study of the embryos. There was scientific speculation that the embryos might harbour vestiges of reptilian teeth or scales, and in fact represent the link between reptiles and birds. The bird's tendency to breed in the dead of night and in one of the harshest climates on earth contributed to this belief. Though Wilson had visited the site in 1902 as a member of Scott's *Discovery* Expedition and again on January 3, 1911, he did not obtain the much-coveted eggs. Those visits were made well before breeding season.

June 28 — We had planned to depart on June 27, the same day as the "Worst Journey," but a Force 10 blizzard blasting over the land from the sea-ice made travel impossible. Outside, wind-driven snow had reduced visibility to zero.

The next afternoon, all five of us left Cape Evans. Robert and John were to go only as far as Home Cove, at the southern edge of the Cape, much as Scott's men had assisted Wilson on his day of departure. To Robert's "three cheers Crozier party," we were soon swallowed by the night, a crescent moon barely flooding the cold and uncertain path before us. Ahead lay adventure. My stomach churned with a curious mixture of excitement and dread. Scott, after watching Wilson's Crozier party melt into the winter darkness, wrote, "This winter travel is a new and bold venture, but the right men have gone to attempt it. All good luck go with them!"[2] I sincerely hoped that we too were the right men to repeat that epic journey.

Our loads of approximately 200 pounds, slightly less than the average of 253 pounds per man pulled by Wilson's party, skated easily across the bare sea-ice, swept clean of snow by the recent storm. An iceberg, with cliffs 300 feet high, was locked in the newly-formed ice before us. It looked startlingly brilliant against the coal-black night.

Mike was in the lead, his toiling figure barely visible. Just past the berg our progress was slowed by crusted snow. The difference between the two surfaces was painfully apparent. On the ice the sledges glided with little or no effort; over snow, brute force was required to break them free of the dry powder which, in the bitter cold, assumed the consistency of sand.

The brightest aurora we had seen to date wavered and rippled to a celestial breeze overhead as we manhauled toward our first goal, the Glacier Tongue hut located five miles south of the Cape. At 7:45 p.m. we arrived at the hut after a tough haul to the top of the glacier. A small refuge, about six by 12 feet, it was used by scientists monitoring a network of gauges measuring strain on the Glacier Tongue. A shelf-like bunk, comfortable for two but accommodating three, was attached to one end while a small table and a couple of Primus stoves sat at the other.

I contacted Cape Evans by radio later that night and was told that a Force 8 blow was in progress. Despite the cold and blizzard just beyond the hut's thin walls, the air inside was balmy from our kerosene lamp and stove. That, plus our first sledge ration, soon had us nodding. We had covered only five miles but we were done in.

June 29 — At 3:00 p.m., under overcast skies, we departed the hut. Descending the south side of the Glacier Tongue we were surprised to see open water between us and Hut Point. We avoided this by pulling parallel to the Tongue, making for Hutton Cliff.

This way we would also steer clear of McMurdo Station and Scott Base. If they were to learn of our journey there would be enormous pressure from DSIR and the NSF to abort what in their minds was a very risky, even useless, venture. We could not forget Bob Thompson's reaction to our being in the Antarctic in the first place. If we were to continue, in spite of a negative reaction, it would place McMurdo Station and Scott Base in the position of deciding when and how to mount a search should they believe us overdue. We did not want or need their support; we wanted more than anything to maintain our independence, so important for the South Pole trek. We would tell them of our adventure on our return.

Hauling our sledges along the cliff face, we erected our tent on the sea-ice just yards from shore. Cherry-Garrard had recorded a temperature of -50°F (-45.6°C) exactly 74 years before. Our temperature, at -22°C, was warm by comparison. The cold that day had frozen the heel and sole of one of Wilson's feet as well as Cherry-Garrard's big toes. Our first tent camp went well, the tent becoming quite cosy with heat from the kerosene lantern and stove. The only problem was that the peak became almost tropical, as Roger described it, while the floor remained locked in a deep freeze. I wrote in my diary that night, "Did not eat one Yorkie bar, one package of biscuits, two salami and hot chocolate." It was days before we were hungry enough to eat the whole of our rations.

The following day was expected to be difficult. To cross Hut Point Peninsula, an ascent of about 800 feet, we would probably need to relay the sledges: hard and tedious work. Mike wrote in his diary, "So much for our ten-mile-a-day average."

June 30 — July 1 — Woke at 11:30 a.m. to absolutely no moon. We decided to wait and didn't actually depart until 7:00 p.m. when visibility improved. For us, as well as the original Crozier party, the convention of day and night had become nothing more than a distant, treasured memory. The pale light of a pearly moon cast its eerie spell over the frigid terrain as we pulled away. Although the temperature had sunk to -28°C, I was sweating profusely, dressed as I was in Lifa longjohns, two Lifa turtleneck vests, a Helly Hansen pile suit and Gore-Tex windproofs, the sweat freezing between my pile suit and the windproofs. Our sweat did not freeze right against our bodies, as had been the case for Wilson's party, due to the wicking properties of modern outdoor clothing.

Moving along the edge of the sea-ice to find an easy climb up Descent Slopes (its name comes from being the only route to Cape Evans once the sea-ice leaves), we found our immediate problem was to cross a large tidal crack between us and the ice edge at the foot of the slope. Hunting around, we soon found where the crack narrowed to two feet and crossing at that point, we lifted each of our awkward sledges over the lip of ice at the base of the incline. Then, with Roger pushing and Mike and me pulling, we fought our way up the rise. Our progress was frustrated by two wide crevasses which we discovered were covered by good snow bridges.

Once we were past the second crevasse we resumed solo pulling. Straining in my harness, I found the 200-pound burden tethered to my heaving body threatened to pull me backward down the slope. I felt pathetic and not much more significant than an ant worrying a piece of picnic refuse across a lawn. At 10:15 p.m. we reached the summit, enclosed in cloud. Mike aired his thoughts.

"You know," he said reflectively, "today was sure more enjoyable for all the work and difficulties than yesterday. That was boring."

"Yes, I agree," I replied.

"And it's curious," he continued, "I was just thinking whether anyone back home could possibly imagine the position we're in. It seems a very strange exploit when one considers the peace of Wimbledon on a sunny summer morning."

Once we were over the crest, our sledges nudged us gently forward down the slope. Roger chose skis while Mike and I remained on crampons. Making camp at the foot of the Peninsula on the edge of Windless Bight just southwest of Sultan's Rock at 4:30 a.m., we finally closed our eyes. My hips, badly chafed from the harness, were sore, but fatigue overcame this minor inconvenience.

Leaving camp at 5:30 p.m. that day on skis, we could see the lights of Scott Base, 15 miles away — a tiny glimmer of warmth in this land of permanent ice and cold. The wind-crusted surface, pitted with scattered pockets of sandy snow, made hauling desperately hard. Lagging far behind the others, I began to question my strength — Roger and Mike had to assist me twice. Was I weak or had I the most difficult sledge?

Mike appeared to be having difficulty as well, but not as much as I was. Although we were both pulling sledges with flat bottoms, mine was burdened with about 50 pounds more than Mike's but a little less than Roger's. Four and a half miles later we hit flags marking the vehicle route from Scott Base to the Windless Bight seismographic hut. I was tired and cold, and the -40°C temperature had sapped what remained of my failing strength.

"We've got to get the tent up right now," Mike said urgently, the cold and exhaustion telling in his voice. "It's too cold to continue.

We're moving so slowly we're going to do ourselves harm. I can already feel my hands and feet going."

"I agree," I said quickly.

Moving feverishly to erect the tent, we had only partly unpacked our gear when our freezing hands and feet forced us into the empty tent with just the stove and kerosene lamp. We had stopped just in time to save our feet from frostbite — we found that our double layer of socks had frozen together.

July 2 — We were away by 9:00 p.m., the temperature an icy -44°C. We switched sledges so that I pulled the Gaybo, which Roger had had designed especially for the expedition after a sledge used by Robert Peroni on his Greenland Expedition. Although it was the heaviest of all, weighing 42 pounds empty, with a Kevlar body, twin-hull design and solid teflon runners, we believed it would still pull more easily than the others. Roger pulled the fibreglass sledge, which was manufactured in the U.S. It weighed only 21 pounds empty but had a flat bottom and was difficult to pull. Mike took over the Ministry of Defence (MOD) sledge, which had brass over wood runners and was also stubborn. After hauling the fibreglass sledge only five feet, Roger declared that pulling it was horrendous, and Mike could barely move his. I had no problem, and moved on ahead — we were all pleased that the Gaybo, as hoped, was proving to be the most efficient. Only one mile later I spotted the hut. Leaving my sledge there, I returned to assist Roger. The time was 10:15 p.m.

Electing to delay our progress for a couple of hours to eat a good meal and dry our damp clothing, we were soon sweltering in a luxurious 15°C. Sleeping bags and bits and pieces of our gear hung from every conceivable post and pin. Four hours later we were still drying and repairing gear and decided to crawl into our sleeping bags for a few hours.

July 3 — 6 — We poked our heads out at 6:00 a.m. ready to depart, but a light snow squall buffeting the hut from the northeast had reduced visibility to almost zero. We decided to stay put. Setting our alarms for 1:00 p.m., we burrowed back into our warm, dry bags. At midday Roger topped up the stove and checked the weather. The wind was still too strong to permit departure.

The next day, which began at 8:30 in the evening, saw Mike accidentally upsetting a pot of snow onto my sleeping bag before pouring a package of dry oats onto the floor and then knocking over a pot of oats soaking in water. Roger, still in his bag, dissolved into laughter, one of the few light moments we all shared on the journey.

At 9:00 p.m. I made radio contact with Cape Evans on the Hughes Aircraft high-frequency radio using a frequency provided to us by the British army.

"Cape Evans, Cape Evans, Crozier party, Crozier party, do you read? Over."

"Crozier party, Cape Evans, loud and clear. Where are you? Over." Robert's staticky response was almost immediate. It was reassuring to know that he was adhering to our radio schedule.

"Cape Evans, we're at Windless Bight hut," I replied. "Do you have a met report for us? Over." I wasn't exactly sure how bad the blow was elsewhere. In the lee of Hut Point Peninsula, our position was relatively calm in comparison to what was happening at Cape Evans.

"Crozier party, Force 12 blow in progress. Force 12 blow. Scott Base as well. Over."

After discussing the severity of the weather, Robert suggested that if the storm were to force us back to base he would be prepared to accompany us on a second try. Roger was quick to tell him that we were not returning.

Weather delays were not only frustrating our patience but using up our food and fuel reserves as well. The longer we stayed, the shorter became our margin of safety. Our concerns were only partly alleviated by the use of some stale biscuits and powdered soup we found in the back of the seismographic hut; it was American property, but out of necessity we felt that we had no choice if our own supplies were to last. We knew that we would have some explaining to do upon our return for it would be obvious that someone had been staying at the hut, but until then we were reluctant to broadcast our whereabouts. I wrote in my diary that night, "We cannot say anything to Scott or McMurdo because of the political situation — they would then be on the alert as a party was in the field in the middle of the Antarctic winter." Knowing that the hut would not be visited until after our return, we eventually elected to leave a note, although no fuss was ever made: the Americans questioned our sanity in eating supplies that had probably been sitting on the shelf for years.

At 8:00 p.m. on July 6 we finally left the hut under partly clear skies, the snow squeaking underfoot in the crisp, dry air. For the first couple of hours we walked blind, the moon in the southwest glowing dully from behind a band of stratus. Sprinkling the heavens above us, however, millions of stars, cold and distant, sparkled over our little earthbound party as we trudged away from the safety of the hut, the bobbing circles of our headtorches advertising our advance across the sea-ice. Our best day yet, we travelled seven hours, pulling 8.1 miles. The storms of previous days had covered the surface with a fine deposit of loose powder snow, over which our sledges passed easily. We stopped at 3:00 a.m. and I wrote "Balmy" in my diary. It was -36°C.

Wilson's sparse journal, devoid of feeling, although he must have been suffering, matter-of-factly records the order of their activity for July 7. Still relaying sledges because of poor surface conditions, he and his party were forced to a stop in thick fog. The minimum recorded temperature the previous night was -75.8°F (-59.9°C). They had advanced only 1.67 miles that day and 1.5 the day before. Wilson, extremely anxious, having promised Scott that he would bring the party back unharmed — Scott was depending upon Wilson to accompany him to the Pole — repeatedly apologized for the conditions, never having dreamt the weather would be so bad.

July 9 — 10 — At 12:30 a.m. we left camp. Ahead, Roger pointed through the semi-darkness to a featureless black hump in the distance.

"That's Igloo Spur way over there," he said, squinting into the gloom.

Between us and Igloo Spur, however, there was still a good day's march. Ahead, in the faint light of my headtorch, a moonscape of sastrugi, rocks and ice stretched uninvitingly before us; a frozen, lifeless hell. Above, almost to compensate for the brutal landscape around us, the southern aurora shimmered and pulsed.

Our camp routine was now taking about four hours. I wrote about it that night, "From stopping, one hour to get inside the tent, start the initial brushing of ice from our clothing and open the last flask of hot soup. Two hours to complete the ice sweep, undress and get the stove going. Three hours for cooking, eating and putting stove away." And by the end of the fourth hour our eyes would be closed to the monotony and the cold.

We left camp at 1:45 a.m. on July 10, our target Igloo Spur, still a faint silhouette in the inky darkness. Headtorches lit, we paralleled the demarcation zone between Ross Island and the Great Ice Barrier pressure ice. Like Wilson's party, we traversed a fairly clear corridor between crevassed land-ice crowding Mount Terror's slopes on our left and heavily crevassed pressure ridges on our right. The two-dimensional contours of Mount Terror and surrounding hills stood darkly beside us. Attaining our goal at 6:15 a.m., after having covered only 6.5 miles, we parked our sledges and hiked down to what was left of the stone hut, known as "the stone igloo," that Wilson's party had erected in 1911. It was almost indistinguishable from the rest of the rock-scattered terrain, which Wilson had christened Oriana Ridge.

A bronze sign, explaining the significance of the site in English, Spanish, Russian and French and asking for the site's protection in the name of the Antarctic Treaty, was posted to one side. Surveying the wreckage in the night was a moving experience. Inside its collapsed walls we found a small wooden packing crate, one sock and a penguin skin, all that remained of the epic journey. I was elated that I was visiting the site under circumstances somewhat similar to those Wilson's brave crew experienced, and at the same time disappointed that time was slowly erasing all physical evidence of their historic trek. This was the hut that Wilson, Bowers and Cherry-Garrard had started to build on July 16, 1911. Seventy-four years ago almost to the day, they had gathered these rocks to fashion the walls of the igloo which was to be roofed with heavy canvas covered by blocks of ice.

On July 22, installed in their new stone dwelling, their tent erected in its lee, they were blasted by Force 9 to 10 gusts and heavily drifting snow. When next Bowers peered anxiously through the door of the hut, the tent was gone, sucked upwards to join the gale raging overhead. Miraculously, their gear, which had been lying on the tent floor, was virtually intact. They quickly retrieved what remained.

During the morning of the following day, July 23, which Wilson recorded as one of the strangest birthdays he had ever experienced, the wind continued to shriek overhead except for brief lulls between violent gusts. These gusts were so powerful that they slowly removed the heavy blocks of ice from the roof, and the canvas began to flap wildly up and down. Its demise was inevitable. Then, into the igloo sifted fine moraine dust, coating everything coal-soot black. Efforts to stop up the holes proved useless. The banging of the canvas grew louder until, as Cherry-Garrard wrote, "The top of the door opened in little slits and that green Willesden canvas flapped into hundreds of little fragments in fewer seconds than it takes to read this. The uproar of it all was indescribable. Even above the savage thunder of that great wind on the mountain came the lash of the canvas as it was whipped to little tiny strips. The highest rocks which we had built into our walls fell upon us, and a sheet of drift came in.

"Birdie dived for his sleeping-bag and eventually got in, together with a terrible lot of drift. Bill also — but he was better off: I was already half into mine and all right, so I turned to help Bill. 'Get into your own,' he shouted, and when I continued to try and help him, he leaned over until his mouth was against my ear. '*Please*, Cherry,' he said, and his voice was terribly anxious. I know he felt responsible: feared it was he who had brought us to this ghastly end."[3]

The indomitable Bowers endeavoured to cheer the little party lying in their snow-drifted bags under the tempest raging overhead. At times they sang, but mostly they thought. They must have known that without shelter their fate was sealed.

Cherry-Garrard lamented, "Now we had no tent, one tin of oil left out of six, and only part of our cooker. When we were lucky and not too cold we could almost wring water from our clothes, and directly we got out of our sleeping-bags we were frozen into solid sheets of armoured ice. In cold temperatures with all the advantages of a tent over our heads we were already taking more than an hour of fierce struggling and cramp to get into our sleeping-bags — so frozen were they and so long did it take us to thaw our way in. No! Without the tent we were dead men."[4]

When the wind abated the next day, they began to search for the tent that had been taken from them at the height of the storm. They were hardly hopeful, but precious little time elapsed before Wilson and Cherry-Garrard heard Bowers' triumphant shout. Slipping and sliding down the slope to join him, they came upon him with the tent. As Cherry-Garrard wrote, "Our lives had been taken away and given back to us. We were so thankful we said nothing."[5]

In the awful silence of that barren windswept hummock my mind replayed those dramatic events. I pictured the relief flooding their grimy faces when they discovered their tent near where I now stood: total despair suddenly replaced by unbridled hope and joy.

We were now anxious to depart for the Cape and, after erecting our tent, prepared our evening meal prior to continuing on. We expected to make the small hut, located at Cape Crozier and used by scientists only during the summer, late that afternoon. We had already located it during our spring traverse of the island's summits and expected no difficulty in finding it again. Most of our supplies, including our tent, were to be left on the Gaybo and fibreglass sledges parked near the stone igloo. They were tied together, over-turned and tethered to three ice screws and a snow stake, and we were confident that even the worst of winds could not budge them.

Loading the MOD with our Hughes radio and enough food and fuel for a week, we stuffed our backpacks with sleeping bags and personal gear. At 2:00 p.m. we stepped into our own harnesses, all three of which were attached to the single sledge, and prepared to drag its light, 120-pound weight across the ice- and rock-scattered terrain ahead.

This was one of the few occasions since Cape Evans that we had been outside at midday and although it was only three weeks past midwinter, the sky was already beginning to brighten. Mount Terror, whose silhouette had been our constant companion for the past few days, was now clearly visible beside us. The light, however, was short-lived and soon the moonless sky blackened to pitch. With headtorches burning hazy tunnels through the darkness, and bundled against -30°C and the searing touch of a light wind, we started off. Roger took the middle, an unfortunate mistake as he was sandwiched between Mike on the right and me on the left. He immediately felt the constraints of this self-imposed bondage, his hair-trigger temper touchy at the sudden loss of freedom.

"We're too far right," Roger snapped. "We're heading for The Knoll. Don't you know where you're going?"

We were on a sidehill and I kept slipping down into Roger's path, continually forcing us to the right.

"You lead then," Mike said, slightly exasperated.

"No! Just tell me which way you want me to go," Roger said impatiently.

Summoning all my strength to contain my emotion, I pointed ahead in the general direction of the hut. A few minutes later we bumped again. This time a shouting match ensued. I yelled at Roger to cut the sarcasm and be more constructive in his criticism of others. Roger, in turn, made it clear that I was not living up to the high standard of performance he expected. Verging on tears, I wondered how two people, at one time the best of companions, could have allowed their friendship to deteriorate to such an extent. Perhaps it was the price one had to pay for undertaking such a demanding trek. I wondered if the price was too high.

Adding to our frustration, the MOD, after striking a large rock, suffered a torn sledge cover. We continued to pull it, and did not notice the damage until about ten minutes later. By then, three of our four gallon cans of fuel had disappeared through the rent side, a serious loss if they were not recovered. The load had also shifted and broken oatmeal packages littered the floor of the sledge.

Roger looked at it angrily. "The centre of gravity's too high. No wonder it tipped," he said.

"We packed the fuel cans upright to prevent spillage," I offered.

Roger, ignoring me, looked at Mike as if it were all his fault.

"Woody and I'll go back and look for the fuel while you clean this up," he ordered.

Within 20 yards I found a dented can of kerosene and within another 20 yards the other two, one leaking. The weather, meanwhile, had begun to deteriorate, causing us some worry. Although we had only seven miles to cover, the risk of travelling without a tent was becoming greater by the minute. To bivouac in such conditions would be to invite disaster.

After repacking the sledge to lower its centre of gravity, we continued in our bumbling fashion, none of us pulling, it seemed, in the same direction. As we moved toward where we imagined the hut to be, visibility worsened, heightening our anxiety. About 4:00 p.m. our situation appeared critical. Navigation, now reduced to a simple compass and a large-scale map, was of little help.

"We should drop down to the coast and walk around the Cape until we find the hut," Roger shouted, his voice barely audible above the screaming wind.

"That'll take hours. I know we're close," I yelled back.

"Look, we don't even know which way the hut is or where we are. Do you want to spend a night out in this?" Roger asked loudly.

"Let's give it a few more minutes," I implored, pragmatism yielding to intuition.

Roger, Mike (background) and Gareth hauling a sledge at Cape Crozier.
(Footsteps of Scott Collection)

Continuing, fearful but hopeful that we must be near our goal, I at last recognized a familiar ridge-line, and there on the other side lay the hut. We were jubilant with relief. Although it was boarded up, we entered with a minimum of difficulty. Inside, there were two bunk beds and a small cooking area containing a few pots, dishes and an assortment of cutlery.

Dinner, cooked by Mike, was followed by a tin of peaches that Robert had stuffed into our food box (Cherry-Garrard had dreamt of just such a treat on the "Worst Journey") and a drink of scotch to celebrate our safe arrival.

Deciding to relax, we all read and updated our diaries by candle-light until early the following morning. The wind, moaning softly outside the hut's thin walls, was losing its strength as my eyes closed. The next day, July 11, we did nothing but wallow in a trough of our own fatigue.

July 12 — Rising at 9:00 a.m. to re-establish a regular day/night schedule, we planned our first excursion in search of the Emperor penguins Wilson had so diligently pursued so many years before. The temperature upon departure was somewhere in the low -20s°C, the sky clear and brightening as we dropped down to the sea-ice over fields of ice, snow and volcanic rubble. With a light wind plucking at our clothing, we carried on through an abandoned Adelie penguin rookery to arrive at the *Discovery* Post.

Leaning precariously from a rough pile of stones, it was note-worthy only for its historic value; it had survived remarkably well in view of what it had endured for nearly eight decades. The post had been erected in 1903 by Scott's *Discovery* Expedition; a cylinder once attached to it advised the relief ship *Morning* that Cape Crozier was unsuitable for winter quarters and that McMurdo Sound had been chosen instead. While we examined the post I reflected on Scott's comment about the improbability of anyone ever discovering it.

July 13 (Friday) — 15 — As Mike observed in his diary, "Not an auspicious day for a risky venture!" Overcast skies, light snow and the belief that a gale was raging on the sea-ice below was enough to persuade us to stay put.

The following morning we left the hut under clear skies, a hint of daylight teasing the skyline to the north. The sea-ice appeared black and brooding below us. Arriving at the shore at roughly the same point as on the 12th, we walked south for approximately 1.5 miles between the Barrier's ragged ice cliffs on our left and Ross Island's basaltic ramparts on our right.

Our descent to the ice was easy in comparison to Wilson's. Frustrated by the drop from the cliff tops to the ice a hundred feet below, Wilson, Bowers and Cherry-Garrard groped their uncertain way between swells of the first and second pressure ridges curling 50 to 60 feet above their heads. A cul-de-sac blocked their path close to sea level and "On all sides rose great walls of battered ice with steep snow-slopes in the middle, where we slithered about and blundered into crevasses."[6] And then, caught in an impossible position that could only be solved by retreat, they heard the cries of the Emperors. "Their cries came to us from the sea-ice we could not see, but which must have been a chaotic quarter of a mile away. They came echoing back from the cliffs, as we stood helpless and tantalized."[7]

They did not reach their goal until the following day when, struggling over much of the same ground, they discovered a tunnel through the tangled pressure ice that emerged above the colony. Where in 1902 Wilson had counted 2,000 birds, in 1911 stood a paltry 100. What had happened to them all was a mystery. The raucous indignation of the Emperors, disturbed by the intrusion, rang against the towering ice cliffs as Wilson stared, fascinated, at the male birds shuffling resolutely about him.

Between each pair of large black feet rested an egg. It was winter and the temperature within that very month had plummeted to -75°F (-59.4°C). In cold that would kill most creatures, the Emperor was incubating its offspring to ensure the chicks were old enough to fend for themselves the following winter. This job of egg sitting is strictly a male occupation. The female wanders back to the sea edge where she continues to forage for food.

While gathering eggs, the object of their mission, Wilson was astonished to find that many of them were in fact lumps of dirty ice — males without real eggs cradled these cold surrogates as lovingly as eggs. The penguins knew the difference, however, for immediately a real egg was abandoned by a disgruntled male, another penguin would quickly discard his ice lump in favour of the egg.

With the precious eggs wrapped in mitts hung about their necks on lampwick lanyards, and the blubber-fat skins of three birds they had killed strapped to their backs, the trio struggled back up the cliff on ropes and made their silent way in darkness toward their primitive stone dwelling. Upon arrival they found that only three eggs had survived the day's march and those were cracked from being frozen. They hoped that what was left would be sufficient for the critical London examination of the embryos. Protected in their stone igloo, with the oily black smoke of the rendering penguin fat curling off their blubber stove, and the flame's orange tongue glowing brightly against their greasy faces, they must have imagined that science would advance a step or two because of their efforts.

On the edge of the Great Ice Barrier, we searched the narrow, icy fjords between the great ridges of pressure ice. At the entrance to the first of these inlets we were attracted to a dark smudge against the Barrier cliffs. Trumpeting their alarm, about 30 Emperors, wary of our sudden appearance, milled about nervously at our approach. Although in adult plumage, they had no eggs. I wondered if they were remnants of the colony Wilson had visited so many years ago.

Determined, we continued to search for signs of a large breeding colony. Walking down one long inlet for about an hour, we found not a hint of their presence, surmising that the colony must have either shifted down the coast or disappeared. I hoped the former.

Mike was disappointed. He felt a fraternal kinship with Wilson — both were doctors by profession — and wanted to see for himself the egg-sitting Emperors that Wilson had gone through hell to find. He was so intent that we decided to renew our efforts the next day despite Roger's reluctance.

The following morning the three of us again found ourselves at *Discovery* Post preparing to step upon the ice, probably for the last time this trip. At Mike's suggestion that we begin where we left off the previous day, Roger voiced a concern.

Mike and Emperor penguins, Cape Crozier. (COURTESY OF ROGER MEAR)

"You're crazy. Don't you recognize the risk? What if we're out there and the weather closes in?"

"Roger," I said, "don't come. Mike and I won't be long."

I had assessed the risks and argued in support of Mike's quest. Roger was clearly as angry with me as I had been with him several days earlier.

"Bloody hell, you're both incredible," Roger spat as he stormed ahead across the sea-ice.

Retracing our steps of the previous day, the three of us managed to locate another small group of about 30 birds, but none with eggs. Finding ourselves two miles from the hut, with the weather beginning to deteriorate, we turned back immediately, Roger walking on ahead. Mike confided to me that with Roger's attitude he did not hold out much hope for a pleasant Pole trip. I wondered if he was angling for a position on the Pole team himself.

July 19 — Our day of departure commenced at 6:30 a.m. I was sorry to leave Cape Crozier as it was so much more interesting than Cape Evans. The landscape was more varied and the Barrier offered adventure as did solving the mystery of the missing Emperors, and the northern horizon, which we so reverently watched for the returning sun, was unobstructed. At Cape Evans, the Barne Glacier would block our view of this spectacular event. In another respect I was anxious to return to base. Preparations for the Pole would completely fill the remaining two months. I had clothing and equipment to modify, letters to write and photographs to take. I also wanted to update my celestial navigation skills, study maps and re-read Scott's and Shackleton's diaries, especially those sections describing wind and snow conditions. Shadowing my thoughts, however, was Roger's mood — he seemed depressed.

Robert was another worry. I suspected that he was uneasy about how he would perform physically on the Pole trek which, combined with his inexperience, might be unhealthy for the rest of us. He was out to prove something. I hoped it would not be at the expense of our lives.

Well rested, fed, dry and comfortable (unlike the original Crozier party where Cherry-Garrard lamented, "The horrors of that return journey are blurred to my memory and I know they were blurred to my body at the time"[8]), we left the Cape Crozier hut at 10:55 a.m., the flush of a new day slowly spreading across the northern horizon. For weeks we had been independent of the sun, living contentedly within the sheltered coronas of our headtorches, the elastic shadows of the real world stretching and shrinking just beyond the circles of our experience. Now that the sun was returning we were suddenly hungry for it, finding our lives once again governed by its influence.

Hauling east of our inbound track, thus bypassing the undulating terrain so characteristic of the area, we arrived at Igloo Spur after having travelled only two hours and 15 minutes, exactly half our inbound time. Upon reaching the Gaybo and the fibreglass sledge, which had not shifted since we parked them several days earlier, we redistributed our remaining supplies and began our return journey to Cape Evans.

July 20 — The temperature recorded overnight by Scott Base was -54°C. Rising at 5:30 a.m., we moved cautiously in the bitter cold which endangered our hands with each exposure. The day's travel was exhausting, the sledges often grinding to a gritty halt against rafts of wind-crusted sastrugi or fields of sand-like snow. Our mile-an-hour average too slow to keep us warm, we donned our down jackets and salopettes for the first time. We were soon sweltering, but without them we were numb. My beard was frozen to my balaclava, making any adjustment excruciating, and my eyelashes became so encrusted with ice that I could hardly see. I had to stop and thaw them periodically.

We stopped for hot soup, a piece of salami, biscuits and chocolate every two and a half hours, and as fast as the warmth seeped into our bodies it was greedily sucked away by the cold. These breaks were not pleasurable; standing in harness and shivering for five or more minutes while we renewed our reserves was often more painful than progress itself.

Making camp at 4:00 p.m., after having covered only 5.4 miles, we were close to freezing; Mike complained that he could no longer feel his feet. By 9:30 p.m., in double bags that were only just warm (the temperature was still below -50°C), we had completed our preparations for sleep. I wrote that night, "Frightening sound outside. Great cracking noise in ice. We can even feel the vibrations. Feels like we are about to get swallowed up in a crevasse. It is the Barrier and its way of relieving pressure."

July 21 — Woke at 5:45 a.m. Rising was a delicate operation. Water vapour generated by the lamp and our breath became hoar frost each night, clinging to the tent walls like stalactites. Disturbing this growth meant a sudden ice shower. As well, between the inner and outer sleeping bag there formed a layer of frost. It was important to brush this off as soon as we were out to prevent it from melting and refreezing.

We were away by 10:30 a.m. Ahead, Mount Erebus, a plume steaming from its yawning mouth, brooded darkly against the distant, brightening sky. Daylight, which had been holding the darkness at bay for about four hours, was becoming an increasingly bigger influence on our activities. Under conditions similar to the previous day's, we had covered only 5.8 miles by 5:00 p.m.

At camp that night Mike unpacked the lamp, accidentally shattering its glass chimney and mantle with his foot. Roger wrote of the incident in his diary, "The news was greeted with little comment probably because we all know the problems that the loss of this light would cause." The lamp represented not just our only source of reliable light but an important heat source as well. Fortunately, we had two mantles left and the lamp would function without the chimney if we were careful. In my diary I wrote, "Can we make it last."

July 22 — 23 — I broke the maximum thermometer while warming it over the lamp. Roger thought that its inclination to record the same temperature three days in a row was a technical fault and that warming it would reset its mercury. Scott Base later confirmed our suspicions that the thermometer was faulty. The minimum temperature recorded by Scott Base on July 22 was -50°C while our thermometer recorded -45°C. Covering 6.9 miles in slightly better conditions than before, I found the MOD unusually slow. A quick look at the brass runners revealed why. The rocks of Cape Crozier had scarred the once-smooth surfaces with pits and scrapes, and the runners now served as better brakes than blades.

We found our inbound tracks for part of the day, which reduced our need to rely on the compass. Roger was in a foul mood, castigating Mike and me at our first soup break for getting too far ahead, and there followed a heated exchange between Roger and me about who was pulling the most weight and who should have which sledge.

Working on his diary the next morning, Roger picked up the argument from where it had been dropped the previous day. I suspected that he was baiting me for some dramatic diaristic prose. Minutes later I lost control of my emotions.

"You're rude, selfish, arrogant, ill mannered, unbearably moody and totally inconsiderate of others," I shouted.

"Woody, why do you always keep everything inside you?" he asked calmly. "You never discuss our problems as they come up. You know," he continued, "I don't think the Pole trip is possible with Robert, you and me."

"Right now I can't help but agree," I replied, the heat still in my voice.

"Well, that may not be a problem for much longer. I've been thinking of pulling out," Roger replied.

"Pulling out! Stop kidding us. You've put too much into this to back out now," I countered.

"That may be, but I'm still considering it," he said.

"Look, I've contemplated the same thing, but this is not the time to be making those kind of decisions," I replied, hoping Roger would drop the issue.

Leaving camp late, we made 9.7 miles before grinding to a painful halt at 7:30 p.m. somewhere in the vicinity of the Windless Bight hut. Despite our fatigue and disappointment at not finding the hut, we were strangely talkative. The release of pressure that morning had done us some good.

July 24 — 25 — "Can see the lights of Scott Base very clearly now," I wrote. With a silver moon pendant in the awakening sky and Hut Point Peninsula clearly visible in the half light, we left camp at 10:30 a.m., anticipating that this would be our last day. It would be a long haul: Scott Base was approximately 12 miles away, more than we had yet travelled in a single day with full sledges. It was not to be. Despite Mike's strong lead with the more efficient Gaybo, Roger and I lagged weakly behind. Upon reaching the flagged route to Scott Base, 8.37 miles from camp, we stopped, totally done in.

Roger left camp at 9:10 the following morning, intending to arrive at Scott Base well before us to thaw the movie camera in anticipation of filming our arrival. During his absence my thoughts turned toward our disintegrating relationship. Although it had reached an all-time low, I still had great confidence in his ability and wondered whether I would attempt the Pole without him.

Mike and I left camp at 11:45 a.m., following Roger's tracks for most of the way. Finally, we pulled our sledges to within 400 feet of Scott Base. Our "Worst Journey" was over.

Cherry-Garrard's "Worst Journey" ended on a much more sombre note: "Antarctic exploration is seldom as bad as you imagine, seldom as bad as it sounds. But this journey had beggared our language: no words could express its horror."[9]

Scott's dramatic diary entry records his impressions of that event: "That men should wander forth in the depth of a Polar night to face the most dismal cold and the fiercest gales in darkness is something new; that they should have persisted in this effort in spite of every adversity for five full weeks is heroic. It makes a tale for our generation which I hope may not be lost in the telling."[10]

Many months later, when Bill Wilson and Birdie Bowers lay entombed in the ice of their defeat, a sombre Cherry-Garrard presented his last link to these brave men, the three Emperor penguin eggs, to the South Kensington Natural History Museum in London. They were received with deference by an officious custodian, but the final objective of the Crozier party was as disappointing as the journey had been rewarding. The eggs, passed to Professor Assheton for the critical analysis, lay untouched due to his untimely death. Only later would Professor Cossar Ewart of Edinburgh University, upon dissecting the hard-won prize, conclude, " ... there is no evidence that feather papillae ever develop into scales or that scale papillae ever develop into feathers. ... "[11]

It would be wrong to suggest that the brutal journey had been for nothing — through extreme adversity, with the vitality of the human spirit shining boldly through, the original Crozier party had at least shown that the courage and faith of humanity can indeed be indomitable. What we had accomplished, although difficult, had paled in comparison, but we were proud to have walked beside these great men, to have sampled their hardships and their joys. This I would keep with me always.

CHAPTER FIVE

SPRING

IN ABSOLUTE CONTRAST to the deprivation of the past month, rest and good food filled our next few days as guests of the New Zealanders at Scott Base. But basking in life's little luxuries was hard work, and I was soon pining for the prosaic order of Cape Evans.

On July 31 we departed for the Cape on foot, having made prior arrangements with three Kiwis travelling by Snow Trac, a New Zealand tracked vehicle, to the Glacier Tongue hut to pick us up en route. Although not formally permitted to assist us, many Scott Base personnel had now become friends and occasionally bent the rules. Arriving at the hut, Mike and I and one of the Scott Base crew elected to walk the remaining five miles to Cape Evans. The final stretch was like a breath of fresh air. The weather was spectacular and, unencumbered with packs or sledges, which were to follow later by Snow Trac, we sauntered across the ice in the casual fashion of gentlemen of leisure.

The sun's recent emergence had recharged our energy, and our fears, cultivated during the long polar night, had withered this far from winter's embrace. The air was ripe with a certain sense of renewal, in fact urgency, which was unmistakable.

At base, I spent the next few days repairing lights, radios and antennas that had malfunctioned or collapsed during our absence, welcoming the opportunity to tinker.

Robert spoke at length with Mike regarding Roger's and my rela-tionship on the Cape Crozier trip. Before revealing any hint of his decision to me, he announced privately to Roger and Mike that he had decided I would not continue to be a member of the polar team. Robert was willing to proceed with just Roger or with Roger and Mike, but felt that my relationship with Roger had deteriorated too far for comfort and safety.

Although I had my suspicions, they were not confirmed until Robert invited me to the caravan, a small New Zealand refuge next to Scott's hut, on the pretence of having me take a picture of him at his work.

"I've had a long chat with Mike regarding your relationship with Roger on the trip," he said, "and believe me, I'm not blaming anyone, least of all you. I know how difficult Roger can be, but I'd like you to consider dropping out of the polar party."

I was not fooled by Robert's use of the word "consider." He had already made up his mind and merely wanted my consent to ease his conscience. I was furious and wondered how much weight his decision held. Mike also was confused about whether the decision was final and wrote in his journal, "The situation here is difficult. The question of the Pole & who is to go on the trip, hangs over us like the sword of Damocles."

On the morning of August 8, while we were all gathered around the table in the hut, Robert broached the subject.

"I think it's time to deal with Roger's and Gareth's hostility toward one another and the implications this'll have for the trek, and," he continued, with hardly a pause for breath, "I want to make an announcement. Mike will replace Gareth as the third team member."

John, anticipating a lively discussion, quickly left the table and quietly set up his camera in the corner to begin filming.

"That's interesting," Roger mused, "and on what do you base this decision?"

"I respect what Gareth has done for the expedition," Robert said defensively, "but I think that the friction between you two will be a real problem."

"But Robert, what about our relationship? It's no better," Roger said.

"Maybe, but Mike's a good mediator," Robert replied, "and I know it will work with the three of us."

The argument continued to ricochet back and forth between Robert and Roger. During a break I gestured to Roger to speak in private. We moved upstairs.

"If you feel that you and I can't make it to the Pole together then I'm prepared to withdraw," I said. "No hard feelings, no strings attached. But I won't accept it from Robert. He's our most inexperi-enced person and knows the least of what it's like out there."

"Do you think our relationship is strong enough to last the 80 days it'll take for the trip?" Roger asked.

"Yes, I do. Since our last discussion on the Crozier trip I've been doing a lot of thinking about what we said. I know we've been pretty close to punching each other out, but we didn't and in an emergency I know I could rely on you and I'm hoping you feel the same about me," I said.

"I don't know at this stage," Roger responded.

"If that's the case I'll withdraw right now," I said.

"I'm not sure that's the right thing to do," Roger replied and then asked, "Do you still want to go?"

Surprised at finding a hint of support, I answered, "Of course, more than ever."

"I'm not in favour of Mike," Roger said, "and even though you and I have some patching up to do, poor relationships don't worry me as much as inexperience. I feel that I could depend on you to perform safely and effectively and be able to take charge of a situa-tion in spite of our personal difficulties."

"Thanks," I said.

"The facts speak for themselves," Roger said, "but now we've got to convince the others. Especially Robert."

As we rejoined the group at the table, Robert, almost immedi-ately, said, "Mike is a confident person. I think he'll fit in with the team better. I believe in my heart of hearts that Gareth is not suitable for the South Pole team and if this's a problem then I'm afraid I'll have to take steps to sort it out. It's going to be difficult, it's going to be painful, but it'll have to be done."

Roger, looking directly at Robert, rebutted. "I feel that Gareth is without a doubt the guy for the job. That gives us the problem of convincing you, but at least we'll leave here knowing that the team is as good as we can make it."

"I don't think that it would be," Robert said. "I'm fairly convinced of that."

"One of the problems, Robert," Roger interrupted, "is that I don't know how you'll fit in with any combination of us three because you've never done any trips with us. You're the most unknown quantity as far as things go."

"I don't think you can change particularly unhappy rifts between people," Robert said, "but you can certainly change if there's some enthusiasm and some love between the people concerned. You can certainly get stuck in and actually go out and do things more than we have."

"It's too late for that now, Robert," I interrupted.

"Our training period is over," Roger added. "We're now looking at the period where we're packing the sledges for the Pole. I have a clear idea of how the dynamics work between Gareth, Mike and me but I've no clue how it works when you're on a trek with that group because it's never happened."

"Looking at the result of the Crozier trip I would say that you're going to be out there in the same frame of mind as you were then," Robert said.

"The result of the Crozier trip was that we actually talked to each other," Roger responded.

"By the end, yes," Robert replied.

"Then, both of you said you'd never do anything together again," Mike interjected. "That was the final line of the argument."

"I think it's insanity for us three to go out, knowing the way we are," Robert continued, "and I don't think that's going to change. But, as I said earlier today, my decision's been made based on six months here and how we interact. I just can't imagine us three getting along that well under pressure."

"Let's get to the real sore point here, Robert," Roger said.

"Okay, I just don't think Gareth's right for the Pole. He's too inflexible. Physically, I think he's up to it but mentally no."

"Please elaborate," I invited firmly.

"Simply, I don't think I could work with you for three months. You've got too many hang-ups. You're too finicky, and I've never really developed a bond with you like I have with Roger and Mike. Our science programme will also look far more convincing if we have a doctor as a member of the party."

"Mike's medical skills are only as good as the equipment he's got to work with. In our case, he's no more valuable than someone skilled in first aid," Roger stated matter-of-factly.

"True," Mike agreed.

"And," Roger continued, "I truly believe that Gareth is far better suited. He's had more experience and he's got a better attitude. I don't think we can decide something as important as this without weighing all the facts."

"I honestly believe," Robert said, "that if the three of us were to go it would end in disaster. Not that I'm afraid of dying out there. In fact, one part of me would quite like it."

The whole room was suddenly filled with silence. I broke it.

"Now you say you're willing to die out there. If that's the case you can count me out," I fumed.

"I also think," Mike said, "that if I were along I'd be able to restore calm."

"I believe that to be the case too," John added quietly.

"Look," Roger argued, "I'm not about to be pushed into a hasty decision. The final make-up won't be certain anyway until three people, whatever combination, begin the walk."

I was anxious about the outcome either way. On the one hand, if I were to go, there was bound to be tension between the three of us. On the other hand, if we chose Mike, I would never be able to forget the missed opportunity.

Hitching a ride to McMurdo the following morning with three American biologists who were in the vicinity, I found the change enormously uplifting. For one day at least I could forget about the trek.

During my absence, Roger took it upon himself to end the dispute.

"I've got more in common with Mike," he told the others. "I can converse with him better, I understand him better, but based on competence, Gareth's got the edge."

"It can't work," Robert fumed. "Mike is by far the better man."

"I've made my decision," Roger said firmly. "Gareth is my choice."

Mike, relieved that a decision had been made, though it was not in his favour, wrote in his journal, "Firstly it would seem that I am not to go to the Pole. This decision somewhat surprised me at the time & I almost felt that it was ridiculous. Now, however, it doesn't seem unreasonable & I find myself almost agreeing that it's the right decision. ... The decision was made & I felt a mixture of relief and disappointment."

Despite Robert's grudging acceptance, I was still on tenterhooks, knowing that the final decision would come the day we left. The fight for position had tarnished my excitement — fate itself could not have chosen more disagreeable companions. This, it seemed, was not uncommon on polar expeditions, although in earlier times it was not considered proper to mention it. The conditions of being isolated from family and friends for months on end, bowed by backbreaking toil and enduring interminable cold were more than enough to set one man against another. Add to that the pressure created by the goals of an expedition and some people would make choices and take positions they would later regret. Men were only men after all, as weak in some respects as they were strong in others. We were no different from those who had gone before except that our modern and well-equipped party had the advantage of knowing how others had failed. I hoped we would not make the same mistakes.

Our access to modern equipment that our predecessors did not have was of some comfort but not much. The element of risk between Scott's expedition and our own, despite the passage of time and the reflections of intelligent men for seven decades, was roughly equal. The weather would be as unpredictable as it ever was, our reactions to the wind and cold were unknown and, lastly, the physical strength required to complete the journey would be little different. Strength was so bound with determination and desire that I wondered if ours was sufficient to match that of the Edwardian heroes for whom there were far greater prizes: international recognition and perhaps historical immortality. However uncontrollable the natural elements were, I hoped that human error would not be a part of our expedition.

We were buoyed by the task of preparing the sledges for departure, and all thoughts and fears of failure dissipated behind stacks of food and equipment, and the lengthy lists of weights and measures that occupied our every waking moment. It was an enjoyable time with much laughter as we sliced pieces of salami and weighed freeze-dried peas.

Roger preparing sledges for the polar journey. (PHOTO BY GARETH WOOD)

A balance had to be struck between what we knew we would require for 80-odd days of heavy work and what we could conceivably transport. One thing in our favour was the Gaybo sledge, although we were still not totally convinced that it could carry the 350 or more pounds Roger estimated we would need or that we could pull such burdens.

Robert provided the perfect opportunity to test the Gaybo's payload and the capacity of its human engine. John estimated that before our final departure from Willy Field he would need at least two days to film the journey's beginning. For those two days we would need stoves, heaters, food, tents, etc. for all of us to remain independent of McMurdo Station and Scott Base. Robert decided he was going to pull a portion of this equipment to a prearranged spot near McMurdo where it would be cached in advance of our arrival. Loading his sledge with an impossible 472 pounds, he covered the 17 miles, albeit not without a struggle, in one day. Although after this stunt he acknowledged the Gaybo's efficiency, Robert was still in favour of a much more classic design with rope trace — the Gaybo had solid trace — for historic authenticity. He seemed so concerned with presenting the right historic image that he had also taken to wearing the khaki-coloured BAS windproofs that resembled Scott's cotton outergear, and sporting a large chest bag of the kind Scott had worn.

Interrupting our attempts to organize were wave upon wave of McMurdo Station and Scott Base employees. After inspecting Scott's hut they would invariably troop en masse into our base to warm up. Although they were all wonderful people with whom we had much in common, the questions, repeated by each group, became tedious, and the frequent visits interrupted our busy schedule.

In spite of this, Roger and I continued with our food preparations. Caloric content was the most significant determining factor in our choice of meals, not texture, colour or taste, the normal preferences. Scott's diet, consisting mainly of pemmican, biscuits and butter, had provided between 4,200 and 4,600 calories per man per day, too little for men manhauling in extreme cold. Wilson was largely responsible for the ration, having experimented with different combinations during the Winter Journey; his conclusions were adopted by Scott for his own preparations. (Scott's idea of an ideal ration was one that just kept up a man's strength and no more.) His diet was also dangerously low in vitamins B and C.

We had been advised beforehand that we would require about 6,200 calories daily to sustain ourselves, but Roger settled on 5,100 calories, a compromise between what he considered an adequate diet and what we could humanly pull. Most of the calories would be derived from fat, much less from carbohydrate and significantly less from protein due to fat's high calorie content for its weight. To avoid monotony we chose four different dinners; each of these, with breakfast and snacks, which would be the same every day (biscuit, butter, oatmeal and chocolate drink for breakfast, and soup, chocolate bars, salami and biscuit for breaks), would approximate our researched daily requirement. Dinner one consisted of compressed bacon bar with potatoes; dinner two, bacon bar with macaroni and cheese; dinner three, rice and chicken with beans; and dinner four, rice and chicken with peas. To save weight, the freeze-dried bean, pea and potato packages were opened, the cardboard directions thrown away and the contents ziplocked into meal-sized quantities. The foil covering the bacon bar was likewise discarded and the fatty contents wrapped in plastic wrap. Chocolate-bar wrappers were also removed, saving us about 1.5 pounds. In all, we made up 81 meals: 26 of dinner one, 27 of dinner two, 16 of dinner three and 12 of dinner four.

Fuel for our stove was also vital. Not only would it ensure hot meals but it was required to melt snow and ice, our only source of water. Taking a lesson from Scott, who found his fuel evaporated

Mike and John unwrapping chocolate bars in preparation for the polar journey. (Photo by Gareth Wood)

due to improper seals, I epoxied soft metal lids beneath each cap. Roger and I estimated that at the outside we would use no more than half a litre per day and we hoped less.

Although we endeavoured to leave nothing to chance, some risks were unavoidable. For instance, we had only one sextant and one tent, both of which would be irreplaceable. Should we be forced to abandon our sledges and tent, each of us carried ultra-lightweight backpacks and bivouac bags that would permit rapid travel on skis. We would still, however, have to rely solely upon our wits for survival.

Toward the end of September and into October the small porch attached to the hut, which was acting as an impromptu refrigerator, was overflowing with boxes of prepared provisions waiting for final loading. While we modified our sledges — we removed strengthening braces to reduce weight — our hut rattled in the thunderous gusts sweeping inland from the sea-ice. Snow continued to drift thickly around our tiny dwelling.

During this period several of us made our last trips to McMurdo and Scott Base before our departure for the Pole. We visited friends and photographed the increasing number of Hercules aircraft flying into Willy Field with food, equipment and the many new scientists and support staff who would usher in another busy summer season. It became apparent that as the flights increased and new officials arrived, our relationship with the two bases began to change. They were less anxious to host our visits and chat on the radio, and we noted a gradual return to the official line of maintaining their distance.

Toward the end of October we made final adjustments to equipment and clothing and loaded our sledges. We planned a short training journey to Cape Royds with full sledges to shake out any equipment problems before our final departure. On October 22 we carried our sledges over the volcanic ash beach to the sea-ice. They moved easily across the bare surface, and several days later we returned to base after a successful trial. The moment of truth was upon us and, as if to mark its significance, the first skua we had sighted in six months soared overhead. Summer had arrived.

CHAPTER SIX

SOUTH AT LAST

O<small>N</small> O<small>CTOBER</small> 25 we left Cape Evans for McMurdo and Willy Field where John and Mike would film our final departure for the Pole. Before leaving, I glanced up toward Scott's hut, undisturbed but for the snow eddying silently about it. I had visions of Scott and his men on their day of departure. Then, they were men just like us; now, memories of them were larger than life, burdened as they were in death with a hero's mask.

Robert later told us that upon entering Scott's hut earlier that morning and pausing on the threshold, he expected a challenge to his intrusion, and lying upon Scott's bunk thought to himself, "This is what you saw, Captain Scott, on the day of your departure." So moved was he that, in tears, he swore that he could feel the spirit of Scott's own ill-fated expedition close about him.

Roger, relieved that we could budge our heavy sledges — the final weight was now 353 pounds each — reminded us that no one had ever pulled these weights such distances. It was a sobering thought. Even more so when I weighed the possible consequences of our recent decision to make the journey without radios or emergency locator beacons.

Roger's rationale, carefully considered, was that the journey could only be truly unsupported if we were totally independent of any and all means of assistance. Our die had been cast with the London fund-raising brochure, published before I was invited to be a member of the polar team, which clearly stated that Footsteps

71

would be "An expedition whose intention is to retrace Captain Robert Scott's footsteps to the South Pole and to restore the feelings of adventure, isolation and commitment that have been lost through the employment of the paraphernalia of modern times. Without recourse to depots, dogs, air support or outside assistance of any kind, two men alone will manhaul the 883-mile journey to the Pole." How could we betray the very feature that had made our expedition so appealing? Although we had an obligation to fulfil I could not help but wonder whether we would survive our temerity.

Just before wrenching my sledge out of its inertia, I again cast a longing gaze toward Scott's hut. "Goodbye and wish us luck," I whispered, hoping that the fate that had befallen our long-departed mentor would keep a healthy distance from our own party.

No joy marked our sombre procession as we pulled away, each bound for our own personal glory. Only four sledges departed, Mike pulling John's, which was loaded with 200 pounds of camera gear, while John filmed our departure; Mike had left his sledge at Razorback Island the day before and would pick it up en route. It was loaded with the extra food and equipment needed to get us to Willy Field.

When we were just the other side of Razorback the sun emerged, returning shadow and contrast to our world. Slogging through deep

Day 1 — Gareth leaving Cape Evans with sledge weighing 353 pounds.
(COURTESY OF ROGER MEAR)

drift, we struggled up the steep slope to the Glacier Tongue hut at 6:45 p.m. and after several brews of tea, melted ice for our evening camp on the sea-ice. At 9:45 p.m. we erected the large dome tent Mike and John would later take back to base. Respectful of our last few days of freedom, they slept in the small dome tent that we would haul to the Pole.

Visibility was poor when we left camp just before noon the following day. Moving in single file, we were guided by John's ghostly figure until, just before McMurdo, Robert swept past in what seemed a maniacal frenzy. Roger wrote of the incident in his diary that night, "JT led most of the morning until RS stormed past as we neared McMurdo, his Union Jack flapping from his sledge. ... Arrived at the diver's hut at 5pm RS dressed in the most filthy shirt & tie. ... "

"I'm just going to make a few arrangements," Robert said to Roger before striding away over the heavily tracked surface.

"What's he up to now?" I asked.

"Oh, the usual Robert," he said. "He's going to talk McMurdo into providing rooms for the lot of us again."

"What!" I exclaimed. "I thought we'd agreed not to."

"I know," Roger said, shrugging his shoulders.

The next few days belonged to John who filmed our daily sledging routine and eventual departure from McMurdo. For this we set up "Cine Camp One" a few miles from Willy Field, using the food and equipment Robert had hauled from Cape Evans weeks earlier. Willy Field was busy and we watched the winter personnel leave, replaced by hundreds of summer staff. As one Hercules after another lumbered in and out, I felt as though I were camped on the approach to a large metropolitan airport. Most of the new staff, I assumed, would remain close to their hermetically sealed quarters during their entire stay, having little or no contact with the elements, unaware of the beauty, oblivious to the danger.

Though he allowed us to use two rooms, the new base commander, Captain Shrite, made it abundantly clear that we were officially unwelcome. After several days of assisting John to film our last-minute preparations for departure, we abandoned the rooms and returned to our tents. Unfortunately, we still could not begin the journey. We had promised Richard Down, our London expedition coordinator, that we would wait for confirmation of our evacuation arrangements.

We had been informed some weeks earlier by Giles Kershaw, our pilot, that the Tri-turbo aircraft to be used for our evacuation was not available for any Antarctic work that summer. We were not the only group whose plans were upset. Giles, with the Canadian mountaineer Pat Morrow and five others, had just established Adventure Network International under whose umbrella they planned to climb Antarctica's Vinson Massif, the last mountain in Morrow's bid to climb the highest peak on all seven continents. Their expedition was left hanging. The owners of the Tri-turbo offered the excuse that they could not risk damage to the aircraft. Giles considered this odd as the plane had been used safely in the Antarctic before, and after persistent questioning he was convinced that the owners were afraid of losing profitable government contracts if they were seen to be supporting a private expedition.

When Richard Down learned that the Tri-turbo was not available, the big question had been how to inform Robert that new evacuation arrangements were being made without revealing it to the Americans, when all communication passed through either McMurdo Station or Scott Base. Although I had developed a code in London for just such an emergency, it was too restrictive for this specific task. Down hit upon an ingenious plan. Prior to our London departure he had given Robert a copy of John Campbell's biography of F. E. Smith, first Earl of Birkenhead, a book that he knew from subsequent contacts Robert was enjoying. Down spoke with Robert on the Scott Base public radio phone.

"How're you getting along with the book?" he asked.

"Fine," Robert replied.

"You know the book I'm talking about? Don't mention its name," he warned quickly.

"Yes, yes, okay," Robert said.

"Well, just get a piece of paper, don't say a word and take down these numbers," Down instructed.

The coded list of words, numbers and pages that followed spelled out a private message that informed us of Giles' belief that the Americans had scuttled the Tri-turbo mission but that London was working on a replacement plan. The message also warned Robert to assume that all communication was being monitored by the Americans and that he was not to discuss any facet of it, once decoded, on radio.

Meanwhile, Giles managed to locate a Twin Otter which would be more than adequate for Morrow's climbing team as well as our own evacuation. The next blow, however, sent Richard staggering. The Chileans, who were supporting the flight, called to advise that after delivering the climbing team, under no circumstances was Giles to fly the aircraft south of the Ellsworth Mountains or proceed to the Pole. To avoid an awkward situation, Giles agreed. It appeared that the Americans had interfered, for the Chileans had been unaware that this was Giles' intention.

Since it seemed impossible to find a charter company beyond American influence, Giles developed a plan that would obey to the letter the Antarctic Treaty members' policy which decreed that a private expedition must be totally independent. He would purchase a Cessna 185 with expedition funds, modify it for long-range flight, crate it, ship it aboard the *Southern Quest* and reassemble it in the Antarctic. We were totally ignorant of all this until just days before our departure from McMurdo.

Giles would later write an account for the expedition's record, "By taking an aircraft on our own boat and operating it from an ice floe there was no stage that anything other than the forces of nature or our own mistakes could prevent us from getting to the Pole." The aircraft would require considerably more fuel than the capacity of its standard tanks to make the 1,800-mile return journey from Cape Evans to the Pole. Additional fuel tanks would therefore have to be installed, and small fuel drums carried on board.

To protect their new plan, now that they knew to what length the American authorities would go, Giles and Richard acted on a "need to know" basis only. Certain precautions were therefore adopted. Even correspondence with John Heap of the British Foreign Office was doctored for secrecy. The impression was given that the *Southern Quest* would be leaving from Melbourne when, in fact, it would load the plane in Hobart. Captain Graham Phippen was brought into the conspiracy, and although he was not happy about keeping a secret from the crew, he waited patiently until the dismantled aircraft was aboard and departure imminent before revealing the plan.

Now idle at McMurdo, we waited anxiously for London's assurance that a replacement evacuation plan was in place. It would have been irresponsible for us to leave without it. When Robert appeared jubilantly at our tent flap with telex in hand, we immediately assumed that our walking papers had arrived.

"Quick, Gareth, where's the code book you made up in London?" he asked excitedly.

Rummaging through my gear I found the book and ducked outside. Robert began to read out the codes.

"LF," he said anxiously, his pencil poised over the telex.

"Aircraft," I said quickly.

"HM," he said, scribbling furiously.

"Cape Evans," I responded.

A few minutes later the message was decoded. Puzzled, Robert stared at it for a few seconds before looking up.

"Well, what does it say?" Roger asked anxiously.

"It says, 'ALL WELL HERE, GOOD TO HEAR YOUR NEWS THIS MORNING. MESSAGE PROMISED AS FOLLOWS: 1) WILL TAKE AIRCRAFT TO CAPE EVANS WITH GILES ON *SOUTHERN QUEST*. 2) ETA AIRCRAFT CAPE EVANS, 14TH JANUARY. 3) ETA AIRCRAFT POLE, 16TH JANUARY ONWARDS, THEN AIRCRAFT BACK TO CAPE EVANS. 4) THEN AIRCRAFT AND *SOUTHERN QUEST* ETC. HOME. 5) JOHN HEAP HAPPY, EVERYTHING UNDER CONTROL. LOVE TO YOU ALL. RICHARD.' "

"I wonder what aircraft he means?" I asked.

"I don't know," Robert replied. "I'll call Richard from Scott Base."

A couple of hours later, Robert reappeared at the tent.

"You're not going to believe this, but we'll be flying back in a Cessna 185," he said, laughing.

"A 185! It can't be, it's too small," Roger replied, astonished.

"Can a Cessna hold us all?" I asked.

"I don't know," Roger replied, "but I think we've got to give Giles the benefit of the doubt. He's got a lot of experience working down here and he knows what he's doing."

McMurdo Station. (COURTESY OF ROGER MEAR)

"Yes, absolutely," Robert replied, satisfied.

Bob Harler, commander of McMurdo's air operations, requested a meeting with Roger that night to discuss our plans. He felt that he should know them in case he had to coordinate a search. When he discovered that we would be travelling without the aid of electronic communication, he was astonished but respectful of our reasoning that we wanted the expedition to be totally unsupported.

Roger, sensing in Harler the need to search even if we were only slightly overdue, asked him not to begin until at least 120 days after our departure. We had estimated that as the outside limit of our food on partial rations. As well, Roger requested that our progress not be monitored by the many aircraft flying to the Pole. It was unlikely anyone would be able to see us anyway; aircraft routinely flew at 20,000 to 26,000 feet, and from that altitude we would be invisible. Later I learned that Harler would have begun his search at 90 days. For him to have allowed three men to die between two American bases would have been considered unconscionable.

I gave little more thought to the prospect of winging back across 900 miles of ice and snow in an aircraft barely large enough to seat us all, let alone carry the extra fuel required. All my energy and concern were now devoted to our imminent departure.

November 3 — Day 1 — 6.85 miles. Our first day dawned bright and clear: a perfect day for the start of our journey. Scott had left from almost the same position exactly 74 years before. Although the weather had been just as spectacular for him, a frostbitten thumb a few hours before his departure had served to remind him that behind the thin veil of beauty lurked danger.

On Willy Field's snow-bound road, a tight clutch of onlookers gathered around our somewhat disorganized assembly. They added a tiny measure of respect to our departure. Compared to the time and effort we had expended to arrive at this point, however, our cheering section was pathetically small.

We grunted and groaned our way to the end of the road. Robert led the way followed by Mike and John — who would accompany us for a few days to capture our activities on film — me and, last, Roger.

Much later we would all have a good laugh reading a New Zealand reporter's account of our departure; the fact that she wasn't even there made the story all the more ridiculous: " ... 150 Americans and New Zealanders crowded around the sled and huskies ... it was all very primitive. The red wooden sled pulled by the huskies turned the clock back to a time when travel was both arduous and dangerous. ... A protective cocoon of well wishers flanked the party for the first 400 metres but finally the huskies were urged on faster. ... "[1]

"Well," Robert laughed, "at least she got our names right."

Stretching before us lay the Ross Ice Shelf, approximately 400 miles of untracked ice bordered to the west by the mountainous Hillary and Shackleton coasts. White and Black islands lay ahead. On a bearing of 356° magnetic, we would move away from White Island to avoid crevasses crowding its rocky shore and then cut back toward Hillary Coast at longitude 168° west.

I struggled with a pair of our ultra-lightweight snowshoes while the others managed on skis. Although we had barely begun, I could already feel a pain in my foot, from an injury I had sustained during an earlier training journey. Weeks earlier, McMurdo's doctor, upon examining it, had advised me that it was most likely a minor stress fracture that could take months to heal. I was purposely staying off skis as long as possible so as not to aggravate it and hoping that I would avoid the painful, blistered condition that had plagued me during previous journeys.

We had only been travelling a few minutes when a fellow on a snowmobile came out to say goodbye. Robert took advantage of the situation to request a favour. Prior to our departure he had been washing his only change of underpants at McMurdo and in the rush he had forgotten them. He jokingly asked the snowmobiler to get them for him and a few minutes later the fellow returned with a plastic bag which Robert put on his sledge. Later that night, to his horror, he discovered that the bag contained a pair of women's panties. There was no sign of his own.

Stopping for our first soup break two and a half hours from McMurdo, we continued until 6 p.m., erecting the tent at 6.85 miles. At Roger's suggestion, seven miles a day was all that we planned to attempt for the first few days in order to accustom ourselves to the effort. We well knew that 12 miles would have to become our average daily travel if we were to complete the journey within our food limits. Less than that and we would exhaust our provisions short of the Pole, and with no means to call for help, we would certainly perish. I had no wish to join the legion of Antarctic dead. We planned to step up our pace on November 6 when we waved our final farewells to Mike and John.

November 4 — Day 2 — 15.21 miles. We left camp at 10:30 a.m. on our original bearing under overcast skies with a slight squall from the south. I was exhausted from the previous day's travel. Occasional sheets of ground drift gave the unsettling illusion that the whole surface was moving and that we were standing still. In reality, considering our present progress and the distance we had yet to cover, this was not far from the truth. Roger led the first stint and I did the next. Using compass only, I was wildly erratic on my first attempt. At our second break, with gusts of Force 4 to 5, we erected the tent to escape the wind. Breaking camp at 4:30 p.m., Robert deferred the lead to Roger due to poor conditions.

Bypassing White Island with a healthy margin of safety, we skied easily over snow-covered crevasses far from its shore. Scott's depot party on February 21, 1911, however did not. Unknowingly running parallel to the crevasses, Cecil Meares' team plunged through a rotten snow bridge. Wilson described the scene: "They looked exactly like rats running down a hole — only I saw no hole. They simply went into the white surface and disappeared."[2] Meares, applying the snow brakes in time, stopped the sledge and then he and Scott jumped clear. Meanwhile, the dogs dangled, yelping, from their harness in the ice-blue abyss. All were eventually rescued.

November 5 — Day 3 — 21.33 miles. Leaving camp just after noon we passed the 20-mile mark and the limit of our first bearing at 4:00 p.m. Scott had also adjusted his bearing here. He reached this point, known as "Corner Camp," on November 5, 1911, only to discover a disappointing note from Lieutenant Evans, who was moving ahead with motor sledges and ponies, saying that the last motor sledge (Evans had deserted the first a few days earlier) was managing only a sluggish seven miles a day. Peering into the distance, Scott was disheartened to see three black dots a mile south; he instinctively knew they were the defunct motor and its abandoned sledges. "It is a disappointment. I had hoped better of the machines once they got away on the Barrier Surface,"[3] he recorded. That the ponies were off their feed was disconcerting as well. Two of them, he surmised, would not last long.

Turning, I glanced over my shoulder. Our ski tracks, framed by the twin impressions of our sledge runners, narrowed to a finite point far behind us. Hut Point Peninsula stood out sharply in the clear air. Soon it would fade from sight and memory, as our thoughts focussed on the monotonous plodding rhythm we were forced to adopt for mobility and balance.

Tomorrow we would part company with Mike and John. Then and only then would I be certain that the Pole would be mine.

November 6 — Day 4 — 28.45 miles. For Mike, who had almost become a member of the Pole team, this was a sad day. He would later write in his journal, "It was all so painful to see them off, but it was a relief — there would be no more tension and there would be the summer to enjoy."

After a long chat while we refitted skins to our skis, we at last departed at 12:30 p.m. I empathized with Mike and his disappointment and silently hoped that he would realize his desire to sledge to the western mountains while we were away.

Shortly afterwards, a Force 3 to 4 blow stirred up a moderate ground blizzard through which we passed easily. In a mere four miles, which we made before our first soup break, Castle Rock and Hut Point Peninsula disappeared from view. Soon, our humble figures would be all that would break the still, white symmetry surrounding us. With little to alter our perspectives and saddled with the emotional trappings of our disparate personalities, our minds began to focus on each other. Tonight it was Robert who was the centre of the discord.

After all our painstaking effort, personal sacrifices and mutual agreement to reduce our combined weights ounce by ounce, it was now coming to light that Robert had brought extra clothing, other odd items and, worst of all, cigarettes with him. Details such as these, immensely important and sacred to Roger's and my sense of practicality and safety, were passed off by Robert's "big picture" thinking with barely a shrug of acknowledgement. Roger and I both believed that hundreds of miles into the expedition we would all be cold and stressed, with our strength waning due to our limited rations. The psychological impact of one of us bringing out an extra pair of socks or other item, beyond what we had agreed on, would be no different from one of us producing a biscuit that was additional to our predetermined ration. To Robert they were just — details.

CHAPTER SEVEN

THE ROSS ICE SHELF

N OW WE WERE totally independent and I felt for the first time that the journey had begun in earnest. We left camp at 9:30 a.m. on November 7 under intermittent cloud, sun and blowing snow. Across the frozen sea, an apparently endless flat plain to the south, we were soon struggling in total white-out. We groped blindly forward on wooden legs, stopping every few feet to adjust our bearings. We covered less than a mile in the first hour. It was at times like this that the doubts of our success hung over me like an immense black cloud. Progress was all and all was progress; without it we were nothing. That thought echoed in my brain.

Five miles east of Minna Bluff we encountered low pressure waves formed by ice pushing against the rocky shore. Cresting the still, frozen peaks, lying rank upon rank, we wrestled with our sledges in each shallow trough filled with grit-like snow. Meanwhile, the frozen sea moved ponderously and invisibly beneath our feet.

Scott, on November 7, 1911, forced to seek refuge in blizzard conditions at the same position, was amazed to see Cecil Meares, a member of his support party who had started late, catch them up. Driving dogs, he had punched through the howling wind and driving snow with little difficulty and having accomplished the same distance in less than half the time, he earned not Scott's admiration for a task well done but an angry riposte that perhaps he had " ... played too much for safety in catching us so soon."[1] Not truly understanding the advantage of dogs, Scott could only express frustration at his own slow pace.

November 8 — Day 6 — 46.89 miles. Abreast of Minna Bluff we encountered great cracks in the ice, a few 30 feet wide and covered by snow bridges. We approached them cautiously, testing them with our ski poles. With each tenuous step I half expected my sledge to crash through. My feet were on fire and I was hoping that they would soon adjust to the rigours of travel. Aggravating the pain and adding to my frustration, the clip holding the skins to the bottom of my skis kept slipping off, causing me to stumble continually.

Erecting the tent at 7:00 p.m., Roger and I were disappointed to see more of Robert's extra gear appear. An additional pile jacket, BAS windproofs, a pair of inner boots, a scarf and kerchief — there seemed no end to it. Roger was determined that since Robert had brought it, he would pull it, and from then on spared him no sympathy during the day-after-day grind.

November 9 — Day 7 — 58.34 miles. Within minutes of our 10:00 a.m. start we reached the southern limit of the Bluff crevasses. The day was magnificent with everything crystal clear. Beyond Minna Bluff we could just make out the Trans-Antarctic Mountains, and Mounts Erebus and Terror, our winter companions, were still visible to the north.

I led the first stint and for most of it climbed an immense pressure ridge, its wind-sculpted surface blasted to a fine polish by the rough-grained snow. Working hard, I began to feel the effects of dehydration, which were only partly alleviated by sucking snow. Again I had trouble with my skins coming off and resorted to snow-shoes for the rest of the day.

November 10 — Day 8 — 61.34 miles. Scott's diary notation for November 10 began, "A very horrid march."[2]

Ours was as well. Blizzard conditions with winds gusting to Force 4 or 5 directly from the south slowed our progress. Visibility was reduced to mere yards, requiring constant bearing checks. Our efforts carried us no farther than three miles in 3.5 hours before we elected to camp; the energy we were using was too great for the distance travelled. I had yet to feel hungry enough to eat all of my meal and left the sausage and butter for later.

November 11 — Day 9 — 74.59 miles. Our best day yet; we travelled 13.25 miles. For most of the day the surface was gentle sastrugi and wind crust over which our sledges pulled with less effort than on previous days. All three of us were now having problems with our skins and walked for the last five hours. The glue we were using was not adhering in the cold.

"I don't know what but there's got to be a better way," Robert said, eyeing his flapping skins.

"What about screwing them on?" I ventured.

"That would damage the skis," Roger retorted. "Besides, what if we want to take them off?"

"Unscrew them," I returned.

Roger scowled at me but said nothing.

November 12 — Day 10 — 86.43 miles. Robert, no longer gung-ho, fell behind by several minutes each break. His face was drawn and pale. He told Roger that he was saving himself: for him any acknowledgement of physical weakness would have been too humbling. I would have felt sorry for him had I not been immersed in my own agony and still angry with him for bringing extra gear.

The pain of my feet threatened to overwhelm me and I began to doubt my ability to complete the journey. I wondered whether I was made of the same mettle as my companions. How hard could I push myself without doing irreparable damage?

November 13 — Day 11 — 93.20 miles. The temperature the previous night was -32°C. As we decamped at 9:45 a.m. in sunshine, gentle winds pressed from the southwest. Dark cloud moved ominously toward us and it was only a matter of hours before it blocked the sun, casting us into a shadowless state in which the snow beneath our feet grew hazy. Hummocks and hollows were lost

Camp. (PHOTO BY GARETH WOOD)

83

in a sea of white, making walking difficult for even someone with an experienced eye. We faced Force 4 to 5 gusts and driving snow by our second break. Calling an immediate halt, we pitched the tent, and once inside, we began to sort out our tangled gear.

Within the tent we moved methodically as we had done on the Crozier journey, each bound to his own tasks, conducted largely without comment. I wrote that night, "Finding this tough going — tougher than I anticipated and still 780 miles to go."

November 14 — 17 — Days 12 to 15 — 142.37 miles. Two hours into the day my skins broke, forcing me onto snowshoes. Overcast skies reduced ground contrast to zero. Following in such conditions was not too bad because one could gauge the posture of the man ahead, but leading was hell.

This was our first day of three, three-hour marches, 1.5 hours a day more than we had previously travelled. I was already exhausted from our normal day's activity and wondered how I would cope with the extra work. We camped at 8:00 p.m.

"To hell with this, I'm screwing my skins on," I said in tired frustration.

"Don't complain if you bugger your skis up," Roger replied.

Although my skins were remaining fastened at the head and tail of my skis, they would slip from side to side causing me to stumble. I thought that the slight drag created by the screw heads would be nothing compared to the benefit of securing the skins once and for all.

The following day the weather changed dramatically: bright sun for most of it with some early morning cloud dispersing by noon. Behind us, Mounts Erebus and Terror were only dark smudges to the north. Against this hazy background Robert struggled with a broken binding.

"I need an hour to repair my binding," he said to Roger at our last break. "Can we stop an hour early?"

"If we start shaving time to repair equipment, who knows how far behind we'll get? Can't you manage on foot for the last leg? We'll fix it tonight," Roger answered.

Robert nodded silently. He was too tired to argue.

The last leg of the day's march was demanding, a fine layer of fresh, dry snow causing very heavy pulling. "God what hard days," I wrote. "Feet still very sore but better I think." Robert arrived at camp about ten minutes late, and in spite of our observations felt that the new snow made pulling easier. Roger's accusation that Robert's tardiness was due to the volumes of contraband gear he had stuffed into his kit at the last moment was met with stony silence.

We were all on edge, and still smouldering from our recent disagreements at base. I felt that our relationships were already teetering on the brink of ruin, and I was frightened by what lay ahead. We were not a team — it appeared that we were three separate expeditions.

The following morning Robert woke first, his wrist alarm piercing the frigid silence.

"Turn that damn thing off," Roger mumbled from deep within his bag. He insisted that our biological clocks would give us all the notice we needed.

At noon, dead reckoning navigation, using the sledgewheel and compass, placed us 2.5 miles from Scott's One Ton Depot where, on November 15, 1911, he and his weary party had gathered strength to continue.

The day dealt me a blister. Only one and a small one at that, but it added to the nagging pain I was already experiencing, and my feet felt shattered. Hauling such heavy burdens day after day did amazing things to one's feet. Robert Peroni, the Greenland explorer Roger and I had met in Italy, had cautioned us that our feet would change in length and breadth by the time the journey was over, but he had neglected to tell us about the pain.

Our bodies now craved all the food we were allotted. I was constantly hungry, my energy requirement finally surpassing my limited food intake. What was too much in the beginning had become too little, and I felt that my energy reserves would soon dwindle to nothing. I also had an insatiable thirst, and although our stools indicated that our bodies were adjusting to the high fat diet, my darkened urine indicated that my fluid intake was too low. Roger appeared immune to dehydration, drinking our normal ration, but Robert and I were always looking to quench our thirst — Robert especially. I wondered if Roger was really fitter and stronger than Robert and me. The difference in our levels of performance didn't make sense. There was too much disparity.

November 18 — Day 16 — 152.6 miles. Today was no different in many respects from the others, except that by position it placed us on top of Scott's last camp. Having reached the Pole on January 17, 1912, he had turned about immediately, expecting that the return journey would be hard but not anticipating that it would cost him and his companions their lives. Our glorious weather was nothing like the fearful blizzard that in late March of 1912 held him, Wilson and Bowers captive in their tent for four fatal days. Without food, fuel or energy to make the last 11 miles to One Ton Depot, each succumbed to the very environment that would have made their feat so worthy had they succeeded.

It was in the tent that the three were found frozen in an attitude of sleep; Scott with his bag thrown open as if to hasten death, Wilson on Scott's left with his hands folded over his chest and Bowers on Scott's right. Before constructing a snow cairn over the tent which still contained their bodies, Atkinson, the expedition surgeon, retrieved Scott's letters and diaries from beneath his shoulder. Scott's last entry told the bitter tale: "We shall stick it out to the end, but we are getting weaker, of course, and the end cannot be far. It seems a pity, but I do not think I can write more. R. Scott. For God's sake look after our people."[3]

And in a letter to a friend, the playwright J. M. Barrie, he wrote, "Goodbye. I am not at all afraid of the end, but sad to miss many a humble pleasure which I had planned for the future on our long marches. I may not have proved a great explorer, but we have done the greatest march ever made and come very near to great success. Goodbye, my dear friend, Yours ever, R. Scott."[4]

Seventy-four years had preserved this position of death in time only, because the bodies of the three were now well beyond that frozen moment. Buried by decades of snow and borne seaward by an icy pallbearer, the Ross Ice Shelf, they were many miles north of us.

Gazing across the barren landscape before me, I was entranced by the delicate streams of sandy snow playing gently down wind-twisted ruts between crusted sastrugi. The land was both hauntingly beautiful and forbiddingly harsh; had it been any other way, I suppose, the Pole would not have been a prize.

On Observation Hill, carved into the cross erected by the surviving members of the *Terra Nova* Expedition in memory of Scott and his brave men, is a line from Tennyson's *Ulysses*: "To strive, to seek, to find, and not to yield." Scott bore that attitude to his death, which said much of him but even more of the Victorian-Edwardian tradition that was his nemesis. His was one of the last of the great expeditions, the dying gasp of those imperial explorations.

November 19 — Day 17 — 164.3 miles. Resting in the sun at our first soup break I looked right around me. Whichever way I turned, my eyes met endless white. Our horizon was unbroken. We travelled as though in the middle of an immense inverted saucer, we at the height looking down upon a smooth white edge. With 24-hour daylight, I expected the landscape to grow monotonous.

During my stint in front, cloud blocked the sun, reducing contrast to zero, so taking an accurate bearing was extremely difficult. Roger, behind me, was constantly checking my accuracy and whenever I turned, his ski pole would be jabbing the air to indicate a correction. Although Roger seemed better able to navigate a straight course than either Robert or me, he was not infallible; on several occasions I wanted to correct his bearing but knew it would only lead to conflict.

That day we paid silent homage to Captain L.E.G. "Titus" Oates who, 74 years earlier on his 32nd birthday, with his feet frozen, crawled from the wind-whipped tent with the comment, "I am just going outside and may be some time."[5] Crippled and in pain, he staggered bravely into death's cold embrace. Whether this was the act of a man crazed with pain and welcoming an end to it or a deliberate move to avoid becoming a burden to his companions, will never be known. Oates was a soldier and indeed a model for the rigid code of honour with which all soldiers were bound. Regardless, it was a heroic act which, I would like to believe, was born of courage and not madness.

Robert was late arriving at camp that evening as he had been for the past few days — something was seriously wrong. He was our powerhouse, the man who had single-handedly hauled 472 pounds of provisions and equipment 17 miles to McMurdo. Sensing something was amiss with his sledge runners, he motioned to Roger.

"Look at these damn things, how they're burred. This has got to be slowing me down," he complained.

"It does look strange, but I don't see how it could make a difference," Roger said.

"Feel how rough it is," Robert invited.

Roger ran his hand over the runner. "Let's see your Swiss Army knife," he said, and when it was handed to him proceeded to scrape a small section carefully with the edge of the blade.

"They'll be fine if you just scrape them down," he said, passing back the knife.

Over the next hour, Robert scraped the runners smooth, wondering about the mystery of the furry surface as he finished the job with a piece of fine emery cloth. The teflon runners had been manufactured especially for the expedition, and we had expected their surfaces to stay glassy smooth for the duration of the journey.

November 20 — Day 18 — 176.52 miles. "Hardest day for me yet," I wrote that night, utterly exhausted. My energy level was low and one shoulder was beginning to ache as I pulled the sledge across the fine, sand-like surface. No amount of harness adjustment seemed to help. I was thankful that except for the one blister I had developed days earlier, which had miraculously dried up, my feet were not unduly painful.

Marching under overcast skies, we hauled over 12 miles with incredible effort, a steady wind at our faces. Shackleton, on the same date in 1908, wrote, "It is as though we were truly at the world's end, and were bursting in on the birthplace of the clouds and the nesting home of the four winds, and one has a feeling that we mortals are being watched with a jealous eye by the forces of nature."[6]

Roger led strongly for the most part despite a heavy cover of loose snow. Falling behind by 20 minutes on the last break, I had no time to recuperate before being asked to lead. The lack of contrast and the deep snow hampered my ability to navigate. To make matters worse I struggled with a tendency to walk a curved track; since a straight line is the shortest distance between two points, I was covering unnecessary ground, albeit only yards. Roger, frustrated, soon took over, being replaced by Robert for the last 30 minutes. What my problem was I was not sure, but I suspected that my energy was not being replenished by what I now considered to be an inadequate diet.

November 21 — Day 19 — 187.99 miles. We reached the halfway mark to the bottom of the Beardmore Glacier, and spent the whole day in zero contrast, a thick ceiling of stratus masking the sun. Robert, using only his yachting compass attached to his chest bag, steered rather well considering the conditions. Roger accused me of navigating a course with as many curves as an English country lane. At our first soup break the most incredible crystals of snow fell directly upon us, each flake a beautifully formed hexagon.

That night, stripping off my polypropylene longjohns and top, which I customarily wore to bed, I had a look at myself. My hips had two angry weals from the sledge harness and I had a rash on my buttocks and crotch. As well, my shoulder was nearly numb and my feet ached like hell. Frost burns, scabbed and blotchy, covered my nose, and my lips were buried in a jungle of scrubby beard. I felt less than whole, both mentally and physically.

Happy with our progress, we agreed to a day off if we reached the bottom of the Beardmore by December 12.

November 22 — Day 20 — 198.18 miles. Roger led off in zero contrast with a Force 2 to 3 wind at our backs. Low stratus imprisoned the sky in a thick grey mat, the horizon becoming visible only toward the end of the day. I led the second session in complete frustration. Roger, believing my track was taking us off course, continually corrected my bearings. In the tent that night Robert produced more illicit gear — this time a pair of gloves. I wrote in my diary that night, "Feet sore and aching but no blisters. Shoulder still goes near end of session but not as bad."

November 23 — Day 21 — 208.3 miles. The day greeted us with bright sun and blue sky, a welcome relief from heavy cloud cover. I led the first leg — my navigation was better in the morning when my energy level was higher — covering 4.25 miles in three hours despite soft snow that caused very difficult pulling.

Robert was 25 minutes late at one break because of a sore heel, and we ended the day early when my ski binding broke. That gave Robert's heel a rest and allowed us to repair gear, a chore that had become routine.

November 24 — Day 22 — 215.05 miles. Fifteen minutes before our second break a Force 4 wind, accompanied by ground drift and eventually snow, forced an immediate halt. Visibility was so bad we were worried that Robert, who was ten minutes behind, would be lost to sight in the ground drift. Covering only 6.75 miles, well short of our daily average, we kept our boots on in the tent hoping for a break in the conditions so that we might carry on with what was left of our nine-hour work day.

While we waited, all of us tending to various pieces of equipment, we cooked our evening meal. Communication was limited to "pass this," or "pass that." Sitting within inches of Roger and Robert, I had never felt so lonely. The fact that the three of us were crammed like sardines into a two-man tent made the tension worse. An errant elbow was sometimes ignored but most often was swiftly reprimanded. We had lost patience with each other. By 5:30 p.m. we lost hope of further progress and, doffing our boots, prepared for bed. I was still very hungry, but sleep overcame this other need.

November 25 — Day 23 — 215.05 miles. "Nowhere," I wrote. Upon waking, we found the wind still gusting strongly with heavy ground drift. Our sledges were indistinguishable from hummocks of snow. Travel was impossible. Spending the day writing in our diaries and sleeping, we ate little: a few crackers, salami, soup and hot chocolate being all that we could afford. We had decided beforehand that we would not consume valuable sledging rations if we were stormbound. At midday, when it appeared that the storm was spent, I stepped outside to limber up. The sun was out and the Barrier was at last silent.

November 26 — Day 24 — 228.09 miles. Most mornings Roger was up first. He would light the stove — he and I shared the cooking duties — and once I was up I would carefully pour the warm water from the previous evening, which we stored in our thermoses overnight, into a pot with three oatmeal blocks and a few ounces of butter. The melted butter gave substance to an otherwise thin gruel. Once we had consumed that, Robert would reach through the vestibule to pack the pot with snow to make more water for hot chocolate, also generously laced with butter, and soup for our thermoses. Then we began the monotonous routine of dressing and preparing ourselves for departure.

Because of the problems with my feet, I took special pains with my socks. Each evening, while we cooked, I secured them with clothes pins to various upper parts of the tent to dry in the heat given off by the stove, but when I went to bed I brought them into the sleeping bag with me or stuffed them into my fibre-pile suit. In the morning, I examined them for moisture. Invariably they were damp. Over feet coated with antiperspirant to minimize sweat, I slipped a light inner sock and then vapour barrier socks, smoothing them down carefully with both hands. I was fastidious in my effort to winnow out any lumps, for even a small one would become a mountain before too long. I then dragged on a pair of heavy outer socks.

Tent and sledges buried by the storm. (COURTESY OF ROGER MEAR)

Although relying primarily on dead reckoning navigation on the Ross Ice Shelf, that day I also used the sextant to compute our position from the angle of the sun above the horizon. The sunshot placed us at latitude 81° 02' south, longitude 170° 15' east. Shackleton, on the same date, claimed, "Tonight we are in latitude 82° 18½' South, longitude 168° East, and this latitude we have been able to reach in much less time than on the last long march with Captain Scott, when we made latitude 82° 16½' our 'farthest South'. We celebrated the breaking of the 'farthest South' record with a four-ounce bottle of Curaçao, sent us by a friend at home."[7]

During our next session, land became visible to the south: the symmetry of the saucer was broken. Shackleton wrote of his astonishment: "It falls to the lot of few men to view land not previously seen by human eyes, and it was with feelings of keen curiosity, not unmingled with awe, that we watched the new mountains rise from the great unknown that lay ahead of us. Mighty peaks they were, the eternal snows at their bases, and their rough-hewn forms rising high towards the sky."[8]

The end of the day saw Robert on his knees, sanding his burred sledge runners again with emery cloth. There had to be an explanation.

November 27 — Day 25 — 239.63 miles. The day was one of the warmest since our departure. Roger and I travelled in longjohns, our salopettes open to our waists, and Robert, feeling the heat as well, rolled up his pant legs. As soon as we stopped, however, the cold quickly returned. It was only -9°C, but in our sweat-soaked clothing it felt much colder to us. Regardless, sipping hot soup while basking in what meagre comfort the sun did provide was a delight we had not previously experienced.

We were now able to gauge our position in relation to the southern mountains, which were gaining in stature from mere smudges on the horizon to ragged, glaciated peaks. This was a welcome relief and took the pressure off our need to rely entirely on compass bearings. I would have enjoyed it more had I not been in such pain. I requested an early halt at 6:00 p.m. Roger reluctantly complied, although not before making sure I understood that with such good weather we should have made 13 miles, not 11.

Curious about the condition of Robert's runners, at the end of the day I turned my sledge over and looked at mine. I recorded in my diary, "Has been a painful day, only 11.45 miles. Roger is very obviously upset by my troubles & is sarcastic tonight — better than usual! Oh well. Scraped one runner ... one is very hairy, the other is perfectly smooth, almost like is on backwards & has a grain. Am told they don't though."

I was beginning to wonder if this wasn't more serious than we thought. Surely it was making a difference to the pulling. During the previous week I had been having trouble with one shoulder. On November 20 I wrote, "Left shoulder giving much trouble ... sledge not pulling efficiently." It seemed that the sledge was dragging on one side and I was pulling harder with that shoulder. My shoulder became much worse and on the 26th I sewed a large piece of closed-cell foam to my shoulder pad. I wondered if the very rough runner was part of the explanation. My request for us all to exchange sledges for a short time was rejected by Roger. In spite of the obvious signs, I wasn't totally convinced that the runners were having a detrimental effect and accepted Roger's decree not to exchange sledges. We were both still angry over Robert's extra clothing and were determined not to give him any relief from pulling his own sledge.

November 28 — Day 26 — 252.18 miles. A problem with the pivot point of Robert's ski binding delayed our departure. The ball joint and one arm of the assembly had deteriorated, leaving us with no alternative but to attempt to replace it. Unfortunately, five of the six screws holding the binding to the ski were impossible to loosen with the only screwdriver in our possession, a Swiss Army knife. More leverage was required. We therefore filed the pick of an ice axe to make a stronger tool, and using our one spare pivot assembly, successfully completed the repair.

My feet were still sore, and I was worried. We were rapidly approaching the point of no return and I sensed in Roger the increasing frustration of being held back by Robert and me. Roger was pulling strongly each day. Robert, despite his tardiness, seemed to have more energy at day's end than I did. Whether I had become psychologically conditioned to my infirmity I was not sure. My legs were feeling weaker and I was finding myself short of breath. I was not looking forward to the glacier climb ahead.

Roger happily informed us at day's end that our average daily travel was up to ten miles, which put us right on target. We could thank better surface conditions for our improved progress.

November 29 — Day 27 — 264.84 miles. I was beginning to feel like a burden on the others. At the second soup break I was a full half hour behind.

"I think you ought to know how I really feel," I said upon arrival. "I'm worn out, my feet and shoulder ache constantly. I'm very worried. I ate all my snacks back there and I still have no energy.

I'm sorry I haven't said anything sooner, but I guess it's obvious from my progress."

"Why don't you change your ration around and eat the biggest part during the day when you're working and the snacks at night?" Roger suggested sympathetically.

"I'll give it a try," I said, unconvinced as I slumped down, exhausted, beside my sledge.

"Perhaps I can take a little weight from you," Robert said kindly.

"Thanks, but I'll manage," I said, buoyed by his offer but suspicious of his intentions.

Roger recorded his opinion of Robert's generosity in his diary that night, "This I feel was a poorly judge[d] offer in that it can only make Gareth feel all the more of a burden, which he is not. ... "

Later in the tent I examined my feet — three blisters. The balls of my feet, however, were giving me the most pain even though they looked normal. My leg muscles, overworked and underfed, were twitching.

I was heartened by the fact that the mountains were growing with each passing day. We had come 265 miles from Willy Field and if all went well for the remaining 130 to the base of the Beardmore, we would have a day of rest.

November 30 — Day 28 — 276.98 miles. A restless night; I spent most of it tossing and turning, much to the annoyance of the others. In the cramped, two-man tent, when one of us moved, we all felt it.

Despite several stops to adjust my boots, I was not too far behind the others. Just before our last soup break, Robert fell back abreast of me.

"You know," he said, "Roger gave me a right bollocking for offering to take some weight from you."

"I'm sorry," I responded. "I appreciated the offer but I guess we all have to look after ourselves."

Robert nodded and pulled ahead. I then realized that what I had just said did not make sense. Were we not in this together?

December 1 — Day 29 — 287.76 miles. My first lead gave us only 3.68 miles. Roger recorded his frustration in his diary that night, "Gareth slow. Repeated stops and much time consumed checking his direction, which he seems to be finding a more difficult task than he ought. Without explanation or reason. Good visibility, good contrast, his compass always agrees, yet so many problems. Basically one of concentration and energy. He is in very low spirits and doubts about his abilities are eating his confidence and as we near our point of commitment these doubts weigh more heavily."

Five times during the day I stopped to adjust my boots to ease the pain in my feet. Finally, when I could take it no more, I requested an early stop after almost eight hours of plodding. Although I felt that I could take more pain, I was afraid of damaging my feet. That night I wrote, "Can see why others & I are worried but can't do more. ... Never thought I would have such severe problems. What a potentially dangerous position to be in."

December 2 — Day 30 — 298.72 miles. One of my better days since departure, my feet required only a few minor boot adjustments. I hoped this would continue, thus allowing me to take more of the navigation from Roger. His impatience with me was caused in part, I was sure, by having to do more than his share of these duties. I also felt that Roger brought a lot of his stress on himself. He often seemed reluctant to relinquish control of the navigation and other tasks, and appeared to have little trust in Robert's or my capabilities. I wondered if Roger trusted anyone other than himself.

Roger's frustration surfaced again later in the day during a break.

"Gareth, everything you say comes across as a moan," he said, "and I'm tired of it."

"Look Roger, I've noticed you often interpret what I say as complaining. When I say that my fingers are cold I mean it as a statement of fact. Would you prefer we not discuss how we feel? Next time call me on it and let's deal with it right away."

"I've tried," Roger replied, "but you just don't listen."

"You know," I continued, "I'll never live up to your ideals, just as you're not living up to mine."

"Maybe, but I don't ask for much — just steady uncomplicated progress."

"And I don't ask for much either, just a little civility and respect."

December 3 — Day 31 — 311.45 miles. For most of the day I continued strongly, keeping well ahead of Robert. However, I soon ran out of energy — every 50 paces I was forced to stop for a rest or a pee — so that even Robert passed me. I arrived 20 minutes late at camp.

During the day we had passed the Nimrod Glacier to our west and the mountains ahead were becoming more prominent by the hour. Looking at our large-scale map that evening we estimated that we were only four to five miles off course — easily corrected in the few more days it would take to reach the Gap. Then the real work would begin, up the Beardmore.

December 4 — Day 32 — 320.41. We left at 9:00 a.m. and I took the first leg, pushing harder than I should have, consumed with the

Roger having a snack at a break. (PHOTO BY GARETH WOOD)

desire to give Roger a break. Within the first 1.5 hours, Roger was a good 600 yards behind me and Robert was struggling to the rear of him. The pace, however, was too fast and my great resolve soon flagged. Roger then passed me. A few minutes later I signalled that I could go no farther. My feet were agonizing and had drained my remaining strength. Both Roger and Robert were clearly annoyed and after erecting the tent, both of them let me have it, their pent-up frustration at my continual stops and problems being ample fuel for the ensuing quarrel. While I applied tape and padding to various parts of my feet, Robert began.

"This has worried me for the past three days," he said dramatically. "We're close to the halfway mark and I'm very concerned that with Gareth's problems we're not going to complete this journey. The implications of this in respect to our remaining food have just hit me and I think that if he or I want out we should go to the American Beardmore base at Bladen Névé or the helicopter refuelling depot at Plunket Point and let Roger finish on his own. I've been thinking about why I wanted to go to the Pole in the first place. Whatever that desire was is no longer important. I would hate to see anyone die out here. I'm willing to go out with Gareth and leave you to do the journey solo," he said, turning to Roger.

"Just what I've been on about for days," Roger said, looking at me. "Your constant boot adjustments are costing us time. Gareth, you've got to cope — mind over matter, you know — just get your finger out. And Robert, you're the cause of delays as well. We can't think of breaking the team up now."

Upset by Robert's and then Roger's attack, I said, "You know that I want this just as much as you guys. Robert, you're the one who wants out, not me. You're having a much harder time than you're willing to admit. And in spite of my problems, you're usually the last to arrive at stops and camp. I know you're worried about me and I may be the cause of our failure, but my feet are painful and I honestly don't know what to do. But, we're not halfway yet and this is not the time to be discussing getting out. There's still time to sort out my problem. I'm damn well not giving up."

Roger wrote of the discussion in his diary that night, "I asked G if a helicopter was available would he get on it. He said that it would take considerable pressure from us two to get him to forsake this journey and get aboard."

Two hours later we were still arguing, using energy that would have been better spent moving toward our goal. Our frustration with each other was probably mostly a sign of fatigue and our concern over the rapidly approaching point of no return. Robert, it appeared, was only now coming to grips with the journey's implications. I also had to wonder if any other group pulling such weights nine hours a day in minus temperatures on an inadequate diet would function any better. I had serious doubts.

At 2:00 p.m. we departed; the drama of the event fizzled and the words became just that — words. Roger led the second leg, setting a punishing pace, which I felt I had to maintain. Two hours later I ran out of steam and stopped to consume a chocolate bar before pushing on into the face of the rapidly freshening wind and blowing snow. Robert, a tiny speck on the distant northern horizon, was occasionally obliterated by ground drift. At our break Roger turned to me.

"You know," he said, "you shouldn't take Robert's criticism too seriously. His anger's a reflection of his own fears. You can see why. If you were so far behind at every leg you'd be disillusioned too."

"I suppose," I responded, "but it's his own bloody fault — with all that extra shit he's carrying."

Roger, appearing not to hear, gazed at Robert's still diminutive figure. "I'd better go back and help him before we lose him," he said, stepping into his bindings and backtracking into the swirling snow. Half an hour later an exhausted Robert, minus his sledge, emerged from the growing blizzard. Roger still struggled with the sledge a little distance to the north. While I went back to help Roger, Robert finished his snack.

Upon Roger's arrival, Robert and I erected the tent in what was now a Force 7 blow. Roger wrote in his diary later that evening, "Pulling Robert's sledge it soon became apparent why he was having so much trouble. Far from easing the situation the 'work' he has done on the runners with his knife has made it much worse, and while on the firmer patches of sastrugi its glide was reasonable, on the drifting sand that was now blowing across the surface it was extremely heavy. As heavy as the sledges were when we began the journey. ... I then announced to Robert that I had a great surprise for him but it would cost him dear in tobacco."

CHAPTER EIGHT

THE GAP

"WHAT DO YOU mean?" we both asked.

"No wonder you're lagging behind. You're right about the runners — your sledge is impossible to pull. Obviously the runners are in worse shape than I thought. We're going to turn them over. That's my surprise," he said laughing.

"With what tools?" Robert asked.

"Your Swiss Army knife," Roger said simply.

With the tension between us temporarily broken by Roger's high spirits, I began the evening meal while Roger and Robert dismantled Robert's sledge. Stowing its contents in the lee of Roger's sledge, they then brought it, minus its trace, into the empty tent. It barely fit. The runners were held by 20 Allen screws; over the course of the next two hours they backed them out and removed the runners. Holding them up to the light we noticed that both had a vee-shaped grain which was facing backwards. Wondering if this was the problem, we turned them over and reinstalled them with the vee facing forward. Considering our minimal tool, the job was remarkable. Robert later recorded, "Pulling this f-ing sledge broke me — first time in my life I've been broken." He went on to describe how he struggled in the rear, " ... concentrated on a lump of ice 100 yards ahead. If I could make that I could do the next one. If I could get there, I could catch them up."

It was ten past midnight when we finally closed our eyes. Outside, a gale continued to rage, boding ill for progress the following day.

December 5 — Day 33 — 320.41 miles. Upon waking, we realized that we would be tentbound for the day. The blizzard, although downscaled to Force 5 or 6 from 7, based on the reading from our light, hand-held anemometer, was still too strong to permit travel. We spent most of the day repairing gear, Roger's anxiety to make some mileage in the slightly calmer afternoon being forestalled by Robert's insistence that he be allowed to finish mending his harness. He and I then repacked his sledge.

Even though we realized that we might be cutting our provisions short, we ate a full day's ration. Roger calculated that we had averaged, since leaving Mike and John, approximately ten miles a day and that we would need to average the same in order to reach the Pole within our remaining food reserves. To provide a safety net for unexpected delays or storms we would have to do better. We hoped that the glacier would provide us with that opportunity.

December 6 — Day 34 — 337.06 miles. The day began with my request for the tent brush, which we used to brush snow and ice from the floor of the tent before leaving each morning. Robert, who carried the brush, could not find it anywhere. Roger and I departed at 10:00 a.m., leaving Robert still sifting through the drift where he had emptied his sledge before turning the runners two evenings before.

I kept pace with Roger for most of the day, and my feet were relatively pain free. We covered 16.65 miles — a record. The conditions were perfect for travel. Our sledges moved easily over the crusted drift deposited the previous day and the temperature, partially due to heavy cloud cover, remained balmy, even rising to +.5°C at one point.

Our southern horizon grew in clarity with each passing day, adding new detail to the glaciers and peaks toward which we moved. To our west, mountains and glaciers, some perhaps unnamed and most unclimbed, pivoted coldly beside us. Roger wrote of them that night, "The many little cwms marked our progress as one sharp arete after another showed us their steep faces, first the north then the south, with a rapidity that was difficult to believe. Such is the scale of life on the Barrier passing 2 small cwms and 3 aretes during a nine hour march is regarded as rapid."

Robert, who throughout the day was nothing more than a speck on the northern horizon, arrived two hours late, without the brush. I shuddered to think that it might have been something vital.

December 7 — Day 35 — 353.13 miles. Robert set a gruelling pace for the first session, moving over the surface as if he had no sledge at all; it appeared that the turned runners had revolutionized his progress. I was very quickly left to toil weakly behind, arriving at the first break three-quarters of an hour late.

"Robert," I said, "humour me. Trade sledges for ten minutes after the break." Very reluctantly he complied. The difference was immediately noticeable and incredible. His glided with little or no effort — mine needed two or three good jerks just to break it free from the frozen surface.

After a few minutes I said, "Robert, how do you find my sledge? Don't you think there's a big difference?"

"Well, it's hard to tell," he replied noncommittally.

It was typical of Robert not to acknowledge the startling contrast and even though I recognized a real difference, I began to question my own judgment. After ten minutes of pulling, however, I knew the difference was real, especially when Robert's plaintive cries for me to return his sledge became increasingly urgent. It was not just in my mind.

At the next break I approached Roger.

"I'd like to stop early. I pulled Robert's sledge for ten minutes last session and there's a real difference. I'd like to turn the one rough runner on mine and see if it helps," I said.

"No," he said curtly. "Robert will help you at the end of the day. We've got to make time now while we can," he said, preparing to resume the march.

Roger was right; progress was more important.

Exhausted, I barely kept the others in sight for the balance of the day. I noted with interest, after inspecting Roger's sledge runners at the break, that they were glassy smooth with the mysterious vee pattern facing forward — the opposite to both of Robert's and one of my runners. Could Roger's sledge have been easier to pull all along?

During the course of the last session I hit the marathoner's wall. I collapsed on the end of my sledge and consumed all that I had left to eat, the brutal work far outstripping my limited energy intake. The sledge and its crippled runner had probably been aggravating my foot problem and depleting my energy from the start. Over an hour before we were to camp, Robert came back to meet me and together we hauled my sledge up to his before continuing into camp.

I removed and turned the burred runner over the next couple of hours. By 1:00 a.m. the job was complete. I fell into bed exhausted but sleep eluded me. I wondered if the turned runner would make a difference. I had a nagging worry that it was all in my head, and in a few hours I would find out. I was frightened.

Gareth turning his sledge runner over. (PHOTO BY GARETH WOOD)

December 8 — Day 36 — 371.07 miles. The moment was tense with anticipation. While I stepped nervously into my harness, half expecting no change in the sledge's performance, Roger and Robert looked on with amusement. Taking one hesitant step forward, and then another, I looked around — the sledge had followed gracefully. The broad grin that creased my face gave it all away — what a difference.

For the first leg I dogged Roger's heels, both surface conditions and temperature being ideal for a fast, clean run. I led the second leg and we completed another six miles without effort. Robert led a little too energetically during the third leg and I was once again relegated to the rear of our trio. Roger, catching him after an hour's chase, gave him hell. He recorded his conversation with Robert in his diary that night, "Don't you realize this is the first opportunity we've had of raising Gareth's confidence? This morning we covered six miles at an even pace and he was right there. It's the first time in days he's ever reached a rest stop in time to sit down before we arrived, and now you go crazy at the front and Gareth is back in his normal position."

Before us lay the long-awaited Gap, named by Shackleton the "Golden Gateway," guarded by the ice-worn spur of Mount Hope to the east and three granitic pillars to the west. Shackleton, who named Mount Hope for the promise it gave on December 3, 1908, wrote of his excitement, "From the top of this ridge there burst upon our view an open road to the south, for there stretched before us a great glacier running almost south and north between two huge mountain ranges."[1]

Through this famous pass we would ascend to the Beardmore, snatches of which we could just make out through the entrance. The Gap, although not quite the geographical halfway point, was the psychological axis of our journey.

December 9 — Day 37 — 387.82 miles. I led all three legs, accomplishing 16.75 miles without strain. Roger, with no pressure to navigate, and wanting to film our approach to the Gap from behind, hauled nonchalantly to our rear while Robert and I moved in tandem.

"I can't believe the difference in my sledge," I said to break an awkward silence.

"Incredible, isn't it?" Robert replied, finally admitting the difference.

"Just thinking about all those weeks of wasted energy makes me angry," I said.

"I know, me too," he agreed.

Close to land the ice was fractured and rippled so that for part of the day we skirted crevasses to both east and west. In the vicinity of Scott's Depression Camp, which he named "Slough of Despond" on

Roger and Robert approach the Gateway and Mount Hope. (PHOTO BY GARETH WOOD)

102

December 6, 1911, our weather was so spectacular we could not imagine the blizzard that kept him and his crew imprisoned in their tents for four consecutive days. Only one day short of the Gap, they experienced an unheard-of +33°F which, combined with driving snow, soaked clothing, tent and everything in it. "What on earth does such weather mean at this time of year? ... How great may be the element of luck! No foresight — no procedure — could have prepared us for this state of affairs,"[2] Scott wrote, and later, "The serious part is that we have this morning started our Summit rations — that is to say, the food calculated from the Glacier depôt has been begun."[3] Scott was already mortgaging his future.

On December 9, 1911, Scott's party began to move again after the blizzard. Hampered by deep, wet snow, the ponies sank to their bellies until PO Evans outfitted the lead pony, Snatcher, with snowshoes. After making no more than four miles, the half-rationed, exhausted ponies were shot where they lay. Scott named that camp "Shambles." From mechanical tractors to dogs and horses, the rest of the hauling, except for two more days with dogs, would belong strictly to the muscle of men.

I was at last becoming content with my performance. With the sledge repaired I believed that I had another 500 miles left in me. My feet were still sore and blistered, but I now felt that they were manageable. The sledge was no longer pulling to one side and the ache in my shoulder was gone. My diet was at last coming close to matching my energy output and I even managed to squirrel away the odd piece of chocolate for reserve.

Since our sledge repairs, nothing more had been said about the runner problems, but we all reflected on what we had learned. It was obvious. Through no one's fault (the manufacturer had advised us that the runners could be installed facing either direction) we had put together only Roger's sledge with the runners facing correctly forward. Our failure to recognize this mechanical problem for 350 miles was a direct result of failing to work together. To think that we could have traded sledges at the first hint of our troubles and recognized the discrepancy made us all complete fools. We could have died because of this obstinacy.

That day was the beginning of my personal journey of learning what it takes to work as a team. As I struggled to realize why it had all come to this, I found myself looking at my two companions with new respect. In spite of the disharmony, we had arrived at our present position only because Robert had the courage to dream, and Roger, stimulated by that challenge, had focussed our energies on the Pole. I hoped they would begin to see beyond my "annoying meticulousness" and appreciate the comfort and support I had provided the expedition with the construction of our base. I wondered if the issue of the sledge runners might usher in a new phase — I had already sensed a positive change in our behaviour toward each other — or would the stress of the remaining 500 miles draw out the worst in us again?

December 10 — Day 38 — 397.43 miles. Although we woke to sunshine, by the time we left camp overcast skies had reduced contrast to zero. This was of some concern, considering that we had yet to pick our way through the last risky miles of crevasses before climbing into the pass that would lead us to the Beardmore. We thought that we might have to rope up, but when we reached the first crevasses the sun emerged, restoring contrast.

Roger, weaving a circuitous path through the complex maze of crevasses, led us to the edge of the icefield three hours later. Mindful that it was our last stop on the Ross Ice Shelf, we ate our snack of chocolate, salami, biscuits and soup in thoughtful silence. For me, it was a time not of happy reflection, but of hope and optimism for easier progress ahead. If the slope rising to meet the top of the col immediately beyond us was any indication of what we could expect, however, we were not going to have an easy passage to the Polar Plateau. Roger began his ascent, but not before asking us to allow him enough time to reach the top so that he might film our advance up the slope. Robert and I took an early break from our second three-hour session and discussed life and girlfriends. I recognized that in spite of what I disliked about him, if it had not been for his relentless pursuit of a vision, I would not have been here, and I thanked him.

We gave Roger a good 50-minute lead before starting up. Once we were moving, the easy surface and the slope — less than antici-pated — made hauling almost pleasant.

Pulling in tandem, we noticed occasional red smears in the snow, not unlike paint.

"What's that?" Robert asked, puzzled.

"Looks a little like red algae, doesn't it?" I responded, shrugging my shoulders and grasping for an explanation.

"It doesn't look like any red algae I've ever seen," Robert said.

"I admit, it does look kind of weird," I replied.

"Look, over there," Robert said excitedly, pointing to a set of tracks in the snow.

"Snowmobile tracks," I exclaimed. "Now I know what that stuff is — oil."

We were shocked, as we had been told in London that no scientific teams would be operating in the area at this time. We surmised that the tracks had been made weeks or perhaps even months earlier. When we were close to Roger at the top of the col, what I saw beyond him immediately changed my opinion. My heart sank — a silhouetted figure was moving in the distance.

"There's someone there, Roger," I yelled excitedly, pointing in the direction of the figure.

Roger, remaining silent, continued to film, his Super 8 camera panning over both my face and Robert's, directly behind me.

"Robert," I said, turning to him quickly, "there's someone over there. There's more than one. God, it's a whole bloody camp."

"My god," he gasped.

Gareth on first sighting the geologists' camp at the Gateway. (COURTESY OF ROGER MEAR)

"Look," I pointed, my eyes welling with tears, my voice cracking. "We're buggered. All this for nothing."

"I don't believe it," Robert stammered, tears coursing down his cheeks as he slumped to his knees in the snow.

The implications of what we had just seen were enormous. The unsupported nature of our expedition was suddenly in jeopardy. The three of us just sat there, deflated. Would we still be able to claim that the journey had been totally unsupported or would this collection of tents be considered a depot?

Slowly we moved toward the three figures waiting by their tents. Pressed to introduce ourselves — Roger had already done so — Robert and I pulled up to them.

"Hi, I'm Robert Swan, the so-called expedition leader," Robert said, offering his hand.

"Hi, Jim Mattison," the grinning figure said, stretching out his hand in return.

"Gareth Wood," I said to Jim and his two companions, John Goodge and Don Depaolo.

"Nice to meet you," Jim said, still grinning. "Welcome to the Gateway. We're delighted, unofficially of course."

We unharnessed and were invited inside for tea and hot chocolate. We were powerless to refuse. Roger wrote of the event in his diary that night, "How we were supposed to walk past this encampment I know not." We decided to accept their hospitality for a maximum of two days and not use any of our rations. We believed that eating their food for two days would have no impact on our performance over the remaining 475 miles, and if we took nothing of their supplies with us when we left and used none of their equipment to improve our gear, the integrity of our unsupported trek could remain intact. Deep down though, we all had our doubts. Our goal had been snatched away from us.

I wrote of our encounter, "Good bunch of guys — Jim, John and Don — all American geologists. There will not be another party here for 10 to 15 years they estimate and they would have been gone several days ago if it were not for a logistical problem. Two others are out on their snowmobiles; Eugene Mikhalsky, a visiting Russian geologist, and Scott Borg, an American."

At their 8:00 p.m. radio schedule they informed South Pole that "Event 100," as McMurdo authorities had named our expedition, had arrived and that all was well. South Pole acknowledged the transmission and then wished us well, advising that they were looking forward to seeing us. Unofficially, of course, I guessed.

That night we were invited to dinner in the large pyramid tent they used as a mess. I stuffed myself — two pieces of steak, two lobster tails, bread and jam, fruit juices, oatmeal biscuits, broccoli, sherry and lots of tea. Everything I had craved over the past month materialized before me. The geologists must have been shocked by our ravenous appetites.

After dinner John showed us the written communique they had received, instructing them to avoid us if at all possible. When Roger hauled his sledge over the summit of the col, it was Jim who had first spotted him. Running through Jim's mind was whether or not he should offer his hospitality and if we would be upset by their presence. With mixed emotions he waited for Roger to reach him, wanting the first contact to be on Roger's initiative and not his own. He was aware of the implications of this unfortunate encounter.

I left the cook tent at midnight, my stomach churning from the variety and quantity of food I had consumed over the past few hours and, lying awake most of the night, listened to Roger retch outside the tent, his stomach refusing what would have been considered a normal meal only 30 days before. The next day we would get our promised rest.

December 11—12 — Days 39 and 40. Woke early the following morning, and my first thought was breakfast. My appetite was insatiable. Both Roger and Robert felt that I was overdoing it, but if

The American geologists' camp at the Gateway. (PHOTO BY GARETH WOOD)

they had not both been suffering violent indigestion, they would have gorged themselves as well. Robert was also unable to keep down the new food.

Using the Americans' fuel to melt snow and heat water, we washed socks and underwear, and had standup baths. After that, we prepared dinner for the geologists in expectation of their 7:30 p.m. return to camp. They had all taken off on their snowmobiles for a day of work, leaving us the general run of the camp, and we considered this the rest day we had agreed on earlier. Although we would not have had the opportunity or the inclination to wash if it were just the three of us, social conventions were now being forced upon us. How we must have smelled to them I can only guess.

In the cook tent, long after the others had departed for bed, I began a cassette tape message to my parents. At 4:00 a.m., surrounded by food, I could not resist making myself a meal. Sleep did not claim me until 5:00 a.m., but by 9:30 a.m. I was again awake and hungry for breakfast. I spent the second day reinforcing my sledge trace, which was fractured by constant wear, and eating. All our traces were damaged, Robert's being virtually irreparable.

I had planned to climb Mount Hope with Roger that day but after doctoring my blistered feet decided against it. Since we were leaving the next day I would have only a few more hours to rest my feet. I watched Roger ski out to the spur descending from Mount Hope and walk its crumbling granitic ridge to the summit. From there he gained a fresh perspective of the Ross Ice Shelf to the north, where we had struggled for the past 30-odd days, and the Beardmore Glacier to the south which we would ascend to the Polar Plateau.

That night both Roger and Robert ate sparingly, wary of the pitfalls of gourmandizing. For them, the only cure would be a return to the strict regimen of bland diet and brutal work. This we would resume the next morning.

December 13 — Day 41 — 409.13 miles. "Finally we manage to take ourselves away from the hedonistic pleasures of the Gateway Hut," Roger wrote of our late departure. Despite his upset stomach, he cooked an immense breakfast of bacon, eggs, toast and hash browns for the lot of us. I ate all that I could and was still hungry at the end of it, but even I recognized that there were limits to hospitality and stole guiltily away from the table to make myself ready for departure. Unknowingly, we had eaten much more than the Americans had anticipated, and later, we would hear stories of how we had left them with almost nothing.

"Strange feeling to be setting off on the next 500 mile leg. Just like leaving Willy Field," I wrote in my diary that night. As we pulled away from camp, Scott Borg filming our departure (Roger returned for the camera once we were out of sight), I had a last look at the Ross Ice Shelf. Whatever lay ahead, to my mind we had already accomplished something significant.

As soon as we left the camp we began to descend to the glacier. Robert sat on his sledge and rode it to the bottom while Roger continued on skis. I, mindful of falling, wore crampons. The weather was fantastic, offering us unrestricted views of nearby Mount Kyffin, and beyond, the Wedge Face, around which the Beardmore flowed. On this side of the Beardmore, and in the Queen Alexandra Range along the western flank of the glacier, lay the mountain called "the Cloudmaker."

It was on this that we set our sights. Within the first few miles we encountered pressure ice. Roped to each other and the sledges, we continued cautiously through a mile of fractured ice caused by the intrusion of the Socks Glacier, named by Shackleton after his lost pony. We were a little worried about repeating his experience.

This is how he described it: "After lunch the light was better, and as we marched along we were congratulating ourselves upon it when suddenly we heard a shout of 'help' from Wild. We stopped at once and rushed to his assistance, and saw the pony sledge with the forward end down a crevasse and Wild reaching out from the side of the gulf grasping the sledge. No sign of the pony. ... Wild says he just felt a sort of rushing wind, the leading rope was snatched from his hand, and he put out his arms and just caught the further edge of the chasm."[4]

Moving uneventfully through the disturbed ice, we stopped between the Socks Glacier and Monument Rock to film Robert holding PO Evans' posthumously awarded Polar Medal. It was near here that Evans, ironically described by Scott on his way to the Pole as a "tower of strength," had died on the return journey.

After suffering falls into two crevasses, Scott wrote on February 16, 1911, "Evans has nearly broken down in the brain, we think. He is absolutely changed from his normal self-reliant self,"[5] and on February 17 Scott recorded his end: "Abreast of Monument Rock we stopped, and seeing Evans a long way astern, I camped for lunch. ... After lunch, and Evans still not appearing, we looked out, to see him still afar off. By this time we were alarmed, and all four started back on ski. I was first to reach the poor man and shocked at his appearance; he was on his knees with clothing disarranged, hands uncovered and frostbitten, and a wild look in his eyes. Asked what was the matter, he replied with a slow speech that he didn't know, but thought he must have fainted. We got him to his feet, but after two or three steps he sank down again. He showed every sign of complete collapse. Wilson, Bowers, and I went back for the sledge, whilst Oates remained with him. When we returned he was practically unconscious, and when we got him into the tent quite comatose. He died quietly at 12.30 a.m."[6]

Although Wilson suggested that Evans died of a brain injury received in a crevasse fall, Roland Huntford, in his book *Scott and Amundsen,* provided a more plausible cause — scurvy. Symptoms of scurvy, caused by vitamin C deficiency, include both weakened blood vessels, which would account for the failure of a wound Evans received to heal, and the general malaise characterized by his lack of enthusiasm, which Scott assumed to be a lack of confidence.

It was fitting that Robert had brought Evans' Polar Medal with him. Both were large men who prided themselves on their physical prowess. That Evans was a "tar" in the truest sense of the word there was no doubt, that Robert was his distant mirror was also apparent.

CHAPTER NINE

THE BEARDMORE

OPPOSITE MONUMENT ROCK we pitched our tent in the lee of the Queen Alexandra Range. To our east lay the Commonwealth Range, lower but no less rugged. Running an icy gauntlet between these two rocky walls, the Beardmore Glacier slides toward the Ross Ice Shelf. Along this serpentine path we would travel to the interior of the frozen continent. The great river of ice descends from the edge of the Polar Plateau, altitude 7,150 feet, 124 miles down to the Ross Ice Shelf, 200 feet above sea level.

December 14 — Day 42 — 425.06 miles. A perfect day for all of us. Stripped to long underwear, we moved steadily forward in bright sunlight, glacier glasses protecting our eyes from the glare. Because we could see our goal, the Cloudmaker, about whose craggy peak hung the inevitable cumulus, we had no need for compass.

I led two sessions at a relaxed pace while Roger, happy to have a day of rest, assumed a rearguard position. He stopped occasionally to take photos and inspect pools of glacial melt around erratics lodged in the ice. Robert, nervous about being in the lead across crevassed ice, remained sandwiched between us during my two stints, leading only when he was sure the surface was solid.

As I looked around, I saw hundreds of sites clearly worthy of a whole day's exploration. I walked as if in a trance, hesitant to even glance at my feet lest I miss a tiny fraction of this remarkable and seldom-viewed land. I recorded in my diary that night, "Position

111

today nearly opposite mouth Alice Glacier. Felt so much fitter & feet are definitely better — if only this left foot would let up."

Scott, manhauling over the same ground 74 years before, made for the Commonwealth Range until, upon reaching the middle of the Beardmore and encountering pressure ice, he was forced to change course toward the Cloudmaker. As he moved closer to the western edge of the glacier, he was able to view some peaks in the east missed by Shackleton. I wondered how he felt, travelling up the Beardmore with Shackleton's stamp on virtually every peak, valley and glacier within sight.

Shackleton, encountering blue ice and thinly bridged crevasses almost immediately, wrote, " ... we have had one of our hardest day's work and certainly the most dangerous so far."[1] Each of them in turn had plunged through fragile snow lids, saving themselves only by their harnesses. "The situation became momentarily more dangerous and uncertain. The sledges, skidding about, came up against the sheer, knife-like edges of some of the crevasses. ... "[2]

December 15 — Day 43 — 444.9 miles. We travelled over névé for most of the day, donning crampons to cross the occasional patch of blue ice and polished sastrugi. Awkward after so many days on skis, I stumbled about, the sharp tines of the crampons catching tiny peaks in the rippled surface. I arrived at camp 25 minutes behind Roger. Robert was nowhere in sight. Opposite Hewson Glacier, just

Robert manhauling on the Beardmore Glacier. (PHOTO BY GARETH WOOD)

112

Manhauling — Scott's 1910-1912 expedition. (COURTESY OF THE ROYAL GEOGRAPHICAL SOCIETY)

north of the Cloudmaker, we ate our meal in silence and, as the weather was fair, bivouacked between our sledges. To have one night's freedom from the close confines of the tent was too precious an opportunity to miss.

Robert, upon arrival two hours later, moved painfully, his pale face drawn from the day's rough ascent.

"God, you look buggered. What's the problem?" Roger asked sympathetically.

Robert winced. "My knee's bad. I caught my foot in a crack and fell. I could hear the bloody thing snap as I went down. It's damn sore, and my back hurts like hell too. I must've twisted it."

"You look pretty bad," Roger said. "Eat your dinner and get into your sleeping bag. We'll take a look at your knee."

Robert had wrapped a bandage around his knee hoping to provide some support. There was little more that we could do. Later, as we lay in our bags under the too-bright sky, Roger and Robert reviewed Robert's options.

"You'll just have to keep moving at your own pace. We can't stop," Roger said. "We'll keep an eye out so that we don't get separated."

"It's that damn sledge. It was all over the place. I think I'm going back to solid trace. There's no control with rope," Robert said drowsily as he closed his eyes to the pain and fatigue.

On this same day in 1911, Roald Amundsen and his four companions reached the Pole. As Amundsen described it, "I had decided that we would all take part in the historic event; the act itself of planting the flag. It was not the privilege of *one* man, it was the privilege of *all* those who had risked their lives in the fight and stood together through thick and thin. It was the only way I could show my companions my gratitude here at this desolate and forlorn place. ... Five roughened, frostbitten fists it was that gripped the post, lifted the fluttering flag on high and planted it together as the very first at the Geographic South Pole."[3]

While Amundsen was celebrating his victory, Scott and his 12 companions were still floundering through deep drift 360 nautical miles to the north. The weather continued to conspire against them, forcing an early stop due to white-out conditions. Scott wrote, " ... but oh! for fine weather; surely we have had enough of this oppressive gloom."[4]

December 16 — Day 44 — 463.15 miles. Reattaching Robert's solid trace while Roger cooked breakfast, I found myself looking forward to the day's advance up the glacier in the clear, mild conditions, and was expecting a smooth surface. Within half an hour I was forced to halt to tape a broken blister. Where this would have caused me great anxiety on the Ross Ice Shelf, I now viewed it with little concern. We completed six miles by the end of the first session, passing close under the Cloudmaker before stopping for lunch on a lateral moraine where the sun's warmth was evident in the surrounding meltwater pools.

It was about here that Scott, on December 17, built his mid-glacier depot, and it was also here that Shackleton camped, bruised and tired after having spent a day tumbling into crevasses and skating over hard blue ice. Unlike Scott, who had crampons designed by PO Evans, Shackleton wore ski boots.

Close to the edge of the Beardmore, we followed its course to the cliffs defining the Cloudmaker fault, where we encountered pressure ice. To avoid the worst of it, we moved in single file. Instead of improving, the surface deteriorated to a frozen chop of crests with troughs two to three feet deep. Over this rough surface our sledges slipped and shied into water-worn hollows and over ridges of frozen icemelt. Nevertheless, we managed our normal speed on crampons, covering five to six miles during each session. (We had taken our sledgewheels off to protect them from the rough terrain, so we could only estimate the distance travelled.)

During the day Robert pulled abreast of me.

"I had a little chat with Roger back there. He's disappointed with the journey now. He thinks it was all ruined at the Gap when we met the Americans. The isolation, the magic, it's gone," he said.

"I can't say that I blame him," I replied. "I'm disappointed too, but it happened and we can't do much about it."

Before Robert arrived at camp that night I told Roger that I thought Robert should start doing some cooking. Just when I thought our relationship might be on the mend, I put my foot in it.

"I'm going to mention it to him tonight," I said.

"No," Roger shot back aggressively. "Robert's not to touch the stove. It's too dangerous. He's not learned how to use it and now it's too late."

"Okay, you're right, I'll operate it and he can do the cooking," I countered.

"No ... aw shit, I don't care, as long as he doesn't touch the stove," Roger replied angrily.

By the time Robert appeared I had been put off discussing the matter that evening.

For the second night in a row we bivouacked, our sledges parked downhill of our sleeping bags, and as the sun circled slowly overhead the steady drone of a Pole-bound aircraft intruded on our silence.

December 17 — Day 45 — 480.90 miles. We pulled away under a canopy of low stratus, which obscured the surrounding peaks but failed to totally block out the sun, and its sharp outline burned through the veil like a circle brand. Although the weather was not as spectacular as the previous day, the +3°C temperature compensated for the low light.

Immediately after departure we found ourselves slowed by rough ice. Robert's trace, which was weak to begin with, separated from stress within the first half-hour. We spliced it with a bootlace and he carried on quite a distance behind us, arriving late for the first break.

"I'm sorry I'm so slow. I can't get used to these crampons," he sighed, easing himself gently down upon his sledge.

"We'll only be on crampons for a couple more days," Roger replied. "Then we'll be back to skis."

We entered the broadest region of the glacier, where to the east the Keltie Glacier oozed from its rocky valley to enter the main flow. Toward the end of the third session, as we gained the top of a small rise, the vista of the upper Beardmore spread out before us. Ahead and in the middle was Mount Buckley, splitting the great

115

river of ice east and west. South of that was another glacial island, Mount Darwin, and beyond that the Polar Plateau, which we would reach in a couple of days.

Leaving together after our second break, I pulled abreast of Robert.

"You buggered off this morning before I could talk with you," I said. "Last night I suggested to Roger that you share some of the cooking duties. He went nuts. He says it's too late for you to start learning to use the stove."

"Too late! Why?" he asked.

"I don't know," I said, ducking the question. "Anyway, he felt that you could do some cooking if I manage the stove. Do you have a problem with that?"

"No," he replied simply.

Shackleton, on December 17, cached warm clothing and extra gear on Mount Buckley to facilitate a light dash to the Pole, seeing an end to the glacier and the beginning of the third stage of his journey, the Polar Plateau. In comparison, Scott, three years later, beset by blizzards and deep snow, trudged about five days behind Shackleton. We had already passed Scott's position of the same date and were closing in on Shackleton's, though it was still a good 1.5 day's march ahead.

Roger helping Robert repair his sledge trace on the Beardmore Glacier. (PHOTO BY GARETH WOOD)

116

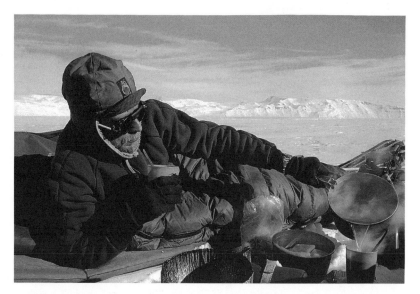

Roger bivouacking on the Beardmore Glacier. (PHOTO BY GARETH WOOD)

That night, taking into account the average error of each of our five watches, I calculated the exact time as I had done every second day since departure. Precise time, to the second, was necessary for navigation, especially for the final leg of the journey where we would rely principally upon sextant and sunshots to calculate our latitude and longitude. On the Plateau, due to our limited amount of food, a few miles could mean the difference between success and failure. Again we bivouacked in the lee of our sledges, but by early morning we were regretting it — a Force 2 to 3 blow and driving snow had drifted us in.

December 18 — Day 46 — 501.67 miles. Robert, buried in snow, woke me early to complain that when I moved my sledge out of the drift earlier that morning it had had dire consequences for him. Roger laughed as he watched Robert's cocooned body wriggling out from under a hummock of snow. Robert, however, was in no mood to see the humour in it. He had been kept awake all night with his aching knee.

Roger was in a similar mood. I recalled my conversation with Robert about Roger's feeling that all had been ruined at the Gap. For him the challenge was gone. He merely wanted to get to the Pole in the quickest time possible, as if the whole expedition suddenly lacked merit. I still felt strongly that what we had set out to accomplish in London had only marginally been compromised at the Gap — it was a matter of degree.

For the first session we donned crampons to cross isolated patches of blue ice. Roger set a harrowing pace that I maintained without pain or hardship. The surface during the latter half of the second and all of the third session was broken occasionally by a few modest crevasses, no more than four feet wide. We crossed them easily as they were well bridged.

Robert, continuing to lag behind, complained of Roger's pace. At our third break Roger and I relieved Robert of the tent and poles respectively. By the time Robert arrived at camp half an hour late, Roger and I had erected the tent in a bowl approximately six miles below Mount Buckley, opposite the Dominion Range and the huge Mill Glacier. To either side of Mount Buckley lay a seemingly impassable field of disturbed ice — to the east, the expansive Shackleton Ice Falls and to the west the smaller Wild Ice Falls.

We were all tired, I more than in the previous few days. It was probably due partly to the increasing altitude but also because none of us were replenishing vital body reserves with our just-adequate diet.

December 19 — Day 47 — 517.42 miles. Our last day on the Beardmore. After covering the first six miles on snow, we hauled onto a large patch of old ice that carried us to the edge of Mount Buckley. From there we struggled up a very steep pitch, the ice corridor between Mount Buckley and the Shackleton Ice Falls.

While Roger and Robert took the direct approach on crampons, I traversed the slope on skis, zigzagging my way to the top. I laboured — two steps forward, pause for deep breath, lean into the harness, two more steps forward, pause for deep breath, lean into the harness — and slowly bypassed the area of ruptured ice to achieve the summit. Both Shackleton and Scott had used the same slope, which Shackleton had discovered in 1908.

Shackleton, relaying his sledges one at a time, without crampons, considered this traverse to be his hardest yet. He wrote, "All the morning we worked up loose, slippery ice, hauling the sledges up one at a time by means of the alpine rope, then pulling in harness on the less stiff rises. All the afternoon we relayed up a long snow slope, and we were hungry and tired when we reached camp. We have been saving food to make it spin out, and that increases our hunger; each night we all dream of foods."[5] They resorted to pony maize to supplement their meagre ration, and their limited and incomplete diet of biscuits, pemmican and sugar was clearly their undoing.

The next day we would negotiate one of the most dangerous ascents of the journey. Although it appeared that we had conquered the worst of the crevassing, beyond Mount Darwin which was just ahead lay an immense cataract of standing waves of ice created at the outflow of that vast ice reservoir, the Polar Plateau.

We attained 6,500 feet altitude that night, the temperature -17°C and threatening colder. I wondered at Shackleton's decision to cache the bulk of his warm clothing on Mount Buckley. While we were working, the cold had little effect on us, but the minute we stopped it crept through our sweat-soaked clothing, stealing precious body heat and painfully reminding us where we were. Despite the cold, I travelled in underwear tops, bottoms and salopettes only.

At camp we were mentally high, silently celebrating the spectacular surroundings and the whole glorious experience. I wrote, "Feel good physically & mentally. We are doing well. Last session in ski & feet still feel good, just a bit sore. This has been real climax to trip. Glad it came in middle." Roger wrote in his diary, "It is 7 days since we departed the gateway and yet the Beardmore lies behind us. We some 2 days now ahead of Scott despite leaving the Gap 2 days behind him. Our progress has been remarkable."

December 20 — Day 48 — 532.8 miles. Bright cirrus, drifting from a great white mass far to the south, stretched fan-like over us as we departed. Circumventing miles of crevasse between us and the Plateau, we bore southwest like Scott, hauling over pressure waves capped with crusted snow. Although anxious to turn south, we were

Roger manhauling at the top of the Beardmore Glacier. (PHOTO BY GARETH WOOD)

determined to avoid the gaping fractures Scott had encountered when he turned south too early. Along the same tumble of ice, Shackleton had discovered a break through which he ventured. He was roped to his companions, and they plunged through snow bridge after snow bridge, unaware of the danger until it was too late. Shackleton wrote, " ... for the ground is so treacherous that many times during the day we are saved only by the rope from falling into fathomless pits. Wild describes the sensation of walking over this surface, half ice and half snow, as like walking over the glass roof of a station."[6] And later, camped on a bridged crevasse, he prayed, "Please God, ahead of us there is a clear road to the Pole."[7]

We moved over crevasses the rest of the day, and at camp that night hoped we would soon leave them behind us. In the tent, Roger and Robert, whose relationship had only recently changed from antagonism to a renewal of their London friendship, chattered brightly to each other. Robert even accepted Roger's lighthearted comments about his clumsiness as he tried to repair his leaking Thermorest mattress. He still remembered with delight Roger's burning a hole in the inner tent while igniting the stove, weeks earlier.

Scott made his final Pole team selections on this day and wrote, "I have just told off the people to return to-morrow night: Atkinson, Wright, Cherry-Garrard, and Keohane. All are disappointed — poor Wright rather bitterly, I fear. I dreaded this necessity of choosing — nothing could be more heartrending."[8] In fact, Scott had just handed them their lives.

December 21 — Day 49 — 549.54 miles. Midsummer day. During the last three-hour session we turned slightly south but before the fractured ice released us completely we were forced to navigate over another series of ominous, snow-bridged crevasses, some over 20 feet in width. We crossed them without mishap.

The weather was spectacular in comparison to what Shackleton experienced on his midsummer day. He wrote, "We have frostbitten fingers and ears, and a strong blizzard wind has been blowing from the south all day. ... We are very hungry now, and it seems as cold almost as the spring sledging."[9]

We dipped into a low valley with little crevassing, its walls just high enough to obstruct our view of the mountains to the north, and turning directly south we faced the Pole for the first time. Scott reached the same position on December 24. Although there were still miles of pressure ice ahead of us, the third and final leg of the journey had begun. We were only 312.5 miles from the Pole.

In the tent that night I wrote, "Feel sad as really enjoyed the Beardmore. ... Beautiful ice scape today with beautiful sastrugi, waves, humps, crevasses with good bridges & distant views of huge crevassed fields. Can still see Dominion Range & top of Bowers & Darwin. What will tomorrow bring?"

Chapter Ten

THE POLAR PLATEAU

"By day the hot sun fermented us; and we were dizzied by the beating wind."[1] That simple line, written by T.E. Lawrence about Arabia, could easily have applied to the Polar Plateau we were just set to traverse. The difference, although seemingly great, was in reality small. Both were deserts, ours no less dry than the earth's greatest sandy wastes. His shifting sand was our driving snow and on good days his fermenting sun cast its relentless rays upon us as well. The wind that robbed his body of moisture was similar to our own. It snapped at our clothing, seared exposed flesh and moaned hollowly in our ears. Within the tent we could escape its icy touch, but the wail of its passage hounded us into our dreams.

December 22 — Day 50 — 564.86 miles. Roger erred in the calculation of our dead reckoning longitude on the 21st, requiring a four-degree compensatory bearing. Memories of the cold we had experienced on our Cape Crozier journey plagued me throughout the day. The temperature the previous evening was -24.5°C, with little change by morning. Although I had known much colder temperatures, to live and work in such conditions without respite was numbing. Under a flawless sky we pressed boldly forward in a Force 3 to 4 southerly blow. My lips and nose bore the brunt of the searing cold, despite the insulation of balaclava and goggles.

Robert announced at our first break that he had also become bored with the march since our meeting with the American geological party at the Gap. Roger, who had earlier expressed similar sentiments, now changed his opinion — the cold and the need for accuracy of navigation had rejuvenated his flagging interest. He recorded in his diary, "The conditions today on the plateau have been a timely reminder of where we are and how much there is yet to do."

Throughout the day we climbed a series of huge pressure waves, each slightly higher than the last. Behind us, sinking beneath the lip of the tremendous ice fall exiting the Plateau, we could still make out peaks of the Dominion Range, copper bright in the afternoon sun. During the last session we started up a steep rise that Scott had referred to on Christmas Day as a submerged mountain. Leading up this slope, I detoured right to avoid a small area of disturbance.

"You're at least 150 yards off course," Roger shouted from behind, pointing forcibly to the east.

"I was just avoiding that pressure ice," I shouted back, nodding across the slope. "We know the deviation. It's easily corrected."

At 9,100 feet we camped. I recorded in my diary, "Really feeling the altitude now ... have been climbing since Buckley Island." Shackleton also wished for an end to the climbing, the altitude and the hard work. That night his thoughts turned toward home, "One longs to hear 'the hansoms slurring through the London mud'. Instead of that we are lying in a little tent, isolated high on the roof of the end of the world, far, indeed, from the ways trodden of men. Still, our thoughts can fly across the wastes of ice and snow and across the oceans to those whom we are striving for and who are thinking of us now."[2]

In our tent that night my mind also turned toward home, although overshadowing all thought was the immense job before us and the worry about a navigational error. Roger and I spent an increasing amount of time ensuring that this would not happen. The end of each day saw us sitting up in our sleeping bags reviewing our navigation. Roger would double- and triple-check our dead reckoning calculations. Then I would don windproofs and dash outside with the sextant to take a sunshot while Roger called out the exact time. I would then also double- and triple-check my calculations before we reviewed each other's work. It was not uncommon for both of us to spend several hours at it, and bed down long after Robert.

We were hopeful that with our remaining 40 days' rations, and even longer of soup, hot chocolate and fuel, we would have a comfortable margin of safety. Barring storms, we estimated that the Pole was no more than 21 days' march to the south.

December 23 — Day 51 — 580.27 miles. The cold, deepened by a persistent southerly blow, necessitated maximum protection. Over balaclava and goggles we pulled our anorak hoods, leaving only small, oval openings to see through. Locked within these tight cells we marched, our faces parallel to the ground to avoid the burning sting of the wind and airborne ice crystals. At each numbing break we ate our ration and drank our cold soup quickly (two of our thermoses were no longer functioning), anxious to resume the relentless plodding, which at least kept us warm.

For the whole day we laboured up one great swell after another, crashing through the crust in the troughs and skating over white ice on the crests. Upon attaining each wind-blasted summit we fully expected a level plain to be revealed beyond it. Toward the end of the second leg we crossed several wide but securely capped crevasses. We probed each with ski poles; they all passed the critical test.

During our last three-hour session we continued upward, each stride of the ski slow and methodical. The rise soon flattened out, and the full, glorious expanse of the level Plateau flooded our vision, overwhelming thought and action. Far to the south, a Wedgwood blue sky met the smooth, white symmetry of the earth's curvature with startling clarity. Although there was still a series of low waves to be negotiated, we had essentially reached the summit.

Shackleton, close to the same position on January 2, mired in deep snow with a broken sledge, struggled against the altitude and a lack of food. "My head is giving me trouble all the time. ... God knows we are doing all we can, but the outlook is serious if this surface continues and the plateau gets higher, for we are not travelling fast enough to make our food spin out and get back to our depot in time. ... Man can only do his best, and we have arrayed against us the strongest forces of nature."[3]

I wrote that night, "Ahead of Scott & Shackleton now — Shackleton for first time. Our average since Gap 16.40 miles per day. ... Shared cooking etc. tonight with Roger. Great meal & feel full but have taken extra biscuit & piece of choc from that saved! What the hell."

December 24 — Day 52 — 595.58 miles. We departed in -24°C under bright sun with virtually no wind. Roger led the first session and I the second. We were 277 miles from the Pole, which at our present pace would take no more than 18 or 19 days. In a matter of weeks we would all be home, we thought, our present anger, frustration and fear overshadowed by our success.

Robert, moving like an express train, led the first two hours of the third session after receiving rudimentary instructions from Roger on how to use the prismatic compass. For the first hour he led well but during the second hour, Roger signalled several times that he was off course. Frustrated, Robert waved me into the forward position while he and Roger hauled side by side behind.

They discussed all manner of personal subjects, including their relationships with me, and Roger recorded his frustration, " ... and been unable to form any bond or even hold a conversation that did not centre on some gripe or other. ... This is perhaps the biggest disappointment of the journey that Gareth with dogged but unjoyous determination waits only for the end of the journey and the end of the expedition."

Had he bothered to plumb the depths of my soul he would have found a man, like himself, with the same joys, fears and aspirations.

Christmas Day — Day 53 — 611.15 miles. Rising at 6:00 a.m. to complete our nine-hour stint early so that we might enjoy what limited festivities we could devise, we were away by 7:35 a.m. I even had it in mind to change my long underwear tops and bottoms, underpants and socks that night. Six hundred miles in the same underwear seemed enough!

The morning was no different from any other — bright sun and clear blue sky except for some thin cirrus, and a slight wind from the south. While Roger and Robert packed the tent I pulled out for the first lead. Alone on the point, I had time to reflect on what this Christmas would not provide. Certainly friendship from my companions, my family, and last, a turkey dinner complete with trimmings. Although we would celebrate with a double ration, it was not a substitute for my family's Christmas fare.

Roger led the second leg with Robert attempting the third. Within half an hour, having covered only half a mile, Roger took back the lead.

"Am I off course?" Robert asked.

"Well, it's not bad," Roger said kindly, "but it's taking too long and we don't have the time."

Robert, miffed, could not help but feel inadequate.

At 5:35 p.m. we camped. The mood was far from festive. Beneath the thin veneer of friendship bubbled a brew of repressed hostility and emotional exhaustion. Forcing a formal civility for the sake of tradition, we downed cup after cup of hot chocolate before consuming a double ration of macaroni and cheese. As well, I ate two bacon bars, two portions of sausage, 11 biscuits, chocolate and butter. While the others complained of being stuffed, I could have eaten the same again. After dinner, Roger surprised us with two teabags he had hauled from Cape Evans just for this occasion. After all, it was a British expedition! Although I wanted only one cup, Roger and Robert squeezed the bags dry before lighting their traditional Christmas cigars. Content, I lay back and watched the cigar smoke drifting through the air.

Polar tradition has it that Christmas is a day when rations are relaxed. Scott wrote of his dinner, "We had four courses. The first, pemmican, full whack, with slices of horse meat flavoured with onion and curry powder and thickened with biscuit; then an arrow-root, cocoa and biscuit hoosh sweetened; then a plum-pudding; then cocoa with raisins, and finally a dessert of caramels and ginger. After the feast it was difficult to move."[4]

In comparison, Shackleton had "hoosh, consisting of pony ration boiled up with pemmican and some of our emergency Oxo and biscuit. Then in the cocoa water I boiled our little plum pudding, which a friend of Wild's had given him. This, with a drop of medical brandy, was a luxury which Lucullus himself might have envied; then came cocoa, and lastly cigars and a spoonful of *creme de menthe* sent us by a friend in Scotland. We are full tonight, and this is the last time we will be for many a long day."[5]

Shackleton, with 500 nautical miles still to go to the Pole and back to this position, had only one month's supply of food left:

The Christmas Day luxury — a cup of tea. (COURTESY OF ROGER MEAR)

clearly inadequate to meet the incredible challenge. Planning to dump excess equipment the following day in an attempt to conserve energy, he and his companions agreed to further reduce their already meagre ration. Marshall, the group's physician, taking their temperatures that night, noted that they were all two degrees below normal. Their inadequate diet, the cold and the brutal work were already beginning to take their toll.

December 27 — 28 — Days 55 and 56 — 645.43 miles. My toenail came off last night and I felt much more comfortable today. Shackleton wrote, "If the Barrier is a changing sea, the plateau is a changing sky."[6] Supporting that observation, wave upon wave of cumulus rolled ponderously overhead as we departed. While Roger led the first session, Robert and I walked side by side behind.

I said, "We've got a reasonable margin of food now. Do you think we should suggest to Roger that we have another double ration on New Year's Day? We could all use it, and I don't think it'd compromise safety."

"Yes, and I'd like to see us have extra biscuits too. We've got plenty," Robert added.

"At least we should be having more drinks," I said. "We've got two full fuel bottles and four gallon containers left."

Robert nodded before changing the subject.

"What're your plans after the expedition?" he asked after a moment.

"I don't really know. I haven't given it much thought, actually."

That was the difference between Robert and me. Robert already had dreams of achieving the North Pole while I was focussed on completing the task at hand.

At camp that night Robert informed me that we would have a double ration on New Year's Day and possibly extra biscuits after that, but the rest we would save. Roger, wisely, wanted to have as much surplus as possible, to prove that we had a reasonable margin of safety and in case we were forced to camp at the Pole. We had no idea what reception we might receive.

December 29 — Day 57 — 679.16 miles. Building toward the east, layers of cirrostratus swept quickly across the southern sky followed closely by cirrocumulus, which dimmed both light and contrast. The surface, pockmarked with the irregularities upon which we depended for our bearings, fused into a solid white sheet over which I again weaved an unsteady course. I could hear Roger and Robert discussing my progress directly behind me.

"Gareth's not trying. He's just not concentrating. In one hour he's thrown away all our good progress," Roger said as he moved forward to take over.

When I checked Roger's track, it was dead on; however, his progress was slower than mine. Perhaps that was my problem; I moved too quickly, always sensitive to Roger's pushing from behind.

After an hour the sun burst through the cloud behind us, unveiling a spectacular full parhelion. The air danced and sparkled with delicate ice crystals, each bearing a tiny spectrum. In the midst of this tinsel-bright storm, the sun's refracted image radiated outward in two golden, concentric halos. I wanted to take a picture with Robert in the foreground but he hurried by, ignoring my plea. Something was eating him.

Beneath this sky, Roger ushered me into the lead at the beginning of the third session. He seemed more impatient than ever to get to the Pole. First, our goal had been ten miles per day, then 15, then 18 miles because it was attainable, and now Roger wanted 20. For him, the journey had not been half the challenge he expected, and the sooner he was quit of it the better.

At camp that night, Roger's frustration with me boiled over.

"I'm disappointed with your navigation. You've been at it long enough. It should be second nature now," Roger complained to

Parhelion on the Polar Plateau. (COURTESY OF ROGER MEAR)

me bitterly. "I'm sick of having to lead as often as I do. I was counting on your support. And you've done nothing to make us like you," he finished.

"Look," I said fuming, "I'm confident of my navigation. No one can navigate to YOUR satisfaction ... and what has Robert contributed to this journey? He doesn't cook and he doesn't sit up every night calculating our position. I don't see you pissed off at him." I continued angrily, "I'd like to have done more, but on the Ross Ice Shelf I just didn't have the bloody strength. It was all I could do to place one foot in front of the other. You had a hell of an advantage over Robert and me with your sledge runners on the right way. And, what've you guys done to build a relationship with me?"

"Well, well, the clam finally opens. I didn't think you had it in you," Roger said condescendingly. "You've never shared a bit of emotion or joy with us. How'd you expect us to react?"

"Your irritating habits are what get me," Robert said, reacting to my criticism. "You're just a bloody old woman. Bed at ten every night, always organizing, cleaning, putting things away, sweeping up. You've never even tried to be one of us."

"You're right," I shot back sarcastically, "I'm only just learning to be a slob."

"And you've never once initiated a project or suggested a trip," Roger added. "You live in your own dark little world where no one can reach you."

"You've provided the energy behind all our training trips, I agree," I said. "But who designed and put together your whole bloody base? Who ensured you had electricity, light and all the other comforts you enjoyed for nine months? You two would be living in a box with candles if Robert didn't burn it down first."

Before anyone could respond to my accusations, I continued, "There's a lot of hate in this tent. Where did we go wrong?"

"I don't know if we were ever right. The pressures in London put a fix to that," Roger replied.

The argument drifted on until 2:00 a.m. when sleep finally dulled our combative natures. I recorded in my diary, "I think the great adventure is no longer for me. I am almost afraid to arrive at the Pole now and certainly afraid to get back to the real world. ... Still a bit confused about Roger and myself. ... During our talk last night, I think I began to see we do have individual traits that are irritating but that we either must accept them or discuss them. They are not a foundation for hatred. Actually shook hands with Roger! Hope there is something here."

December 30 — Day 58 — 696.12 miles. With Robert leading the first session, I pulled abreast of Roger. We spoke at length about our conversation the previous night, and although resolving nothing, it improved our painful relationship. We could now discuss anything, without the bitterness that had clouded most of our talks to that point. I also told Roger that Robert's failure to do any of the cooking, despite his agreement on the Beardmore to do so, annoyed me.

December 31 — Day 59 — 712.14 miles. The day began with Roger asking Robert to cook breakfast. Watching him foil Robert's every excuse was amusing.

Leading the second leg, I crossed an area of rough sastrugi, not unlike the frozen chop of the Beardmore. The contrast and shadow made for excellent navigation.

Roger wrote of our healed relationship that night, "Things are good now I think between Woody and me. But less so between RS and G. ... Now it's my relationship with Robert that is as bad as it's been. The atmosphere in the tent is calm but subdued. Robert is not quite as content as he likes to have us believe, brooding on something."

As I closed my eyes, I could not help but reflect on the reversal of Robert's and my relationship with Roger. The pressure created by the close confines of the tent and the hard work made tight bonds,

Robert. (PHOTO BY GARETH WOOD)

Roger. (Photo by Gareth Wood)

but at the same time it took nothing more than an innocent remark to upset everything again.

New Year's Day — Day 60 — 727.71 miles. We departed camp at 7:00 a.m. and continued through the field of rough sastrugi, some of which were four feet high and 20 feet long. Searching for level ground between these icy furrows, we were always conscious of losing sight of the fleeting shadows we relied upon for our bearings. Despite the rugged terrain, I was happy now that Roger and I were on better terms.

We pulled side by side for three hours, celebrating a wonderful reunion of our friendship — an appropriate beginning to the new year. Roger wrote, "I felt so happy and close to Gareth. In the end it was too much. I stopped and unable to speak leant forward with my head on my ski sticks and cried, cried with relief and joy and all I could say was 'you have no idea how hard this journey has been for me and now your faith and trust in me has given us both the opportunity to salvage all from the blackness of the past months.' We both slipped and cried for a moment, Gareth in his tears saying 'I am so happy.'"

I had real love for Roger at that moment and could not remember being as close to any other man. How sad, I thought, that we waited till the end of the journey.

January 2 — 3 — Days 61 and 62 — 758.85 miles. For the third day in a row we faced incredible sastrugi, around and over which our sledges were tossed and jostled. My feet, battered from my trying to maintain my balance on the rough surface, again became a serious problem. I was now resorting to Valium at night to reduce the pain, sleep being vital to solid performance the next day.

By the start of the second leg, the sastrugi which we had traversed for 56 miles began to subside. The rugged terrain had taken its toll on our equipment. My skins were again failing and Roger's trace required patching with metal cut from an empty butter tin. If I had learned anything on this expedition it was to be resourceful.

Shackleton, at the same position on January 6, 1909, planned the following day to be his farthest south. Every day forward jeopardized a day's return. He lamented, "I would fail to explain my feelings if I tried to write them down, now that the end has come. There is only one thing that lightens the disappointment, and that is the feeling that we have done all we could. It is the forces of nature that have prevented us from going right through. I cannot write more."[7]

For the next two days Shackleton was prevented from moving at all. Besieged by a blizzard and frozen by temperatures plummeting to -70°F (-56.7°C), he and his three companions shivered in their bags while waiting for the break that would allow them one more day's advance to the south. They were hungry, having for weeks had insufficient nourishment. Marshall, taking their body temperatures a couple of days earlier, recorded that they had fallen to 94°F.

Roger led the whole of the next day. That night, camped at Shackleton's farthest south position, I assumed all the cooking duties to give him a break.

It was here that Shackleton, on January 9, 1909, after finally being liberated from the storm's embrace, carried the Queen's Union Jack and a brass cylinder containing stamps and official documents for his last march south. At 9:00 a.m. he erected the flag and claimed the Plateau for Britain. He then turned back toward Cape Evans. He wrote, "While the Union Jack blew out stiffly in the icy gale that cut us to the bone, we looked south with our powerful glasses, but could see nothing but the dead white snow plain. There was no break in the plateau as it extended towards the Pole, and we feel sure that the goal we have failed to reach lies on this plain. ... Whatever regrets may be, we have done our best."[8]

Scott, reaching the same position exactly three years later, noted that everything ahead was new. How wrong he was — Amundsen had already been and gone, and was within 17 days of arriving jubilantly back at his ship, the *Fram*. His black flags, snapping steadily in the brisk southerly breeze, lay triumphantly ahead of Scott.

January 4 — 5 — Days 63 and 64 — 783.51 miles. Toward the end of the second leg, we hauled into the face of a Force 4 blow. Ahead, the ground drift came at us just above the surface, blasting past our ghostly figures, swirling and settling on our sledges and in the lee of each icy ridge of low sastrugi. Behind us, all record of our presence was quickly erased. Above, cloud cover reduced contrast to zero. Navigation, now more critical than ever as we closed on our goal, was virtually impossible despite a vastly improved surface. Roger called the day at 8.33 miles.

Departing at 7:45 the following morning, we were thankful that the storm that had kept Shackleton tentbound for two days would not plague us. The flat surface was covered with a fine layer of gritty snow which slowed our progress. Although we still faced a Force 3 blow, the sky was clear, and the contrast, although not good, was better than the previous day. Glinting in the air above our heads, millions of ice crystals coalesced into a solar halo.

My feet were again causing me agony. Each day I bathed the weeping blisters in white gas, as we had little antiseptic, before applying fresh dressings. Although they did not heal, at least they were manageable and I suffered no infection, and I was thankful for that. Considering the years of hiking and climbing I had done before the journey, I was surprised by my foot problems. I had thought my feet were tougher.

CHAPTER ELEVEN

SOUTH POLE

THE CLOSER WE advanced to the Pole, the more anxious I became. Although my relationship with Roger was the best it had ever been, there were already signs of its crumbling. We were emotionally exhausted and I felt empty now that our goal was at hand.

My feet were still in pain from several blisters, and against my better judgment I began to use the occasional painkiller to anesthetize the ache at night and dull my senses to the agony during the day. I was too close to the Pole to worry about any permanent damage.

January 6 — Day 65 — 799.73 miles. I began to lead the first session only to be forced to a halt within ten minutes to tighten my boot. Roger moved right by me, taking over without comment. Forty minutes later I had just caught up with him when Robert, far behind us, hoisted his poles in a large X, signalling us to stop.

"Why don't you carry on," I suggested to Roger. "I'll wait. He probably just needs the repair kit. We'll see you at the break."

For once, just sitting and waiting was a joy. The day was the most beautiful we had experienced on the Plateau — bright sun, blue sky and absolutely no cloud or wind. Robert arrived all too soon and lifted a broken pole. As Roger carried the only spare, an adjustable, which he used for the camera tripod, I attached Robert's handle to one of the long tent stakes and we carried on.

During the second leg I led for 2.5 hours. My course was true, but I felt like a staggering drunk through most of it. I wondered if I was experiencing a delayed reaction to the painkiller I had taken earlier that morning. When I stopped for the noon sextant sight, which took me a full ten minutes, Roger passed me and assumed the lead for the last half-hour of the session. While he led the third, Robert and I walked side by side behind.

In the tent that night I calculated my noon sunshot. My estimated position confirmed our sledgewheel and dead reckoning latitude and longitude. If we had deviated a mile or so in the last 300 it would be acceptable given our navigational technique, but could still be critical. The American Amundsen-Scott Station at the South Pole, we had been told, could be seen from 17 to 18 miles away in good visibility. I estimated that we would be well within that range. With only 73 miles to go, we would soon find out.

Checking my feet just before bed, I knew that the painkiller had been working. The bandages were crusted with dried blood, and my socks were stiff with it as well, and I had felt nothing. Too tired to change the bandages, I left them until morning.

January 7 — Day 66 — 815.79 miles. Robert, as usual, was already dressed and packed by the time I had the oatmeal ready. After bolting his breakfast he hurriedly left the tent before we could suggest that he assist with preparing the soup. Despite the head start, Robert was usually last to leave camp.

Robert (foreground) and Roger stop to check a compass bearing. (PHOTO BY GARETH WOOD)

Before departing I downed a different painkiller, hoping to avoid a reaction like the one I'd had the previous day. I led the first session on a ten-degree bearing. I was uneasy, knowing that Roger was just behind me checking my bearings. The pressure necessitated quick compass work and a hasty stop for a boot adjustment and pee. I thought it had been a good session, but Roger arrived fuming.

"You've been following a nine-degree bearing for the whole bloody session and I've been signalling all morning," he complained.

Taken off guard by the old Roger, I wondered what to say without making the situation worse. He surprised me though, at the end of the break, by asking me to lead again. I was hesitant, considering his mood. Close to the end of the session I began to feel nauseous. Breaking out in a cold sweat, I staggered and my stomach cramped. Reaction to the pill was my immediate thought. With only ten minutes left of the session, Roger took over.

At the break I tried to eat, but couldn't. I spat out a mouthful of crackers. The mere thought of food soon had me vomiting to one side of my sledge. Robert screwed up his face in disgust.

"Do you want me to put up the tent?" Roger asked, concerned.

"No, I'll be all right. Go ahead," I replied weakly.

Despite having nothing to eat or drink I began to feel better almost immediately and skied the next three hours without incident. The painkiller had obviously been the cause of my upset stomach. Taking backup bearings for Roger, I discovered that he was meandering between nine and 12°, but decided against mentioning it.

After my reaction to the painkillers I stopped taking them. Pain and I had travelled together for over 800 miles over the Ross Ice Shelf, up the Beardmore and across the Plateau, and I had taken painkillers only to make the last few days easier, now that we were confident of our success. We hauled 6.48 miles during the last session, an incredible 2.16 miles an hour.

January 8 — Day 67 — 831.96 miles. The day began with Roger offering to dress a bleeding blister between my toes. I was grateful for this act of kindness.

Roger decided he would lead all three sessions. He was like a racehorse stretching for the finish. The anticipation of ending the journey excited me as well, but I would have been content with a slower pace. I followed, checking Roger's bearings and occasionally taking back bearings on Robert behind me. The Plateau was amazingly beautiful. I wrote about it that night, "With the sun behind later in the day, ice crystals on the ground glistened as if someone had sprinkled diamonds on the surface." The air glinted with these ice particles as well and through it all the usual sundog blossomed in the tranquil sky.

At the start of the third session, clouds building on the horizon directly ahead threatened bad weather. Within minutes they scudded over us, eliminating surface contrast as they advanced. The light was suddenly dim and a slight wind began to press from the south. I wondered whether Roger would stop, but hauling resolutely on, he was determined to make 18 miles or better. Almost as fast as they appeared, the clouds dissipated, revealing a flawless sky.

Taking a sunshot to determine our latitude and longitude, I found that my calculations placed us on course, but compared to the sledgewheel we were 4.31 miles out. With the Pole only 41 miles away, four miles could be critical. To confirm our position I decided to take three sights a day until the Pole was sighted. Although this would mean late nights working through tedious calculations, I considered it necessary.

Scott, reaching roughly the same position on January 14, 1912, wrote, " ... there are practically no signs of heavy wind here, so that even if it blows a little we may be able to march. Meanwhile we are less than 40 miles from the Pole. ... Oates seems to be feeling the cold and fatigue more than the rest of us, but we are all very fit. It is a critical time, but we ought to pull through. ... Oh! for a few fine days! So close it seems and only the weather to baulk us."[1]

Roger, still irritable, recorded his thoughts that night, "But most of all I look forward to the space that will be available and the news and loving people to break this working but stale triangle. ... We await the flags and pomp. I would like to finish quickly and return to normality and end with this Footsteps of Scott and quietly digest the event of this momentous business."

January 9 — 10 — Days 68 and 69 — 858.96 miles. Roger led the first session in limited contrast, which by the second leg was reduced to nothing. Only a hundred yards into the third, he called the day and we erected the tent in light snow. It was impossible to proceed. With nothing to do but eat, we cooked a double ration of bacon bar, salami fried with butter, and macaroni and cheese.

Later, recalculating our sights, Roger and I struggled to determine our exact position. By 9:00 p.m. we arrived at what we considered was a plausible latitude. At 10:00 p.m. I took another sight, which confirmed our latitude at 89° 34.7' and longitude at 157°. Dead reckoning was 89° 36.19'. We were close.

Scott, establishing his last depot on January 15, wrote, "It is wonderful to think that two long marches would land us at the Pole.

We left our depôt to-day with nine days' provisions, so that it ought to be a certain thing now, and the only appalling possibility the sight of the Norwegian flag forestalling ours."[2]

Into the second hour of Scott's afternoon march, Bowers caught sight of what he thought was a cairn. Arguably, it might have been sastrugi but within half an hour they determined that the black speck was manmade. A few minutes more confirmed that it was a black flag. Amundsen had beaten them to the Pole — the surface, even after a month, was still gouged with the runners of his sledges and trampled by the paws of his dogs.

Scott wrote of this worst of all possible events, "It is a terrible disappointment, and I am very sorry for my loyal companions. Many thoughts come and much discussion have we had. To-morrow we must march on to the Pole and then hasten home with all the speed we can compass."[3]

The following morning, Robert prepared the soup, allowing me to eat my oatmeal at my leisure. I enjoyed the break. Leaving camp at 9:30, we fully expected to make excellent mileage. The weather was clear, our goal was close at hand and the temperature, at -14°C, was moderate.

A Hercules aircraft, clearly visible, appeared to land just below the horizon. We wondered whether we had been spotted. If nothing else, the aircraft confirmed that we were heading in the right direction. My sight that evening placed us only 14 miles from the Pole. It was near enough to taste.

In the tent that night, Robert coated himself with antiperspirant and rubbed sun lotion into his bronzed and sun-blotched skin. He even changed his underwear and put on new socks. It looked as if he expected someone to smell him. I decided to wait for a cup of tea and a shower before I dressed for dinner.

I wrote in my diary that night, "Relationships again becoming strained last few days — guess is nearness of Pole. Yes, I want it to be over too." The harmony we had experienced for a few days was rapidly disintegrating. Supplanting it were old grievances that left us all depressed and irritable. We were all worried about our reception at the Pole.

As I left the tent to take another sight, Robert was discussing what he would wear for photographs at the Pole. He eventually elected to sport a scarf about his head, and when he tried it on I heard Roger joking that he looked like Peter O'Toole in "Lawrence of Arabia." Robert was not amused.

January 11 — The Pole — 872.99 miles. Waking at 5:07 a.m. for a pee, I disturbed Roger who thought it was time to get up.

Although he made motions to get ready, I fell back exhausted. I had been up until 1:38 a.m. plotting sights and double-checking my calculations and needed at least another hour of rest.

Robert made the soup again. Leaving camp at 8:10 a.m., we marched south into a Force 4 blow and drifting snow. Visibility was virtually nil, forcing Roger off course. We erected the tent at 4.78 miles, Robert and I attempting to tame its flapping corners while Roger quickly pounded in the stakes. Just short of the first break, we drank our soup and crawled into our sleeping bags to wait out the storm. I felt alone. We had no words, each of us captive of his own thoughts and intently focussed on a future that would exclude the others.

It was not until 5:30 p.m. that visibility improved enough to permit travel. First outside, I stacked Roger's gear beside his sledge as it was passed to me by Robert. While Roger was busy sweeping out the tent, I led off. Contrast was adequate for navigation and I was able to make good distances between sights. Wind continued to drive snow at us from the south. Drifting into my anorak hood, it collected coldly about my neck.

Ahead, the horizon was indistinct because of blowing snow, but the sky, except for some isolated stratocumulus, was clear. Only two hours into the session, navigating on a five-degree bearing, I heard Robert shout from behind.

"Over there, look!" he cried excitedly, pointing his ski pole at the vague outline of what appeared to be a building about a mile away and to our right.

I stared, excited and relieved. We had made it! About half an hour later we were close to a tower, perhaps previously used as an automatic meteorological station. Red flags marked the site and leading away from the tower was a route lined with green flags. We assumed that the Pole lay at the end of that route. While Roger and I pulled nearer the tower, Robert, anxious to complete the journey, veered off onto the flagged route as if to entice us to follow. After a hundred yards he looked back to see that Roger and I were preparing to stop for a soup break. He sat down on his sledge to wait. Both Roger and I noticed that he was anxious to lead his team to the Pole.

Roger, manoeuvring his sledge right next to the tower, lost control of it when it slipped into a wind-scoured hollow. While he was extricating it, his traces broke. Instead of mending them for the three remaining miles of the journey, he asked me for my spare rope trace — his was packed too deeply to find easily. After our break we were soon moving down the track, Robert ahead, me next and Roger last.

We had travelled only a short distance when Robert flung his poles into the air and dropped to his knees as if in fanatical prayer. Low on the horizon a large domed structure was just visible through a hail of blowing ice crystals, the sun glinting dully on its pearl-grey panels. Antenna masts and a tall orange building quickly materialized beside it. My immediate thought was how like a space station this isolated settlement looked. It was not only an astonishing display of humanity's arrogance but a magnificent example of our endeavour. Science, I felt, was its cover, territorial imperative its mandate.

Turning to Roger I smiled and said with a sigh, "At last, we've done it."

At that point Robert got out his chest bag with his Paddington Bear sticking from the corner, much like the bag Scott had worn *sans* the teddy, and after putting that on, proceeded to tie the "Lawrence" scarf about his head. Hauling in front, he stopped when the dome did not appear to be getting any closer.

"How long do you think it will take us to get there?" he asked.

"About 30 or 40 minutes," Roger replied.

At that point Robert slowed to let us catch up and together, side by side, we moved down the flagged route. When we were a short distance from the dome, Roger stopped to film our arrival and after a few minutes returned to retrieve the camera and tripod. Robert, meanwhile, with anorak hood down and face bare for the momentous arrival, was beginning to feel the cold. The wind was blowing strongly.

"Can't we just get on with it?" he pleaded anxiously.

Roger, as if in direct opposition to Robert's impatience, methodically packed up the camera before stowing it aboard his sledge. It took all of five minutes, but for Robert it must have seemed an eternity.

Hauling our sledges around the dome we searched for an entrance that would take us inside. We looked with amazement at the manmade structures around us. I made first contact with a muffled figure hurrying by on an errand. He stopped and gaped as if we were from another planet.

"Hi, we're the 'Footsteps of Scott Expedition.' How do we get in here?" I asked, as if I was seeking directions to the nearest bus stop.

Suddenly recognizing us, he smiled and shook my hand excitedly. "We were expecting you guys around the 17th," he said. "The entrance's over there. Follow me."

It was 11:53 p.m. and as he led us down the ramp into the darkened interior of the dome, I felt as though we were entering a

140

Nearing the Amundsen-Scott Station at the South Pole. (COURTESY OF ROGER MEAR)

cave. After months of continuous sun, even minimal darkness was a profound change. Beyond the entrance lay a number of insulated metal buildings and as we approached them, the news of our arrival spread like wildfire. Soon, people were spilling from doorways, whistling, shouting, cheering and congratulating us.

They were all in awe, and I was somewhat taken aback. For me the journey had become routine and I no longer considered it much of an achievement. The perspective we had lost, however, returned with a rush as we were bombarded with introductions, questions and general excitement.

Lee Schoen, the officer in charge, gripped each of our hands in turn, welcoming us to Amundsen-Scott Station, and the National Science Foundation rep, Dr. John Lynch, stepping forward, said somewhat jokingly, "I've been instructed to invite you in for a cup of tea."

Thank god, I thought, wondering how far they were willing to stretch their hospitality. I hoped that we would not have to rely upon our sledge rations. Now that we had arrived, I didn't think I could stand one more meal of bacon bar and macaroni.

Dropping our harness where we stood we were guided toward a nearby building, which turned out to be the mess. We were drinking coffee when Schoen, obviously upset about something, approached us for the second time. He had devastating news.

CHAPTER TWELVE

SUNK

WHILE BITTERLY COLD winds had been moaning through the black Antarctic night, piling drift upon drift against our base hut at Cape Evans, the *Southern Quest*, caressed by warm Pacific breezes, was lying snug in her berth in Sydney Harbour, Australia. The crew, who had worked so diligently to get her seaworthy for the southern journey, deserved a rest. However, there was still much to do. She was scarred from the polar ice, her holds needed cleaning and restoring, and her engine required overhauling. The crew had only six months to get her shipshape before she was to return to the Antarctic to pick us up.

Steve Broni, a Scottish ornithologist who had signed on in South Africa on a whim, was promoted to the position of bosun. Supervising a team of volunteers, he slowly worked through the 240-job list Captain Graham Phippen had thrust into his reluctant hand. While Broni scraped paint, Phippen was busy organizing an Antarctic Exposition to describe our journey and life in the Antarctic. It was held in the Sydney Opera House, and the proceeds were used to overhaul the *Southern Quest*'s engine.

The ship was ready by December and took a group of Australian archeologists of "Project Blizzard" to Antarctica to restore Sir Douglas Mawson's hut at Commonwealth Bay. Mawson, an English-born geologist who was a stalwart champion of Australia's Antarctic interests, was with Shackleton's 1908-1909 expedition; he was also a member of the parties which were the first to climb Mount Erebus in 1908 and to reach the South Magnetic Pole in 1909. Later, he led his own expedition to Commonwealth Bay to map the coast directly south of Australia.

On the return journey from Commonwealth Bay, encircled by pack-ice, the *Southern Quest* was holed. Steve Broni, commenting to the skipper some time later that the bow was not recovering quickly enough in the light sea, was sent below to check. Upon opening the bow storage locker he could hear the ominous slap of water in the compartment that held the anchor chains. It was already six feet deep and rising. The pumps were engaged immediately and kept running 18 hours a day for the remainder of the voyage. Although the ship was in no immediate danger, the compartment being isolated behind a watertight bulkhead, the incident was alarming.

After the ship was dry docked in Hobart, Tasmania, for repairs, the Cessna that Giles planned to fly to the Pole was swung aboard. The plan at first had been to box the fuselage and wings to prevent Giles' ambitious plan from leaking out, but as the fuselage was too long — it barely fit on the after deck — it was merely wrapped in polyethylene to protect it from salt spray. The boxed wings were then lashed to a container on the forward deck. Accompanying the aircraft were Giles and two Alaskan aircraft mechanics, Ed Saunier and Rick Mason, who would assemble the plane on the ice.

Once repaired, the ship was moved to nearby Port Huan, and from there on December 28, 1985, she departed for the Ross Sea. On board were six Austrian climbers who were to attempt a first ascent of Mount Minto in the Admiralty Range. They were led by the same Bruno Klausbruckner who had visited us in Switzerland during our equipment trials. He and his team, with two tons of gear including snowmobiles, were to be dropped off on the outward journey and retrieved on the return. However, as the pack-ice was too thick, the ship couldn't get any closer to Cape Hallett (where they were to disembark) than 20 to 25 miles. Phippen decided to drop Giles and the aircraft off first before continuing with the Austrians to find a route through the ice. Crossing the sea-ice at that time of year would have been a risk, one that the Austrians were hesitant to take.

The weather was exceptionally calm and those crew members who were off duty basked on deck in the sun. Not far north of Franklin Island, the *Southern Quest* met heavy pack-ice; otherwise, the Ross Sea was clear. That night the ship encountered open pack-ice. Butting small ice cakes from her path, she followed a jigsaw pattern through open leads. The ship was ideal for this sort of work. Small and manoeuvrable, she could move slowly or speed up quickly.

Meanwhile, at the expedition's Cape Evans hut, Mike and John made radio contact with the *Southern Quest* at 9:00 p.m., fully expecting her to be off Cape Hallett. They were surprised to find her a quarter of that distance away. Mike was especially excited because on board was his girlfriend, Thea, whom he had not seen for a year.

Early next morning, January 9, saw the ship battling through thick pack-ice looking for a level floe on which to unload, assemble and launch the aircraft. The floe had to be flat and long enough to provide a runway for the ski-equipped Cessna. Easing the ship beside a small floe, Phippen summoned Ed Saunier for advice on whether a slightly larger floe would be suitable for the proposed runway. Ed nodded tiredly and toddled off to bed, leaving an exhausted Phippen, who had had little sleep since the ship entered the ice, to continue the search.

About 6:00 a.m., just north of Beaufort Island, the ship encountered a solid barrier of pack-ice. From the bridge the ice appeared to stretch only a few miles, but the sky told a different story. Reflected on the undersurface of the distant clouds was a whitish light, familiar to sailors as "ice blink." Phippen estimated that the pack-ice extended beyond the horizon. It seemed impossible that anything short of an icebreaker would be able to make its way into North Bay that year.

Nosing the ship into a floe about two miles long, with enough flat terrain to carve out a rough runway, Phippen set the engine to dead slow. The propeller slowly churned the frigid water and, with a watch at the bridge, the skipper descended to the ice by way of a Jacob's ladder to inspect the floe. It looked perfect, and he invited the others down for a second opinion. The time seemed right. The long stretch of good weather could not be expected to last. With the others in agreement, Phippen set about mooring the ship. Anchoring timbers were set into trenches hacked into the ice.

By 9:30 a.m. the unloading of the aircraft, christened *Admirable Byrd* by the crew, had begun. With the help of volunteers, the Alaskans had the machine put together early the following morning and while they were testing the engine, Giles was summoned to conduct his pre-flight check. A short distance away, Steve Broni and a few others had hewn a makeshift runway with mattocks from the rugged ice.

The plan was for Giles to ferry the aviation fuel necessary for the long flight to the Pole to Cape Evans and near Willy Field where it would be stored. He wanted two fuel dumps in case one became inaccessible. Several trips would be required to transport all of it.

Steve Broni wrote, "We were all tense as Captain Giles taxied the aircraft to the far end of the runway for the first take-off. ... Would the aircraft be able to get up enough speed on her skis? Would the engine perform properly in the sub-zero temperatures?

"There was a moment's silence during which we all held our breath and crossed our fingers. Then the little engine whined, and the aircraft accelerated across the ice-runway. The skis rattled and thumped as the plane shot past the ship. There would be no second chance; with skis instead of wheels, the plane had no means of braking. Beyond the far end of the runway lay an area of open water, then another ice-floe dotted with sharp ice-ridges.

"Just when I felt sure the plane would run right off the end of the ice-floe, the skis lifted from the ice and the little plane shot low over the broken ice-floes. Slowly it climbed into the clear blue sky, then turned and made a low pass over the ship."[1]

Exhausted after working through the night and into the early hours of the morning, the crew stopped for breakfast and a rest. After months of usual days and nights, it would take them a few days to acclimatize to 24-hour daylight.

It was only an hour and a half later that Steve, checking the mooring lines at the bow of the ship, heard the distant whine of the returning aircraft. Within minutes the diminutive speck to the south materialized into the Cessna. The crew stepped quickly down the Jacob's ladder, its jostling rungs clanging hollowly against the ship's steel hull and, rushing pell-mell onto the runway, shooed curious Adelie penguins left and right as Giles made a slow, sweeping pass from the north. Examining the landing strip before circling back, he began a low approach.

The skis had just touched the ice when the engine roared and the machine lifted clear for a second attempt. Around it went in a wide, lazy circle, sunlight glinting from its metallic skin, and once again it lined up to land. This time Giles cut power at the floe's edge and the Cessna dropped down hard upon the floe. The aircraft barely slowed its breakneck pace on the icy surface despite Giles' waggling the tail in an attempt to slow the momentum. At the last moment, when it appeared that the plane must surely shoot straight off the floe and into the sea, it suddenly veered right and careered into an icy hummock.

Before the crew could get to the aircraft, Giles and Rick Mason, his passenger, were already out and bending over the landing gear. The right ski was shattered. The rest of the plane was undamaged and because the ski was fibreglass, it could be repaired. Rick removed it and took it back to the ship. It would be hours, however, before the fibreglass was cured.

Meanwhile, the forces of nature were conspiring against the flying operation. The floe to which the ship was moored split, severing the far end of the runway from the main part. Although there was still enough room to design a new runway at an angle, if the floe continued to calve the aircraft would be prevented from taking off, and since the Cessna was assembled it would be impossible to bring it back aboard. There was a sense of urgency about the ship as everyone waited anxiously for the fibreglass to set up.

Twelve hours later, the ski was installed and the aircraft loaded with barrels of fuel. Once again the plane lifted off perfectly, swinging back over the ship before gaining altitude toward McMurdo. Giles had found that landing the fuel-laden Cessna on the sea-ice at Cape Evans was too dangerous as the plane was difficult to stop. Although the Americans had denied him use of the Willy Field ice runway, they did permit him to land and store the fuel to one side.

Before Giles returned for the next load, landing inhibitors in the form of three giant canvas tarps were spread across the far end of the runway and beyond them, garbage bags filled with snow were arranged in ranks. They were designed to prevent the aircraft from overshooting the floe upon landing.

On Giles' return, Adelie penguins again dotted the runway. They appeared unconcerned that the *Admirable Byrd* would be landing amongst them. The crew quickly chased them off again and waited anxiously to see if the tarps would work. The aircraft skidded down the runway as before but its progress was arrested by the tarps just feet from the water's edge. Three more flights were made to transport the rest of the fuel, although the runway was redesigned several times as the floe kept breaking up.

On January 11, at 7:30 a.m., with the last of the fuel aboard, Giles and Rick waved their final farewells. They flew to the fuel depot near Willy Field to prepare the aircraft for the long polar flight and to await the news of our arrival at the Pole. After they left, the plastic bags, tarps, fuel drums and debris were collected and taken back to the ship. The crew still had to have breakfast and the ship's engineers had about an hour's work ahead of them to make the ship ready for sailing. The work of the previous couple of days had been rewarding but intense, and Phippen suggested a well-deserved break. With a football belonging to Daryl "Dibble" Jones, one of the Australian deck hands, a game was started on the ice. While it was in progress, the floes began to shift silently about the players. Although the weather was still stable, a slight wind had begun to press from the east.

At 11:15 a.m., with the ice anchors dug from their frozen trenches, the ship began to steam north toward Cape Hallett to drop the Austrians off. Then the *Southern Quest* would return to the pack-ice to construct another ice runway pending our arrival at the ship. Before being disassembled and winched aboard, the Cessna would return to Cape Evans to pick up Mike and John. The ship would then proceed to New Zealand where we would disembark for London. The *Southern Quest* would wait in New Zealand pending news of the ice breakup at Cape Evans before returning to remove the hut and equipment.

The ship bulldozed great plates of solid ice from its path, its progress hampered by a ten-knot wind that drove the floes together, narrowing some leads and sealing others. Graham Phippen, who had been on the bridge since late morning because he did not wish to pass the responsibility of the ship's safety to anyone else, nosed the ship into a floe at 6:00 p.m. and rested for an hour before having a bite to eat and a mug of tea. He also needed time to consider his next move. He felt that barging through the large floes would unnecessarily jeopardize the ship.

Somewhat refreshed, he climbed the mast and from the barrel gained a fresh perspective on the pack-ice ahead. He later recorded his thoughts on tape, "I could see this narrow lead between two large floes that stopped short a hundred yards from a series of open leads which led to open water. So I thought, I'll have a look up there to see if it might lead on. I didn't want to go further to the west because that was taking me closer to the island, and further to the east I knew that the ice was coming from that direction so there was no point, no way out there. So I went up this narrow lead between the two floes and the first three points of contact were very easy. They didn't take any breaking, we just went straight through them, but the last one was tough. We lodged our bows between these large floes and we just couldn't get out."

Steve Broni, exhausted after having worked around the clock, had kicked off his boots and collapsed fully clothed on his bunk in his tiny cabin just aft of the engine room. Although the grinding of ice against the hull at first kept him awake, the noise settled into a steady rhythm and he drifted off. At 7:30 p.m. he was rudely shaken awake by John Elder, one of the Australian crew.

"Steve! Quick! Skipper wants everyone topside. We're stuck in the ice. We need your help to try and free her."

Annoyed at being disturbed, Steve wondered what the fuss was all about. The ship had been stuck before and it had never been a panic. As he emerged from the dark confines of his cabin to the bright Antarctic day, his opinion changed. From bridge to bow the ship was pinioned between two large floes driven together by a steady, 15-knot wind from the east. A mere 50 yards beyond lay open water, and aft, the ship's stern lay in an open lead. Across the ice was strewn a rainbow array of tents, boxes of food, clothing and the ship's inflatables. Clearly, the ship was in trouble and the crew had been busy.

Around him activity was frenetic. The crew, with picks and shovels, were hacking at the ice trapping the bow while seawater was being pumped between the hull and the floes. A line stretching from the forward winch to an ice hummock aft of the ship was taut, trying to pull the ship backward. A great boil surfaced at the stern as the propeller churned uselessly in reverse.

While Steve was busy on the forward deck, the hatch cover on Number 3 hold exploded open like a champagne cork, the large wing nuts securing it to the deck popping skyward. An ominous "crack" followed and under Steve's feet the thick deck plates shuddered and swelled. Number 3 hold had ruptured, and into it poured tons of seawater. Although alarming, this did not necessarily mean an end to the ship: all holds were isolated and watertight.

Turning to Steve, Phippen said, "Quick, get your personals from your cabin and get the hell back up here fast," he said.

Steve rushed into the ship, not knowing what to expect. His cabin was deep within its bowels, and if the ship went quickly he would be caught.

"I remember," he recorded later on tape, "I had all my slides from the first half of the expedition in one hand and my diaries in the other and I heard this incredible bang and water sloosh against the bulkhead on the other side of me. It was the engine room blowing. And all this smoke started to pour down the stairway and I heard 'for God's sake get out.' There was a fire in the engine room. So I just dropped everything and climbed the stairs. As I passed the engine room, the engineers were pouring out and by the time we got to the front alleyway, just where the

148

bridge was, we were up to our knees in water. Outside, the skipper was on the bridge yelling at us all to stand still so that he could take a head count."

When Phippen was convinced that everyone was off, he and the mate, Dave Iggulden, climbed down to the ice. Just before that they had to physically drag one of the Austrians out of a forward hold where he was trying to retrieve his radio equipment.

The crew watched in disbelief as the *Southern Quest* settled into the water by the stern. With a horrific screech and wrench of twisted metal, her red and rust-streaked bow rose higher and higher as the weight of her stern dragged her down. A great surge of water invaded the bridge and blew out the windows. As she finally slipped beneath the surface, air trapped in the hull boiled upward like a last defiant gasp.

Passengers and crew were numb. This was not the first Antarctic expedition to be stranded on a floe and probably will not be the last, but this was happening to *them*. Steve Broni recalled, "When it was all over the skipper called for three cheers for the *Southern Quest* and John Elder, this Australian reporter, had an old brass trumpet and he played the 'Last Post.' There were a lot of tears."

With the ship went more than just memories. Our evacuation from Antarctica and the removal of our hut and equipment from

The SOUTHERN QUEST sinks, on the very day Roger, Robert and Gareth reach the South Pole. (COURTESY OF STEVE BRONI)

Cape Evans were suddenly in jeopardy — what had been feared all along had just become a reality.

A helicopter was already being dispatched from the American icebreaker *Polar Star* in response to Dave Iggulden's 11:37 p.m. radio signal giving the stricken ship's coordinates. The crew now stood on the ice, only 17 miles from Ross Island.

The sinking of the SOUTHERN QUEST. (FOOTSTEPS OF SCOTT COLLECTION)

CHAPTER THIRTEEN

NO ALTERNATIVE

"I'M SORRY TO have to dampen your spirits right now," Lee Schoen said, "but we just got word over the radio that your ship was crushed in the ice and has sunk. The crew's safe, but beyond that I don't know much more."

We were too stunned to speak. Robert broke the silence.

"Can we talk to the crew?" he asked.

"I'm sorry," Schoen said, "all voice communication has been restricted until further notice."

We had lost our only means of getting off the continent. It was urgent that we contact Richard Down in London to begin organizing our air evacuation using the fuel we had stored at Cape Evans, but with no access to radio communication, we felt our future was totally in the hands of the Americans. We wondered about Giles and whether the aircraft and fuel had been saved and if so, whether he would still be coming to pick us up. Our success, a tremendous high, was crushed by this worst of all possible news.

Powerless to affect events so far away, we continued with our own limited agendas. The first item on our list was to wash, find some clean clothes and then, at Schoen's request, see Dr. Brad Craig, the base physician. Schoen wanted us to have a quick physical and while we were there Dr. Craig weighed us. The three of us looked like starved prisoners of war. My bony figure weighed 20.6 pounds less than my departure weight of 180.5 pounds. Roger, originally 153.56 pounds, lost 17.3 pounds, while Robert dropped 25 pounds from his 182-pound starting weight.

I was then escorted back to the mess for a beer and a meal. Although I was not particularly hungry, the food was so different and so tasty that I could not stop eating. I felt that I had to sample everything in sight. I wasn't tired, in spite of having had little sleep the night before. My body was still reacting to the adrenalin rush I had received upon arrival. At 4:30 a.m., however, more out of convention than necessity, I retired to bed, leaving Roger in the virtually empty mess to mull over the expedition's future. He wrote, "The journey shrinks in proportion to this event, our walk a non-event. ... It's as though with the ending of my task the expedition hits trouble, the news of *Southern Quest* came through 5 mins before we walked in through the tunnel. That door should have been the ending but it was only another beginning."

Rising at 8:00 a.m., I had another shower, more for pleasure than cleanliness, got dressed and at 9:15 a.m. walked over to the mess where the station commander had organized a Sunday brunch meeting for 10:00. Dr. John Lynch dropped by to confirm that the ship had indeed sunk but that all hands had been safely airlifted off the ice to McMurdo.

Wilson, Scott, Evans, Oates and Bowers at the South Pole. (COURTESY OF THE ROYAL GEOGRAPHICAL SOCIETY)

Robert, Roger and Gareth at the South Pole. (Footsteps of Scott Collection)

Immediately after eating I wandered over to the dome's entrance and stared out across the Plateau stretching before me. I now viewed this scene with detachment. What had been our home and the focus of our energies for the past 70 days was nothing more than a featureless landscape, a desolate, trackless waste of ice and snow.

Later, standing by the true Pole — a barber pole placed there by the Americans and surrounded by the flags of the treaty nations — for photographs, I recalled that brave men had died trying to reach this point. At least we had been spared that calamity. Photographs complete, our thoughts returned to the plight of the *Southern Quest* crew.

As we were to learn later, even as the last bits of flotsam were swirling over the *Southern Quest*, renamed by the crew the "*Sunken Pest,*" the crew started taking an inventory of the survival gear strewn haphazardly on the ice. They split into groups and divided food, clothing, sleeping bags and gear among three canopied life rafts and two inflatables. They had 15 days' provisions and adequate equipment to meet any challenge the sea and ice might throw at them for a 17-mile journey across the pack-ice to Ross Island and another 37 miles along the coast to Cape Evans.

Fortunately, they did not have to test their skills against the elements. While we were enjoying the hospitality of the Americans at Amundsen-Scott Station, the ship's people were gathering at McMurdo where they had been flown by the *Polar Star*'s rescue helicopters. The disastrous turn of events had occurred so quickly that it was only at McMurdo that the crew had time to reflect on the past few hours. Even then, they had little knowledge of what had gone on behind the scenes.

While the ship was being crushed in the ice, Giles and Rick, who had just finished the Cessna's long-range fuel system, were on one side of Willy Field loading the aircraft with food, fuel and survival gear for the long flight to the Pole. Their next move depended entirely upon the weather. Reports indicated that although the conditions at the Pole were poor, they were favourable at Beardmore Camp on the Bladen Névé, 120 miles west of the Beardmore Glacier. Giles had it in mind to fly to Beardmore Camp and wait there for the weather to clear before proceeding south.

Turning to Rick, he said, "When we're finished here let's go have a coffee. After that we'll talk to the weather people before making a move."

It was late in the evening and as they tidied up, a lone figure walked purposefully toward them from the buildings at Willy Field.

"Looks like someone's coming," Giles said. "I'll just go and see what he wants. Be back in a minute."

A feeling of grave portent swept over him (at that point no one had heard from us) as he walked anxiously toward the person coming out. It was Jules, a friend of Robert's and one of the Willy Field staff.

"You're wanted urgently at Scott Base," she said excitedly. "It seems there's a big problem with your ship. Come on, you can call from here."

Hurrying back with her to the Willy Field complex, Giles rang up John Parslow at Scott Base. The ship, he was told, was holed in the engine room and taking on water. Beyond that, Parslow knew nothing. Running back to the aircraft, Giles and Rick stripped it bare of the extra fuel, 80 days' rations and survival gear, which had taken them more than three hours to pack, in just eight minutes flat.

Flying toward the ship, Giles was informed by radio that a helicopter rescue mission was in progress and that he was to stay clear of the area. Giles acknowledged the transmission and cautiously approached the scene. Banking north at Cape Bird, he picked out Beaufort Island dead ahead. As he drew near he expected to see the ship — from his vantage point it would be nothing more than a red speck in the vastness of the pack-ice — a familiar beacon on his many fuel flights. For a moment his eyes focussed briefly on what he thought was the ship and then his attention was diverted to the camera he was fiddling with in his lap. When his gaze returned to the scene, whatever had attracted him was gone.

Calling South Pole radio, he asked them to confirm the ship's position. At that point he was told that it had sunk. Below him, scattered over the ice, was the colourful array of gear and in the distance he could see two large, red-and-white Coast Guard helicopters approaching.

The crew of the *Southern Quest* was picked up and whisked away to nearby Beaufort Island and to Cape Bird. When all of them were transferred safely from the ice to terra firma they were evacuated to McMurdo. The survival gear, except for personal items, had to be abandoned on the ice.

Once all the crew were accounted for at McMurdo, the officer in charge, Captain Shrite, allocated two canvas Nissen huts for their use. His no-nonsense attitude suggested to the crew that they were now under his control. The air was thick with tension, neither the crew nor the Americans trusting the other.

Though we appreciated the hospitality we were receiving at the South Pole, our enjoyment was tempered by the fact that we were being gagged. Not only were we denied radio communication with McMurdo and the crew, but the Americans were not providing us with any additional information. We were especially anxious for news of Giles and the aircraft. Lee Schoen and Dr. John Lynch believed that Giles was still intending to fly. It was not until evening that we were advised that this was not the case and that we would be airlifted out on a special flight in a Hercules the following day.

The next morning we were requested to have our sledges ready for loading on a pallet and were cautioned at the same time to have no contact with a group of visiting U.S. congressmen who would be arriving by Hercules to tour the South Pole station. Though the congressmen arrived at the same time as we departed, we didn't see them because we were hustled aboard our flight before they deplaned. Just before that, however, we met Dr. Peter Wilkniss, head of the U.S. National Science Foundation's Polar Program, who had arrived on the Hercules with the congressmen.

Cornering us in the dome's tunnel, he launched into a great speech, devoid of emotion, in which he reiterated American policy on private expeditions. He asked no questions and gave us no opportunity to speak. I later wrote, " ... very officious manner. It all seemed so prepared and while speaking he avoided looking directly at us. Have never witnessed anyone speak to another like this." He then requested that we board the Hercules. I suppose he expected us to argue, but with no information from the crew or Giles, we complied.

As we entered the aircraft, one of the flight crew standing by the entrance asked me if I was one of the Footsteps team. I immediately thought, here we go again, another speech, but when I said yes he gave me the thumbs-up sign and a wide grin. Once we were aboard he told us that the flight was scheduled and that no special concessions were being made for us.

The 3.5-hour trip to McMurdo was enjoyable. The crew shared their food with us, and the 25 other passengers were eager to hear of our journey. The dour mood set by Wilkniss evaporated in the friendly confines of the cabin. Between conversations I took the opportunity to steal glances at the frozen expanse far below. The altitude smoothed the wrinkles from the Plateau, which only a few days before had challenged our endurance.

As we approached Willy Field, Robert came to life.

"We should be out first," he said, guessing that the ship's crew would be there to welcome us.

I had little desire for the glory Robert sought so actively. Our arrival at Willy Field was scant cause for celebration in the present circumstances. My heart was tugged by the sight of the whole crew

Roger preparing to board the Hercules at the South Pole. (PHOTO BY GARETH WOOD)

and a good contingent of U.S. and New Zealand personnel waiting expectantly for our arrival. With tears in my eyes I embraced and kissed those I knew well and shook hands with the others. It was an emotional moment filled with joy and hope for new beginnings. What struck me as odd was that there were no officials from McMurdo on hand. Not that I expected them to welcome or congratulate us, but as they seemed to be orchestrating our every move, I had anticipated some sort of acknowledgement, if only to reinforce their government's position.

After the excitement had subsided, the three of us were led into the kitchen of Hut 5 by Peter, Graham, Rebecca and Giles for a briefing on the expedition's present status. We were aghast at what the Americans were suggesting.

Graham told us that shortly after the crew had arrived at McMurdo, Shrite and Wilkniss summoned them to a meeting. There, Shrite advised them that they would be airlifted to Christchurch within 48 hours on a dedicated humanitarian flight. He emphasized his government's policy of no support to private expeditions and said that we would be billed $30,000 for the flight. Wilkniss then asked Giles not to fly our aircraft to the Pole as he would bring the polar team to McMurdo at no cost to the expedition. Giles, who had responded that he was capable and ready to fly to the Pole, had tried, unsuccessfully, to get assurance from Wilkniss that our airlift from the Pole would not be considered a rescue mission.

"I really had little choice," Giles said. "We would be damned for turning down Wilkniss' offer and taking the risk, but on the other hand I was sure that if we didn't fly we would be damned by the press for having you three rescued from the Pole."

"We asked for permission to talk to you several times, but they turned us down each time," Peter interrupted. "And," he added, "I'm convinced that communication was secured for one reason only, and that was to prevent you from influencing decisions with respect to the expedition's future."

"I called John Heap from Scott Base," Giles continued, "and he suggested that I not fly. I still wonder though if I made the right decision."

There were now less than 24 hours before the flight was due to leave for New Zealand. To simply leave the continent without securing the partially packed and dismantled base was both absurd and irresponsible. We represented a long list of worthy contributors, and if our expedition was to maintain its credibility we would have to act in a manner deserving of their trust.

We searched for alternatives. Expedition HQ in London informed us that it would take them several weeks to organize our air evacuation using the 40-odd drums of jet A-1 fuel I had stored at Cape Evans for just such an emergency. We had enough rations to winter the entire crew until we could be evacuated by ship the following season, but it would have been ridiculous to consider this, given the Americans' offer of the flight to Christchurch. It was clear to me that only one option remained.

"We don't have to let this happen," I said. "If necessary we can leave a small party behind to come out with the base and Cessna next season. I designed and outfitted the base and feel confident that I can make it work for another year."

I felt a lump in my throat as I forced myself to continue.

"I'll stay behind," I said quietly.

"You'd actually rewinter?" Roger asked, looking at me incredulously.

"Yes, if that's what it takes," I replied, terrified by the implications of what I'd just offered. "It's the only solution that makes sense. Then, we won't be seen to be abandoning our commitments and responsibilities. Robert can't do it. He's the expedition leader and he's needed in London to continue fundraising. Mike has to write up the scientific programme. Roger, you're committed to writing the official account of our journey and John has to produce the documentary film. Both the book and the film are needed for fundraising. That leaves me, but I'm hoping that two of the crew will be interested in staying with me."

We moved to the mess and while we were busy talking, the visiting U.S. congressmen whom we had been told to avoid at the Pole trooped boisterously in. A few, who were honestly interested in our venture, came over to shake our hands and wish us well. Several requested photographs and gave us business cards. In the end it was decided that Roger, Giles, Peter and Graham would try to negotiate with Shrite one of two things: delaying the flight, or flying the majority of the crew to New Zealand now and allowing two or three expedition members to remain for a few days before flying out to New Zealand on a later flight. Either of these two scenarios would allow us to secure our base and aircraft. If they failed, they would have my offer in reserve. They learned quickly, however, that he would not delay the flight.

"Personally I think you're a swell bunch of people," Shrite began in his slow drawl, "but professionally, my government has said that we won't support private expeditions. We'll provide you with a humanitarian airlift out of here and that's it. And you don't have to get on it, but you must vacate my base very shortly because we do not want to support you."

"We're not actually looking for any more support," Graham said. "Anybody who stays behind to secure our base doesn't need to live at McMurdo. We're just asking for a small number of our people to tidy up our affairs here and then go out on your next flight."

"From my standpoint I won't let that happen," Shrite retorted. "I'll launch that flight tomorrow and that's the only option I'm giving you people."

"What happens if our plane stays at Willy Field?" Giles asked.

"That plane will be destroyed sometime with 90-knot winds. There's no doubt in my mind," Shrite answered.

"That's why we just can't leave it," Giles responded.

"Exactly the same situation applies to the base," Roger added. "We want to secure it so that we can return at a future date to remove it. The alternative is that a small group of us rewinter."

"The environment will certainly suffer if we allow our base and aircraft to be destroyed in the winter storms," Giles said.

"Well, those are issues all right, but we don't support what you're doing," Shrite said. "We have no respect for it. We're in scientific support down here and you had an adventure which didn't come out quite right and we don't want any part of it. The plane leaves tomorrow and I've arranged space for all of you on it. I've told you about it. I hope you get on it. If you don't, you must vacate my base and do your own thing. But it won't be at my expense nor will I feel responsible toward you. This is it."

Shrite's intractability left us no other option: a small group of us had to rewinter. Curiously, Shrite accepted that decision rather than allow us the few days we needed to secure the base and the Cessna.

The weight of my decision to remain another year, which I had yet to fully digest, plus physical fatigue — I had not really slept since January 11, our last night in the tent — soon had me hunting for a bed. While I slept, Giles called John Heap at the Foreign Office in London from the public phone at Scott Base to inform him of our decision. Heap accepted our reasoning.

After talking to Heap, Giles flew Roger to Cape Evans so that he could recover his diaries and other personal items, in addition to allowing him a final night at our base. I had asked Giles to bring Mike Stroud back with him to McMurdo so that I could consult him about our medical needs for the next year, but he returned alone.

Meanwhile, Steve Broni, at Phippen's request, was searching for a room in which to have a crew meeting. Just before that, Phippen had approached him with an offer.

"We've decided we're going to winter another party. Would you be interested?" he asked.

"You're damn right I would," Steve replied in his broad Scots accent.

Steve organized a meeting in the mess, which at that time of night was virtually empty. Robert made an eloquent speech, the intent of which was not only to update the crew on our decision to rewinter but to request two volunteers as well. To everyone's surprise, besides Steve, two other *Southern Quest* crew members, Tim Lovejoy and Lynn Davis, also expressed a desire to remain. The following morning I met with the three of them.

"I don't know you that well," I told Steve, "but since Graham Phippen recommended you that's good enough for me."

After expressing my preference for only one other due to the small size of the base hut, and feeling incapable of making any more decisions, I left Tim and Lynn alone to decide who it would be. Just before I went, however, I told each of them what it would be like, especially the cold and dark of the long polar night. Lynn came with a great recommendation and I had little doubt about her ability, but she had some metal in her leg from a motorcycle accident and we were both concerned about how this old injury might be affected by the cold. Also, because Lynn was a woman, I was worried that her presence might lead to future complications. I was secretly hoping that Tim would be the one. The situation was awkward as both wanted to overwinter, and just as I was about to make a decision in Tim's favour, a tearful Lynn came out and said, "It's going to be Tim." I felt sorry for her. Later, I reflected on how badly I had handled the situation. I should have demonstrated better leadership by choosing the team myself rather than placing the burden on them.

As the three of us gathered at the helicopter pad with my sledge and Steve's and Tim's few belongings — the Americans had decided to airlift us to Cape Evans on their way to pick up Roger, Mike, John and Thea — the prospect of remaining behind suddenly shook me. It was as though I had just woken from a nightmare only to find it was real. I looked around me at the crew who would be safely in New Zealand in a few hours, and my polar companions who would be in England in a few days. I suddenly felt quite empty. Just before we left, Wilkniss approached us.

"Could I see you in private for a moment?" he asked.

Steve, Tim and I followed him into a nearby hangar.

"I want you to know that I'm dead against your staying," he said. "We're predicting a very severe winter here this year. If you were to fly out with us now to New Zealand you could come back another year. Don't you think you'd like to reconsider?"

"No, I'm sorry, we won't," I responded. "We've got to stick with the hut until we know that it'll be evacuated. The expedition is committed to leaving the area the way we found it. It would be irresponsible to do otherwise."

"There's already a lot of other junk out there anyway — from Scott's hut," he said.

"That may have been true in 1912 but you can't call it junk now," Steve said, obviously piqued.

"Unofficially, I beg you to reconsider. It's a waste of another year of your life. Think about it. If you want to be in the Antarctic, come and work for one of the programmes," he suggested.

I smiled to myself — it was highly unlikely that he would ever allow us to be employed in an American programme.

"We're staying," I answered.

"Well, I have to inform you that after we fly you out to Cape Evans you can expect no assistance whatsoever from us in the next year. You'll be forbidden to enter any building at McMurdo and our staff will not be permitted to visit you. And I want you to sign this," he concluded.

He resumed his official mask as he passed me a one-page document that read: "I have been informed of the policy of the U.S. government for the U.S. Antarctic program not to render any support to private expeditions, except in emergency, life threatening situations. I have today refused such assistance, in particular evacuation from Antarctica. I accept full responsibility, understand that I forfeit any further U.S. assistance rendered in the present emergency. I agree that I will indemnify and hold harmless the United States of America and its agents and employees from any and all claims, actions, or proceedings which may result from the assistance provided by the United States Antarctic Research Program."

"All right," I said, scrawling my signature at the bottom before walking out of the hangar toward the waiting chopper and the sad farewells. Steve and Tim signed and followed me.

During the helicopter trip to Cape Evans I gained a fresh perspective on the area. I had never seen McMurdo or Cape Evans from the air. Both looked incredibly bleak. Ten minutes later the spell was broken as the helicopter settled gently onto the black volcanic ash beach beside the hut. Wilkniss, who had accompanied us, came in to inspect our base.

"You've got 20 minutes," he said gruffly to Mike and Roger before moving back outside.

Hugging Mike, John, Roger and Thea, I barely had time to ask Mike to appraise the base's medical supplies before they were being encouraged aboard the still-running helicopter. With tears in my eyes I watched it lift off, turn and make directly for McMurdo. I was sorry that I had not had more time with Roger. There was so much to discuss about the journey and our friendship. Though the expedition supported my decision to remain, I worried that I would be excluded and forgotten. Robert and Roger would share the excitement in London.

The machine was only a dark speck in the bright sky when I broke my stare and turned to Steve and Tim. "Well guys, this is it. Home sweet home for another year."

CHAPTER FOURTEEN

OSTRACIZED

THERE WAS MUCH to do. The hut and equipment had been left
in various states of disrepair as Mike and John had anticipated being evacuated and had started to pack up the base, thinking
that it would be dismantled. The plane also required moving to
shore from where Giles had left it on the sea-ice and we had to take
a food inventory.

My diary for January 15 reads, "Up 8:00 a.m. Didn't sleep well.
So little snow around and so warm. Skua Lake looks pretty with a
waterfall between Scott's hut and ours running in a stream to the
beach. Skuas everywhere."

I found myself feeling very lonely and still struggling to come to
terms with my decision to stay — I really didn't want to be here.

At 10:00 a.m. the silence was shattered by the racket of a helicopter landing close by. Steve and Tim were still in bed. Across the
beach strode Captain Shrite, all smiles and snapping pictures left
and right.

"Hi," he said brightly. "Just thought I'd drop by and see how
you're doing. Beautiful day, isn't it?"

"Yes," I answered warily.

After some small talk, he asked, "How's your medical kit?"

"Good," I answered. "Mike Stroud, our doctor, put it together."

"What about your food and fuel?" he inquired.

"I organized that myself. We've got enough food for five people
on full rations for a couple of years and we've ample coal and plenty

of kerosene. Come on, I'll show you," I said and I led him around the outside of the hut to our various food and fuel dumps.

"Well, don't hesitate to use the radio if you've got an emergency," he advised amiably as he stepped back aboard the helicopter. His visit had lasted only half an hour.

I assumed he was satisfied with our resources and interpreted his relaxed manner as a positive sign. I hoped that we had made a favourable impression and, as long as he perceived us as not being an economic threat, I felt that there would be no problem.

Moving the Cessna from the sea-ice to the shore proved more difficult than I had imagined. Tide cracks, which I thought would close under the pressure of the north wind, remained open between the machine and the shore. With a system of ropes and blocks, and a few sheets of plywood on planks bridging the gaps, we winched it slowly shoreward. Despite a tense moment when one of the planks slipped and the plane teetered precariously over the water, we completed the job without mishap. The machine would still have to be weatherproofed and secured against the winter onslaught, but we had plenty of time for that.

The next few days were a blur of cleaning, repairing equipment and organizing the hut. My fastidiousness had Steve and Tim wondering what they were in for, but I felt that in time we would all settle into a comfortable routine, each assigned to his own responsibilities.

Moving the Cessna from the ice. (Photo by Gareth Wood)

On January 18 we overheard a transmission between the *Polar Queen*, a Norwegian ship, and Greenpeace's *Gondwana*, which was in the area trying to get in touch with us. Our attempt to contact *Gondwana* the following day was thwarted by poor radio connections. I had heard that Greenpeace was planning to set up a base in the vicinity and wondered if it was to be this year. Pack-ice that was heavier than usual was probably frustrating their attempts to reach shore.

In the middle of the afternoon of the next day, Jules and a small party arrived with two VIP Inuit to visit Scott's hut. We had a great chat and I was able to catch up on the latest scuttlebutt from McMurdo and Scott Base regarding our expedition. When Jules heard that we were about to start handwashing all our laundry, she immediately offered to take it back to Willy Field and wash it in one of their machines. I could pick it up on a later trip. I don't think she knew what she was in for, because Steve, Tim and I quickly scoured the hut for all the dirty clothing and linen we could find. Jules and her companion left a few minutes later with about 100 pounds of laundry strapped to the backs of their skidoos.

On the morning of January 22, Greenpeace's tiny chopper, large enough for only the pilot and one passenger, touched down next to the hut. From behind the perspex emerged Jerry Johnson, the expedition leader, and Dave, the pilot. Over a cup of tea they told us that Greenpeace had planned to set up a base that winter but would now content themselves with an air reconnaissance of Ross Island with a view to establishing something permanent the following year.

Because they wanted a presence on the continent, Greenpeace had thought that a straight exchange of personnel with us, three for three, might have been the best way to get a hut and equipment while simultaneously solving our evacuation problem. We learned from Jerry, however, that Footsteps was not interested in doing a deal that year. I was somewhat embarrassed not to have heard this first from our own people in London. I guessed that it was just not politically appropriate for us to develop an association with Greenpeace at this time. They were still feeling their way in the Antarctic and had yet to make their intentions known. After a quick tour of the area, including Scott's hut, Jerry and Dave gave us a few bottles of liquor, a box of fruit, chocolates and some frozen meat, the last of which we were especially grateful for.

In spite of no longer being hungry, I had gained ten pounds in as many days and my appetite was enormous. I continued to sample every kind of food in the hut just for the taste. Other parts of my recovery were not so rapid. My feet were still sore and now swollen since our arrival at the Pole. At night I would prop them on pillows to alleviate the pain. Despite this minor inconvenience, I was beginning to feel more content, and was fully occupied every day.

I now set to work preparing our wish list for London. Although the items we requested were not essential, they would simplify our lives. We needed a new grate for the stove and some generator parts. I also needed to send London an inventory of our food and fuel as well as to assure them of our good health and our ability to see out the next year. The last incoming flight of the summer to Willy Field would occur in late February and if I was to provide London with sufficient time to meet that deadline, they would need to receive a telex of our supply list within the next few days. I was not relishing a trip to Scott Base, knowing the political climate, but the public post office's telex facility was our most consistent link with the outside world.

My preparations were interrupted by Dr. Kitt Taylor who arrived on the Greenpeace helicopter. I had asked Dave, the pilot, on an earlier occasion to pass a message to their doctor that I would appreciate some medical advice with respect to my feet. Dr. Taylor thought it was a perfect excuse to visit Cape Evans and after examining my feet he told me that the peripheral blood vessels had been damaged, allowing blood to seep into the surrounding tissue and causing the swelling I was experiencing. I was relieved to learn that the condition was only temporary.

On January 27 I left Home Cove on skis for the 17-mile trip to Scott Base. Loaded on my sledge was a tent, sleeping bag, stove and food for the few days it would take to send a telex to London, answer any letters that might have arrived, wait for acknowledgement of the telex and make whatever radio-phone calls were necessary.

The trip was uneventful and by 4:00 p.m. I was at Scott Base where I tracked down the officer in command, Peter Cresswell, to explain the purpose of my visit.

"What're you doing on base?" he asked curtly when I arrived at his office.

"I just need to use the post office and public phone," I replied.

"Where are you staying?" he asked.

"I've got a tent and gear on my sledge just the other side of McMurdo." After an interminable pause, I asked, "Is there anything else?"

"No," he responded rudely, signalling an end to the interview.

Other than the OIC, the staff seemed anxious to extend their friendship and hospitality toward us. The morale, I learned, was very low, the ostracism of Footsteps and Greenpeace from Scott Base occupying the centre of a raging debate. It had started over two small incidents which we never thought would escalate to the point of controversy. First, just after the *Southern Quest* sank, three of her crew had been asked to leave the Scott Base bar by the OIC after being invited there by base employees, and second, Greenpeace had been denied use of the post office for not giving sufficient notice of their arrival. The official statement with respect to both of us read: "We have been advised by our government that we are not to have communication with you except for safety reasons or on strictly humanitarian grounds."

Several Scott Base employees had held private meetings to discuss the issue, the result of which was telephone interviews granted to New Zealand newspapers criticizing base policy. One Scott Base employee had been fired and another returned home early. This caused a great stir, the ripples reaching McMurdo as well.

I vowed to keep our visits to the public post office to a minimum to avoid any further controversy. While we deeply appreciated the concern shown by the many personnel at Scott Base and McMurdo Station, I wanted to avoid any accusation that we were directly affecting their operations.

After sending the telex I walked back to McMurdo and searched out Captain Shrite to let him know that I was in the vicinity. On the way I bumped into Bob Harler, head of air operations, and discussed the events surrounding the sinking of the *Southern Quest*. He explained that McMurdo is one of the few bases in the Antarctic with the resources to assist in distress situations and is therefore continually diverting funds from its scientific operating budget for this reason. The Americans were caught in a difficult position, since they could never refuse a humanitarian request, and they didn't know what to do about it. Their patience had been wearing thin, even before the sinking of our ship.

Although I was apprehensive about meeting Shrite, I felt it was my responsibility to reassure him that I understood the political situation and the restrictions he had placed upon us. He appeared somewhat relieved at my statement and asked after my health, even commenting that I looked much better clean shaven. He also suggested that I perform radio checks with South Pole anytime I wanted. I left his office feeling that I might be able to work with him after all; only a few days earlier I had thought that he could be nothing more than a bitter adversary.

Having just met with Shrite, I felt guilty travelling to Willy Field to pick up the laundry which Jules had taken from us a few days earlier.

The following morning I received a reply to my telex: "REALISTIC DATE OF ARRIVAL IN MOST ITEMS LAST FLIGHT. PRESS REACTION VERY FAVOURABLE HERE IN U.K. ... PLEASE CONTINUE MIKE'S MEDICAL PROGRAMME WITH TOOLS AVAILABLE. LETTERS TO FOLLOW. PARENTS ETC. IN GOOD ORDER. GENERAL/USUAL PANIC. IT IS AWFUL TO BE BACK, LONDON STINKS. ... THANK YOU FOR YOUR EFFORT. ROBERT."

Reading the message made me wish that I had chosen to depart with Roger and Robert. I longed to be back in stinky London.

When I got back to the tent later that day in preparation for returning to Cape Evans, I was stunned to discover the inside crammed with a pile of frozen meat and some beer which I could only guess came from Scott Base. I later learned that it had been delivered on the pretence of a garbage run. I wondered if they thought we were starving and began to worry about the repercussions to these individuals should they be caught. Although I was grateful, the heavy sledge, which reminded me of the weight of my sledge on the polar journey, played hell with my feet as I struggled, exhausted, to drag it along the shore — I was prevented from getting onto the sea-ice by a wide tide crack. Eventually I chose to unload the sledge and, dragging it empty for a kilometre through a jumble of rafted pancake ice, finally found a crossing. It took me five trips, back and forth, to lug load after load of meat and beer back to the sledge. On one trip, a bag split, spilling its frozen contents onto the ice. Although overwhelmed with the kindness and concern shown by the providers of our gift an hour earlier, I was now tired and frustrated, and my feet hurt. I cursed our benefactors as I grabbed a large pork loin roast and hurled it as far as I could into the tide crack. I gathered the rest, and with one more trip had retrieved the entire load. I moved rapidly over the sea-ice, my body fuelled only by my determination to get to base as quickly as possible.

Just past Inaccessible Island I glanced down at my ski tips. Tiny geysers of water were spouting up beside each ski from the pressure of my weight on the ice. Thin ice! I froze instantly, terrified to move in any direction. As my mind raced for a solution, the ice beneath my feet rose and fell with a gentle undulation. My first reaction was to back up but the sledge dug in, making that impossible. Moving around in a shallow turn I headed directly back toward Inaccessible Island.

As I moved rapidly but cautiously away from the danger, frightening images of killer whales smashing the ice from below spurred me on. I remembered reading about Ponting, Scott's photographer, who, on January 5, 1911, had such an encounter. While the *Terra Nova* was moored to an ice floe preparatory to unloading, Scott and Ponting saw six or seven killer whales in a state of agitation around the stern of the vessel where two of the expedition's dogs were tethered. Ponting, grabbing his camera, was running toward the edge of the floe when the ice beneath his feet heaved up, splitting into several pieces. While he scrambled to safety, Scott could hear the dull thuds of the whales butting the ice from beneath and as both of them watched in horror, between the smashed fragments the whales' glistening black heads rose, their eyes focussed on the terrified dogs which, fortunately, had not fallen in.

From Inaccessible Island I headed directly for Turk's Head and shore, the ice beneath my feet still thin. At 3:00 a.m. I stumbled through the door of the hut, having completed the crossing by land. Steve got up to help me unload the sledge and transport the meat to Home Cove where we buried it to keep it frozen. My feet were very swollen and after several cups of tea I limped off to bed.

A week later we had a surprise visit from Greenpeace and the day after that one from an Italian expedition which was considering establishing a permanent base at Terra Nova Bay the following year. Despite the generosity of all these guests, I found their visits unsettling. One of the joys of the Antarctic is its solitude, but since my return I had lived the frantic pace of a man on the outside, hardly in keeping with the natural rhythms around me.

Following the Italians' departure we began to prepare for a return to the post office to pick up the supplies I had ordered on my last visit. On February 23 we set off; I hauled the sledge while behind me marched Steve and Tim, each carrying a full rucksack. Descending to the sea-ice, which we hoped would be thick enough for travel, we avoided the longer and more arduous route by land. Four and a half hours later we camped near Hutton Cliff where Mike, Roger and I had camped on our winter journey eight months earlier. Both Steve and Tim were played out.

"My god, I'm exhausted, and thirsty," Tim said wearily. "I think I've a little better appreciation of what you went through on the polar journey."

We started late the next morning with Tim hauling the sledge. Steve and I were soon far ahead of him. Another 4.5 hours put us below Crater Hill, but above the road leading into Scott Base. There on a level surface we erected the tent and crawled into our sleeping bags for a short nap. At 7:00 p.m. we went down to Scott Base to check the mail and our supply package.

At the post office we ran into Jim Rankin, base engineer and newly appointed winter OIC. After introducing ourselves I explained that I had a small problem.

"This is embarrassing," I said, "but I need to use the washroom and there isn't one here."

"Well," he said, looking thoughtful for a moment, "post offices usually have facilities, don't they?"

"Yes," I agreed quickly.

"Okay," he said, "we'll take the washrooms off the out-of-bounds list."

A few days later we departed for Cape Evans. The sledge was heavy with the stove and generator parts that had arrived on the last flight to Willy Field. Hauling it was desperately difficult, especially through the light drift dusting the surface. Both Steve and Tim took turns but on the hills they required assistance. On March 3 we arrived, exhausted, back at the hut. There would be no need to return to McMurdo until late May when we would ask London to parcel-post any small items we required for repairs around the base. These would arrive via the midwinter air drop which would occur at the end of June.

The rest of March was consumed with innumerable chores. The light was beginning to fade and we still had to organize some of the outside stores for convenient access during the winter. While Steve and Tim winched the plane farther up the beach, I dismantled the wind generator and repiled our coal. We also stored the best of our sledges, all our extra polar clothing, sleeping bags, camp stoves, etc. in a box tent erected in the yard. It would serve as a temporary shelter in case of fire.

Snow was beginning to drift around the hut and we had already experienced winds of up to Force 9. Our gravel beach disappeared beneath a shelf of ice extending into the sea and pancake ice was forming in North Bay. I was hoping that Wilkniss' prediction of a harsh winter was only that, a prediction, but it was difficult to ignore the signs at our doorstep.

On April 6 I could see the crescent edge of permanent ice stretching from the Cape to Inaccessible Island. Whether it would hold or not, we couldn't know. The weather was cold enough to freeze the sea in calm weather, but the slightest wind would blow the ice out.

Several days later I climbed Wind Vane Hill to check on the sea-ice. It had not only held but was growing into the Sound at a rapid rate. On the morning of April 14, however, I found that it had broken up under the pressure of a southerly wind the previous night. The wind was both powerful and pervasive. It controlled and shaped the land, building and cutting drifts, ripping at the sea-ice. We were intruders in its path, insignificant and humbled by its authority.

CHAPTER FIFTEEN

LEOPARD SEAL ATTACK

WITH THE LONG Antarctic night only days away, snuffing light from our tiny world for approximately 70 days, Steve, Tim and I made one final excursion for the season. Our plan was to visit Cape Royds to see Shackleton's hut and, if time allowed, investigate a nearby Adelie penguin rookery. We had been anticipating the trip, and in fact had been ready for days, but heavy southerly winds, dense fog, cold and snow had kept us basebound and not in the best of spirits. I suppose I was experiencing all over again what we had suffered the previous winter but I was none the wiser for having gone through it. Cabin fever has a diabolical way of concealing itself from its victim.

About noon on April 15, under clear skies and with fair weather ahead, we set off for the Cape. Once across the Barne Glacier, we planned to follow the coast around to Backdoor Bay behind the Cape and then cut across the sea-ice to the Cape itself. The trip was only about seven miles one way and would take no more than four hours, weather and ice permitting. At best we expected to be away three or four days.

Carrying rucksacks instead of towing sledges, we hiked northwest into the orange glow of the setting sun, our crampons scuffing jagged holes in the wind-sculpted surface. Poised on the lip of night, the sun bathed the stark, white landscape with a delicate flush, offering little physical warmth but great anticipation, even then, of its return. Transfixed by the interplay of soft light and long shadow, we basked in the thin comfort it radiated across the frozen expanse before us. The memory of this day would serve us well in the contrasting blackness to come.

Although the glacier was crevassed, the crevasses were visible and their snow bridges secure. We had ropes but I did not consider them necessary. From the Barne summit we looked back across the 17-mile gulf separating us from McMurdo Station. The view was spectacular. The glacier had changed little since Scott first stood upon it with Victor Campbell, Tryggve Gran and Edward Nelson, three members of the *Terra Nova* Expedition, on January 15, 1911.

Reaching a rocky area on the far side of the glacier, we removed our crampons to walk the bare coast to Backdoor Bay before crossing the sea-ice. The coal-black coastal rocks sharply defined the glacier's brilliance. There were no shades of grey to soften the harsh reality of this unforgiving land.

Arriving at Cape Royds and the New Zealanders' scientific hut about 4:30 p.m., we settled in for the night after having a cursory glance around. Close to Sir Ernest Shackleton's 1908-1909 expedition hut, the uninsulated eight- by 16-foot, plywood affair that the Kiwis used for studying a nearby Adelie penguin rookery had two eight-inch-square windows, a small counter complete with four Primus stoves, two bunk beds and some shelves stocked with tinned food which we did not require, having brought our own. Although rather austere, it suited our simple purpose and certainly those of the scientists for whom it was erected.

"My god it's cold," Tim commented as we huddled over the hut's kerosene stoves as well as our own. "You'd think they'd insulate these shacks, wouldn't you?"

"I guess it's not necessary," I answered. "The scientists are only here in the summer."

"Small bloody comfort," Steve said, "but it's warmer in here than it is outside."

"Thank god for small mercies," Tim said dryly.

After a meal of noodles, sausages and beans, we retired to our sleeping bags for some well-earned kip. As I lay in my bag, Shackleton's nearby hut, barely visible in the gathering winter darkness, pervaded my thoughts. What history had taken place at our doorstep! That the hut was here at all was only due to an extraordinary set of circumstances.

When Shackleton's attempts to land at three more favourable sites failed, he was forced to settle at Cape Royds as a last resort. His first choice, an inlet on the edge of the Ross Ice Shelf, had been abandoned when he discovered that several miles of the ice shelf had calved since his last visit. Shocked at the change in the landscape and his own failure to predict it, Shackleton steamed east toward King Edward VII Land but was turned away there by heavy pack-ice which threatened to imprison the *Nimrod*. McMurdo Sound, his third location, now appeared to be his only option unless he chose to return to New Zealand.

He wrote of his predicament in a letter to his wife, Emily, on January 26, 1908, "What a difference a few short hours can make in one's life and work and destiny: Child o' mine I have been through a sort of Hell since the 23rd and I cannot even now realize that I am on my way back to McMurdo Sound and that all idea of wintering on the Barrier or at King Edward VII Land is at an end that I have had to break my word to Scott and go back to the old base, and that all my plans and ideas have now to be changed and changed by the overwhelming forces of Nature."[1]

Shackleton was devastated by having to break his word to Scott but, confident in his resolve, he elected to press on. When he arrived at McMurdo Sound he found miles of ice lay between the *Nimrod* and shore. However, no more than seven miles east of there he at last found success. There lay a bare rock outcropping known as Cape Royds, named for Scott's first lieutenant of the *Discovery*, Lieutenant Charles Rawson Royds.

On February 3, 1908, with the *Nimrod* lying just offshore, Shackleton and two of his shore party, Adams and Wild, ran the ship's tender into the ice of a small bay just behind the outcrop. The small crescent of water would later be named Backdoor Bay. Nearby was a convenient dock of ice that they considered ideal for offloading stores. Jumping ashore near the very spot where we lay, they also determined that the solid rock just beyond the ice was well suited for their winter quarters. The Cape was not ideal for beginning the polar journey as it was cut off from the interior by heavy ice flowing down Mount Erebus, leaving the sea as the only avenue of travel. Scott, like Shackleton, had recognized these same shortcomings.

When we awoke, the morning was clear with magnificent views of Mount Erebus, Cape Bird, Cape Barne, the Barne Glacier and the western mountains, including Mount Discovery. After porridge we spent the entire day exploring and photographing the surrounding area. Later, returning to the "box," as we called our little shelter, we lit two stoves for a couple of hours of relief from the intense cold and, after preparing supper, read before getting into our sleeping bags for the night.

We decided to leave the following morning, but not before visiting Shackleton's hut and the Adelie penguin rookery. Although entry to the hut is strictly controlled by the New Zealand government, which is responsible for its safekeeping and maintenance, a rusted lock offered us an informal, albeit surreptitious, invitation.

The hut was exactly the way I'd imagined. It was dark, with windows boarded against the endless wind and blowing snow, and the historic reverence of the moment washed over me as objects now belonging to history materialized in the gloom. Just as I had when I visited Scott's Cape Evans hut for the first time, I felt enveloped by the aura of the men who had eaten, slept and worked within these confines. Glancing over to Shackleton's room, I almost expected "the Boss," as Shackleton was known to his men, to come out and greet me. Campbell, upon visiting the hut in 1911, wrote, "The whole place was very eerie, there is such a feeling of life about it. Not only do I feel it but others do also. Last night after I turned in I could have sworn that I heard people shouting to each other."[2]

Surrounding the rough, central table were once the cubicles of Shackleton's men. The dim light now revealed they were gone. Next to Shackleton's room was Adams and Marshall's "No. 1 Park Lane." Beside that was "The Gables," the den of Marston and Day, and across the room was Joyce and Wild's "The Rogues' Retreat."

Above me, suspended from the rafters, swung two Nansen sledges; through one snaked now-useless gas lines from an acetylene generator perched over the door. Across the room were the front skis of Antarctica's first motor vehicle, a 15-hp Arrol-Johnston, and at one end of the hut stood the stove around which the men must have gathered for warmth and communal comfort. It was built by Smith & Wellstood of Scotland, the manufacturers of our own little Esse stove. I could imagine its radiant heat cutting through the brittle cold of the hut's interior. Upon it still sat a colossal snow-melting pot and a large frying pan in addition to other pots and pans. Behind and around it were stacked boxes of wholewheat biscuits, a large tin of Colman's Mustard, a box of Hunters Famed Oatmeal, Colman's corn flour, bottled salt and Bird's Egg Custard among other necessities.

Steve could hardly contain his amazement.

"My god, look," he said, pointing to a case of bottled fruit. "I wonder if it's still edible?"

"It looks good," Tim commented. "The labels are still bright."

"It should be," I speculated. "It's been in a deepfreeze for close to 80 years!"

The remainder of the hut was ascetic in its simplicity. In a bid to reduce expenses and freight, Shackleton had brought no furniture, planning to build it all from empty packing crates. The crates serving as chairs and shelves still bore the British Antarctic Expedition 1907 stamp. Despite the passage of time, the hut appeared to be in a state of readiness, as if expecting a returning party.

Shackleton recorded the effect of their first storm, "During our first severe blizzard, the hut shook and trembled so that every moment we expected the whole thing to carry away, and there is not the slightest shadow of a doubt that if we had been located in the open, the hut and everything in it would have been torn up and blown away. Even with our sheltered position I had to lash the chronometers to the shelf in my room, for they were apt to be shaken off when the walls trembled in the gale. When the storm was over we put a stout wire cable over the hut, burying the ends in the ground and freezing them in, so as to afford additional security in case heavier weather was in store for us in the future."[3]

It was also from this very hut that Shackleton and his three companions departed on October 29, 1908, to begin their "furthest south" journey which would end in defeat. Disappointed at his failure to reach the Pole, Shackleton would find some solace in Robert Browning's poem "Prospice," which became for him and his wife a signal comfort in his darkest days.

> Fear death? — to feel the fog in my throat,
> The mist in my face,
> When the snows begin, and the blasts denote
> I am nearing the place,
> The power of the night, the press of the storm,
> The post of the foe;
> Where he stands, the Arch Fear in a visible form,
> Yet the strong man must go. ...

Outside, partly buried in the grimy snow, were the remains of the expedition's stores. From disintegrating laminated boxes, weighed down with large chunks of black lava, spilled candles, glass jars of salt, large tins of corn and other unnamed substances. Leather harnesses hung here and there: the brass hardware, now coated with a thin green patina, looked strangely festive against the hut's weathered siding. Bales of hay, still smelling fresh, were toppled over doghouses while ponies' feedboxes hung from what remained of the stable.

Expedition boxes were stacked behind a rusty wheel. Designed for ease of handling and stowage, 2,500 of these 15- by 30-inch boxes made up the bulk of Shackleton's stores. A portion of the stores had been offloaded at Backdoor Bay onto the jetty of ice that had not yet "gone out," but Shackleton noticed just in time that a crack was beginning to form between his 30 tons of supplies and the land. He called on all hands to redouble their efforts, and the stores were quickly moved to safety. Half an hour later the ice jetty calved into the frigid waters of the bay.

As we left the hut to explore the nearby Adelie penguin rookery, I could not help but wonder at the stamina of those heroes who, without benefit of modern science, had tested themselves on this most formidable of continents.

Upon arriving at the rookery we were disappointed to find nothing but guano and a few carcasses. The Adelies seek the higher temperatures of the pack-ice during the winter, and had already migrated. They would not return until October when, drawn by the sun and in their best soup-and-fish, they would wobble and weave across the pack-ice to the colony like so many tipsy gentlemen. The males arrive first to clean and repair the pebble nests in preparation for breeding. The Adelie, a small bird averaging 12 pounds, is adept in the water, often gracefully leaping five feet or more from the water surface to the top of a floe. Their hilarious nest-building antics, or pebble-stealing, for they are natural thieves, have entertained many an Antarctic visitor.

Returning to the New Zealand scientific hut, we prepared to depart for Cape Evans by burning our paper rubbish and packing empty cans for disposal later at base. It was April 17 and our pre-winter diversion was over, but I was happy to return to the routine of base life and our preparations for my second winter on the continent. My mind was thus occupied as we shrugged on our packs and began to pick our way across the barren rock outcropping of the Cape to Backdoor Bay.

"Why don't we cross the bay rather than take the shore route," I suggested. "The ice is old, it's got to be at least seven or eight feet thick. It'll be faster."

"Do you think we'll be able to cross that crack over there?" Tim asked, pointing across the bay.

"I don't think it'll be a problem but if it is, we'll just follow it back to shore," I replied.

"Yes, I guess so," Tim agreed.

Pancake ice was already beginning to form in the outer bay due to the cold, calm weather we had been having and a slight south wind wafted over us beneath an almost summer-blue sky. The air, around -30°C, was not warmed by the fading sunlight weakly illuminating Cape Royds behind us. All things considered, it was a perfect travel day.

Being familiar with the area from the trip we had made just before leaving for the Pole, I took a different approach to the sea-ice than either Steve or Tim. Once on the ice I crossed the bay toward the black volcanic monolith of Cape Barne. Ahead, the low sun catching the seaward edge of the Barne Glacier gilded its 200-foot emerald face. Beyond, the black back of Inaccessible Island was just visible in the distance. Looking around I realized that I was ahead and slowed my pace accordingly to let the others catch up. The going was easy and as I moved over the ice I had no idea that I was being stalked from beneath its surface.

Ahead was a working crack which was slightly more than one stride in width — too far to comfortably cross without jumping. It was covered with a very thin layer of unblemished ice. Innocently, I stepped closer. Would it hold my weight, I wondered, or would I have to jump. Stretching one foot down, I probed it with the tip of my crampon, much as I'd done with dozens of other working cracks in similar circumstances. Suddenly, the surface erupted as the massive head and shoulders of a mature leopard seal, mouth gaping in expectation, crashed through the eggshell covering. It closed its powerful jaws about my right leg, and I fell backward, shocked and helpless in its vise-like grip. Feeling myself being dragged toward a watery grave, I locked my left crampon onto the opposing edge. I knew that once I was in the water, it would be all over.

"Help, help, Steve, Tim, help," I screamed repeatedly. It seemed an age before I finally caught sight of their running figures.

"Kick it, kick it, kick it, get the bloody thing off me, hurry, hurry for Christ's sake, you bastard, you bastard," I yelled hysterically, my gloved hands scrabbling fruitlessly for purchase on the smooth ice behind me as I strained against the seal's prodigious weight.

For one tiny fraction of a second our eyes met. These were not the pleading eyes of a Weddell seal nor the shy glance of a crabeater seal — they were cold and evil with intent. What fear the seal must have recognized in my own during this brief moment of communication, I can only imagine.

"Bloody hell, it's a leopard seal," Steve shouted breathlessly as he leapt across the crack to attack the brute from the opposite side.

"Get the bloody thing off me, kick it, for Christ's sake," I screamed again.

"Aim for its eye, its eye," Tim shouted, his voice verging on panic.

"Bastard! Bastard! Bastard!" Steve chanted in rhythm to his swinging boot.

"Get its eye, blind it," Tim shouted again.

I watched, dazed, as the front tines of Steve's cramponed boot made small, fleshy wounds in the side of the beast's head near its eye. Fifteen or 20 times his foot swung with crushing impact. Blood streamed from the wounds and spattered to the ice with each sickening smack of the boot. The impact of the violent attack vibrated through my body. Stubbornly, the beast continued to grip my leg which appeared tiny in its jaw. I felt as powerless as a mouse caught by a cat.

"It's backing off," Tim shouted triumphantly as the seal suddenly released its hold and slipped slowly back beneath the surface.

Numbed, confused and mesmerized by the concentric ripples slapping the edge of the bloodstained hole, I stared entranced at the spot where the frightening beast had disappeared.

"Quick, get him back from the edge," Tim gasped.

Arms had just grabbed me when the seal's monstrous form leapt once more from its watery lair. Lunging at me, it crossed the ice with an awkward gait, streams of bloody water cascading to the ice around it. Its large, interlocking teeth crushed down on my plastic boot.

"My god, we've blown it," I gasped. "Kick it, kick it, for Christ's sake, kick it," I shouted, the fear in my throat threatening to choke me.

"Its eye, get its eye," Steve shouted as he and Tim again booted its head with the lance-like front tines of their crampons.

Irrational thoughts careered madly about my brain. What would the ice look like from beneath the surface? What would death be like? As if divorced from life already, I pictured the seal swimming down with my limp, red-coated body in its jaws. I could see pale green sunlight filtering down through the ice as I descended into the gloom of certain oblivion. It all seemed so real, so peaceful — a silent movie with myself as the reluctant hero.

Tim's tugging at my shoulders pulled me swiftly back to reality — finally vanquished, the animal had retreated to its nether world. They skidded me quickly over the ice a safe distance from the crack. I stood up shakily.

"Lie down, let's have a look," Steve implored, motioning me down.

"No, I'm all right. Thank god it's not broken," I gasped, as I tested my wounded leg by stumbling backward, away from the terror I had just experienced. Glancing down at my torn clothing I saw blood on my leg — whether it was mine or the seal's I was not sure. I unzipped my outer Gore-Tex and fibre-pile pant.

"Oh my god," I trembled, horrified at the blood and puncture wounds on the front and back of my leg just below my knee.

"Let's have a look," Steve repeated.

"The back of my leg — my longjohns have been pushed right into it," I said.

"We can't do anything here," Tim said, "but slap a wound dressing on it. We'll get you back to base and treat it there."

"Shit, we've only got two dressings," Steve said, rummaging through the first-aid kit.

"Here, use this glove, it'll do till we make it back," Tim offered.

Applying the dressings to the front puncture wounds and the glove to the back, I replaced my outer clothing and leaned into my ice axe, testing the strength of my leg.

"Do you think you can make it?" Steve asked.

"Yes, I think so, but we'd better hurry. It'll be stiff soon," I responded, adrenalin still pumping wildly through my system.

"Do you want a painkiller before we start?" Steve asked.

"Not yet, but keep it handy. I had a bad reaction to a painkiller on the Plateau. I don't want to add that to my problems," I replied, wincing as I took the first hesitant step. "Let's just get the hell out of here."

For over three hours I punished myself across the Barne Glacier to Cape Evans using my ice axe for support. For the most part I was moving rapidly, almost too fast for Tim and Steve.

"Woody, slow down, my feet are sore," Tim begged, in jest.

By the time we reached the glacier edge, 300 yards from the hut, my leg was swollen and stiff.

"Tim, can you help me off with my crampons? I can't bend my knee," I asked wearily as I sat heavily down upon the gravel.

With the assistance of the others I limped to the hut where we consumed several pots of tea while waiting for the hut to warm. I was terrified by what else I might find beneath my bloody clothing.

"I'm going to have a thorough wash before I begin," I said. "I don't want to increase the risk of infection."

Removing all my clothing except my bandages, I washed myself at the sink in warm water and put on a clean shirt, sweater, socks, slippers etc. With all the medical supplies I would need laid out before me, I began to unwrap the bandages. Steve and Tim stared curiously.

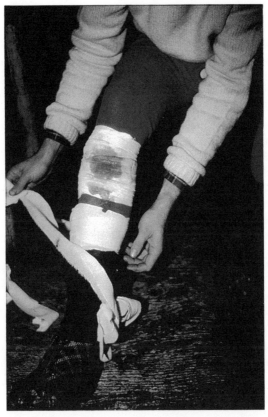

Gareth preparing to treat the wounds caused by the leopard seal's attack.
(Courtesy of Steve Broni)

"I'll have to cut these longjohns off, I can't get them over my knee," I said as I took scissors to the blood-soaked cloth.

"Here, let me help," Steve offered.

"No, I can do it myself," I rebuffed him unkindly.

Once the longjohns were cut away, my wounds were exposed. The top was the most wicked, a three-inch-long gash just below my knee, right down to the bone. I felt slightly nauseous as I viewed the grisly pink sheen of the bone membrane weeping at the pit of the ragged tear. The others were deep punctures, much like I thought bullet wounds would look. With warm water I began the slow and painful process of cleaning and removing the fragments of clothing pressed into my leg by the seal's teeth. Pain was now coming on in throbbing waves. Two hours later I had done all that I could. I retired to bed, pale and weak, after taking a painkiller, with a pee-bottle and a bucket in which to be sick if I reacted badly to the drug.

Changing the dressing the following morning I was suddenly concerned about infection, and also there was a big flap of skin and muscle which loosened alarmingly whenever I flexed my leg. I could do nothing more myself: I had already exceeded the limits of my medical knowledge. I decided to call the American base to satisfy myself that I had done everything I could to prevent infection; it was humbling, but necessary for my well-being. I knew that the episode would be blown out of all proportion and I was later proved right.

"South Pole, South Pole, Cape Evans, do you read? Over," I called somewhat nervously. I wondered, as I made contact, whether, with the current political climate, this would reinforce the American opinion that private expeditions were incapable of functioning on their own.

"Cape Evans, Mac Relay. Go ahead. Over," they responded.

Surprised that McMurdo answered and not South Pole — normally McMurdo was too close for proper radio communication — I downplayed the problem.

"Mac Relay, Cape Evans. One of our party has had a minor seal bite. If it's possible could I please speak with Dr. Dalton. Over."

"Cape Evans, Mac Relay. Is it important? Over," the radio operator asked.

"Yes. Over," I responded, contradicting myself.

Dr. Dalton, the base physician, came to the radio a few moments later.

"Go ahead Cape Evans. Over," he said.

"I've been bitten on the leg by a leopard seal and have suffered puncture wounds and a laceration below the knee. Over," I replied.

After requesting a brief description of my injuries, Dr. Dalton asked, "Is the bone exposed, and if it is has it been scratched? Over."

"The bone's exposed but I don't think it's been scratched. Over," I responded.

"Good. What have you done so far? Over," he asked.

"I've cleaned and dressed it and started a course of tetracycline. Over," I replied.

"What strength? Over," he asked.

After I described the dose, he suggested that it be doubled for three weeks and that I update him on my progress in a few days.

Later we began to read about leopard seals. In *Reader's Digest's Antarctica, Great Stories From the Frozen Continent*, a picture caption states, "The teeth of a leopard seal are clearly adapted for seizing and tearing flesh. Despite the fact that they are fierce predators, leopard seals have not been known to make unprovoked attacks on human beings."[4]

I beg to differ and history does as well. On January 1, 1916, a little more than a month after Shackleton's *Endurance* was crushed by pack-ice, one of his crew, Thomas H. Orde-Lees, was attacked by a leopard seal. Alfred Lansing, in his vivid account, *Endurance, Shackleton's Incredible Voyage*, recorded the event, "Returning from a hunting trip, Orde-Lees, travelling on skis across the rotting surface of the ice, had just about reached camp when an evil, knoblike head burst out of the water just in front of him. He turned and fled, pushing as hard as he could with his ski poles and shouting for Wild to bring his rifle.

"The animal — a sea leopard — sprang out of the water and came after him, bounding across the ice with the peculiar rocking-horse gait of a seal on land. The beast looked like a small dinosaur, with a long, serpentine neck.

"After a half-dozen leaps, the sea leopard had almost caught up with Orde-Lees when it unaccountably wheeled and plunged again into the water. By then, Orde-Lees had nearly reached the opposite side of the floe; he was about to cross to safe ice when the sea leopard's head exploded out of the water directly ahead of him. The animal had tracked his shadow across the ice. It made a savage lunge for Orde-Lees with its mouth open, revealing an enormous array of sawlike teeth. Orde-Lees' shouts for help rose to screams and he turned and raced away from his attacker.

"The animal leaped out of the water again in pursuit just as Wild arrived with his rifle. The sea leopard spotted Wild, and turned to attack him. Wild dropped to one knee and fired again and again at the onrushing beast. It was less than 30 feet away when it finally dropped.

"Two dog teams were required to bring the carcass into camp. It measured 12 feet long, and they estimated its weight at about 1,100 pounds."[5]

As soon as word of my misfortune spread, leopard seal paranoia struck Antarctica. Overnight, scientists at McMurdo Station and Scott Base, who earlier had shown only moderate caution, were suddenly mindful when conducting their affairs on the sea-ice. This fear infected our own party as well. Tim recorded in his journal, "I went out to empty the bucket this evening and fear of what [might] emerge from the sea meant I kept well back from the edge. A few days ago I might have lingered to watch the phosphorescence, but now the dark and the eerie noises of the sea-ice and of course the fears I've already mentioned make it less of a pleasure. I think a good deal of the problem is the suddenness of the event. From the stillness and calm of a beautiful day the sudden violence of the attack remains deeply imprinted on my mind, and of course in the others."

To the leopard seal I was no less a prey animal than a penguin or a Weddell seal. Later, seeing films of leopard seals waiting beneath floes for careless Adelie penguins, I shuddered at what might have happened. The seals grab the hapless Adelies by their rumps and flail them against the water, literally jerking them from their skins. I also recalled reading that *National Geographic* photographer Jannik Schou, while photographing Adelies and leopard seals in the Antarctic, almost became a meal for one huge brute that lunged at him with jaws wide, following him over the ice for a distance of about 30 feet.

My weeping leg was a constant reminder for many weeks after the attack. Toward the end of May, however, I was walking again and my thoughts drifted toward working constructively around the hut, taking meteorological readings, repairing equipment and organizing replies to sponsors. The limiting factor was no longer my wounds, but the descent of winter darkness. But even darkness had its delights. On clear nights, the silver moon, bathing an already sterile land with the pallid light of winter, captured our gaze. And where its reflection pooled on the iridescent back of the Barne Glacier, our imaginations caught visions of Scott, Amundsen, Shackleton and other Antarctic heroes, struggling within the silent, frigid confines of their dreams.

CHAPTER SIXTEEN

HUT POINT

THE ADJUSTMENT REQUIRED during the first few days of total blackness was greater than I remembered. The eyes still searched the lost horizon for the tiniest ember. Great store was placed in being able to differentiate the ragged crests of the western mountains from the greater mass of the sky above. In a few days even that would be impossible.

Despite the onset of the long night we were all adapting well. There was no false loyalty like the previous year, little argument or recrimination and no one vying for anyone's friendship. There was nothing that important at stake. We were just three men in a hut in the Antarctic night facing our boredom and being little challenged by the domestic chores that we had to do each day.

In 24-hour darkness we left for Scott Base on June 3 to send our telex to London HQ for the scheduled midwinter supply drop which would occur at the end of the month. We were requesting a small amplifier for our radio.

On the morning of June 4 we entered McMurdo after erecting our tent just out of sight at Hut Point. While I searched out the winter officer in charge, Lieutenant Commander Rachko, Steve and Tim walked over to Scott Base to begin booking our radio calls. Rachko appeared quite happy to meet me but was careful to offer no assistance beyond asking how we were and if I would like to consult Dr. Dalton about my leg. Dalton removed several pieces of dead flesh from my wound before dressing it again, but there was little more required.

The next day, after making several radio-phone calls and sending our telex, we left the base for our tent at 11:00 p.m. in slight-to-moderate wind and blowing snow.

Peering outside on the morning of June 6, I knew that we were going nowhere. Driving snow had reduced visibility to zero. I slept until 3:00 p.m. when I got up to read. Air currents within the tent, however, made lighting the lantern impossible; the lamp glass had been shattered the day before. I finally managed to light it in the protection of the stove box. By this time the walls were bellying heavily under fierce gusts. After reading awhile I extinguished the lamp and drifted restlessly back to sleep.

At 11:00 p.m. I was jolted awake by something covering my face. I panicked momentarily, my arms windmilling to ward off whatever was trying to suffocate me. Sitting up quickly, I realized what had happened — the tent wall had collapsed. Either the guy had given out or the windward tent poles had inverted under the tremendous pressure of the wind. I suspected the latter — the same thing had happened in the wind tunnel in London when we were testing the tent.

"Get dressed now. Put everything on," I yelled to the others above the banshee screech of the wind. "Steve, you first. Tim, put your back against this wall while Steve gets ready."

Taking turns supporting the collapsed wall we rapidly dressed in our Gore-Tex windproof salopettes and down jackets. I crawled out to assess the situation. As I rose, the full force of the blast struck me, forcing me down onto all fours. The ice stung my eyes, blinding me. With my headtorch on, visibility was no more than a foot or two. Groping my way around the outside of the tent, I found that one of the stakes had pulled out, slackening a guy. The poles on the windward side had then inverted, bringing down the wall. The nearness of McMurdo had made me sloppy. The best site available for the tent on the rocky point was a wind-scoured scoop. It was impossible to dig the tent in and the pegs would only penetrate six to eight inches before hitting gravel. I should have built a wall of rock and ice around the windward side for protection.

I thought of tying a rope from the sledge to the collapsed wall, but after trying unsuccessfully to get the rope from the sledge, I abandoned the idea. The others were shouting at me unintelligibly, their words whipped away by the wind.

"We'll collapse the tent, weigh it down and make for the *Discovery* hut," I yelled directly into Steve's ear. The hut could not have been more than 50 yards away.

186

We had just started to loosen the still-secure guys on the windward side when the tent was torn from our grip. I grabbed the nearest corner and was dragged over the sledge before being forced to release it; the tent tumbled off into the dark and windswept night.

"Hold hands and don't let go. We're going for *Discovery* hut. Follow me," I screamed at the others.

I led them into a partly protected gully about 20 yards wide, but once we crested the ridge the gale forced us to our knees. The wind drove steel-hard ice crystals into our eyes until we were forced to shut them tight. My hood, ripped back by the blast, exposed my head to the cold and the accumulating snow froze into my hair and over my eyes. Every few feet I was forced to stop and clear the ice from my eyes. If we missed the hut, we were in trouble. I knew that the *Discovery* hut was surrounded by a chain and post enclosure and once we were inside that we would be safe.

Crawling and stumbling forward — even the lights of McMurdo were obscured — we eventually fell over a section of the chain about 2.5 feet above the ground. I immediately went limp with relief — we had been delivered from a fate too horrible to consider. Once we were inside the fence we groped our way toward the walls of the hut and, feeling around them with searching hands, located the door. It was locked but was easily forced. Exhausted, we fell into the hut's dark interior. This was the oldest hut on Ross Island, built in 1901 by Scott who used it as a storeroom and refuge, having elected to winter on his ship, *Discovery*. It seemed made to order for us and we were thankful for it.

On February 28, 1909, a hungry and weary Shackleton and one companion, Wild, had staggered to this same unoccupied hut after completing their "furthest south" journey. There they passed a cold night, as we did, before attracting the attention of their ship, the *Nimrod*.

Early on the morning of June 7, a slight lull in the storm allowed me time to race to a small American scientific hut just below *Discovery* hut. I knew that there would be a heater in it which I lit before dashing back to get Steve and Tim. At noon the weather cleared sufficiently for me to hurry over to the site of our tent camp. About 25 yards farther along the shore I spotted the tent, partly buried in a deep drift. I returned to the hut to get Steve and Tim, and we started to dig it out before being forced back to the hut by the return of the wind and driving snow.

At 2:00 p.m., during another short lull in the storm, we walked over to McMurdo and tracked down Rachko under the pretext of asking for an updated weather report. We told him that we thought it was crazy for us to sit out in a small tent for days when just a few yards away there was a huge scientific station. He was obviously relieved to see us as he thought we must be pinned down somewhere between McMurdo and Cape Evans. He had no idea we were still at McMurdo and offered us a room immediately. Wind speeds of 93 mph had been recorded. The following morning we were up early and walked down to the Point to dig out our tent and equipment.

On June 10 we departed for Cape Evans. Although the weather was still not ideal — 30-knot winds and blowing snow — Rachko appeared agitated, suggesting that it was time we left. Organizing ourselves immediately, we headed straight for our sledges at Hut Point and by 9:30 a.m. were off across the ice. Blowing snow drove directly at us, stinging our eyes, but in our favour was the slight hint of daylight to the north. We could just make out the dark bulk of Mount Erebus and the rocky landscape of Tent and Inaccessible islands ahead. Heading directly for the islands, I suddenly noticed that the snow crust had changed from white to grey.

"Stop!" I shouted to the others. "We're on thin ice."

Sea fog swirled ahead, a sign that open water was nearby. I plunged my ice axe into the crust. Instead of the usual pinging sound, the point of the axe sank easily into the surface with a wet "smuck." The hole immediately filled with water. Moving slowly ahead in as short a turning radius as possible, much as I had done on the earlier trip when faced with the same situation, we headed toward shore and solid ice. Less than half an hour later we reached the Glacier Tongue hut, all of us drained of energy. From the elevation of the hut we looked out over the sea-ice. A large chunk had blown out in the storm. Within minutes of our arrival, the wind picked up and visibility was once again lost. Our timing was perfect.

We lit two stoves to cook a meal and warm the hut. A couple of hours later Tim began to feel ill and then almost passed out. I immediately recognized what was wrong. In our exhausted and well-fed stupor we hadn't left the door open wide enough to let out the carbon monoxide fumes given off by the stoves. I quickly threw the door open and dragged Tim toward the entrance. He recovered quickly, but to be sure Steve and I stuffed him into a sleeping bag near the door with a toque on his head. He stayed there for an hour.

The weather throughout the next few days was brutal. On June 14 the walls of the Glacier Tongue hut were vibrating so forcibly under the raging onslaught that I was concerned for our safety.

"We're going to have to repack the sledge so that our bivouac bags are on top," I said worriedly. "If this hut goes we're in trouble. Get on your down jackets, salopettes and boots too just in case."

My stomach was twisted in a tight knot all that day as we lay fully dressed on the bunks while outside the wind tore and ripped across the Glacier Tongue, rocking the hut back and forth on its four anchor posts. By late evening the gale abated enough that I felt safe undressing and slipping into my sleeping bag.

The following morning we were up early and departed in clear weather, hoping that we would make base before the storm resumed. We covered the distance in a little over two hours. A few hours later the wind and driving snow returned — I estimated Force 11 or 12. The hut's walls were bowing in and out with the tremendous pressure of the wind and every once in a while an airborne chunk of ash from the beach would land with a dull thunk. Sleep was impossible and my concern over damage to the south-facing windows had me out of bed early to board them up. With Steve's help I also heaped sacks of coal around the cables anchoring the hut, fearing that they might be uprooted.

Two days later we dug ourselves out and on June 21 began to prepare for our midwinter celebration. The sun would now begin its journey south and we would soon see the beginnings of daylight on the northern horizon. Tim prepared the meal while Steve and I decorated the hut with flags and balloons. The table, adorned with our seldom-used tablecloth, was heaped with delicacies Tim had baked including chicken vol-au-vent, mince tarts and home-baked crackers spread thickly with fish and shrimp pate. While we sampled Tim's treats and drank scotch, a roast of beef sizzled in the oven, its aroma pervading every corner of the hut. For one night at least, all our cares were forgotten.

June slipped into July and with every day's passing, a few more minutes of light were added to our daytime hours. By the middle of the month the horizon blushed with orange and red so that the stars to the far north were difficult to see. On days with a full moon we managed a few chores outside without the aid of a torch. On July 21 we received a radio message that a Kiwi dog team was at the Glacier Tongue hut and would be coming to visit. Jim Rankin, the Scott Base officer in charge, wanted to talk with us but would wait until the dog team arrived so that he could use the VHF they carried. About midnight the barking of excited dogs travelling fast over the sea-ice woke Steve, who in turn woke me.

By the time we had dressed, the dogs were already lolling about on the ice below the hut, their breath steaming in the frigid air. As we helped tether them, I wondered how many years it had been since dogs had worked at the Cape. Only feet away, the mummified remains of one of Scott's dogs, still on its chain, lay beneath mounds of drift. We talked with the drivers until 4:00 a.m., catching up on Scott Base news and a recent surprising development that Rankin told us about by VHF. Apparently Robert, in a telephone interview with a New Zealand newspaper, had expressed his disappointment over our ostracism from Scott Base. The resulting public outcry was responsible for overturning that policy so that we were now officially welcome to visit Scott Base whenever we were in the vicinity. While silently rejoicing at this small concession, I was nevertheless determined to keep our visits to a minimum to avoid straining the new relationship.

The dog drivers departed just after lunch the following day, leaving me with the rest of the afternoon to absorb the immense pile of mail they had left. I had letters from people I had not heard from for many years, but nothing from the expedition outlining our evacuation plans. Our future was still uncertain.

I was now looking forward to leaving the continent, but how was a big question. I was impatient to know and decided to take advantage of New Zealand's change in policy to try to find out. On

Tim Lovejoy and Steve Broni opening midwinter mail. (PHOTO BY GARETH WOOD)

August 14 we travelled to the Scott Base post office and placed a call to Robert in London. He revealed that he was in the process of trying to organize our evacuation with "90° South," an expedition led by Dr. Monica Kristensen, a Norwegian glaciologist, to recreate Amundsen's polar journey. Their ship, the *Aurora*, was just leaving Norway for Punta Arenas, Chile; from there it would be sailing first to New Zealand and then to the Bay of Whales in October. After dropping Monica off it was to return to New Zealand to pick up Bruno Klausbruckner and the Austrian climbers who were still intent upon climbing Mount Minto. Leaving them at Cape Hallett, the ship would sail directly for Cape Evans to collect us, after which it would pick up Bruno and return to New Zealand. It all sounded so simple, but if there was anything I had learned from two years in the Antarctic it was that things are never what they seem and nothing is ever simple.

I asked Robert about a backup plan.

"We're working on that. Greenpeace will be in the area. That's a possibility. Graham's also searching for a ship which we could possibly lease and Giles has a plan to fly a Twin Otter in from Punta Arenas. Don't worry, something will come together. We'll get you out, trust me," he said, trying to sound confident.

The next morning, after collecting our mail, which included the linear amplifier for our ham radio (which we were to use to keep our evacuation plans private) and a very odd telex from Amanda Lovejoy, Tim's sister, in Sydney, I searched out Rankin. He showed us volumes of messages he had received from the Department of Scientific and Industrial Research advising that, subject to the discretion of the officer in charge, we were not to be denied "normal hospitality." I wrote in my diary that night, "Officer in charge said he was prepared to offer us an evening meal and a room for the night. We can't win either way. If we refuse we look foolish, if we accept we risk the accusation of 'assistance.' We accepted."

Amanda's message was obviously written in a code with which we were unfamiliar and was much too clever for our simple minds to decipher. It read,

To: Tim, Woody and Stevie
Midwinter Greetings 2 All at McMurdo and Scott.
Mum Back from Mombasa Sun and/or Mon at about 8 p.m. Our Time.
Info You Requested
1) Barclays 566885911525
2) Nat West 1336563737

3) CLYDESDALE O/D 15,505 PNDS

WE R STARTING WITH BARCLAYS AND WORKING R WAY DOWN, HANG TEN ON EACH.

4) WHATS 100?

5) HOPE JENNY CAN COPE

6) ASSURED OF A GOOD RECEPTION BY "SHIP PARTY". DON WILL B THERE.

OODLES OF LOVE ETC. AMANDA

It took a phone call to unravel the cryptic message. The 8:00 p.m. "our time" was the proposed ham radio sked time, the list of bank account numbers gave the three frequencies we were to use and "hang ten" meant ten minutes on each frequency. The "whats 100?" referred to the transmitting watts and "ship party" was the call sign. "Jenny" was our generator and "Don" was the Sydney radio operator. We all had a good laugh and concluded that Amanda had been watching too many spy films.

After visiting McMurdo's meteorological station the next morning to trade information about the extent of the sea-ice around Cape Evans, we departed for base at noon. The sky was clear, the full moon brilliant and although there was not a hint of wind, the temperature hovered somewhere in the low -40s°C. Three and a half hours later we made the Glacier Tongue hut and after a meal and short sleep left for Cape Evans at 9:00 p.m., arriving two hours later. I was extremely tired and needed little coaching to find my bunk.

We were now hanging on the edge of twilight waiting for the first appearance of the sun which was guaranteed to rejuvenate our flagging spirits. On August 21 I suggested a trek to Inaccessible Island from which we would have an unobstructed view of the dawn. At the bottom of the blood-red sky we watched the fiery orb slowly cast off the bonds of winter. Not a ray of warmth escaped into our frozen world but the event kindled an interior warmth that no cold could extinguish. Still breathing -35°C air through our ice-encrusted balaclavas, we returned jubilantly to the hut, the sight of the sun etched indelibly on our minds.

The balance of August drifted by. Steve now pottered about the hut and Tim was seldom away from his reading chair. I was little better. We often saw scientific parties travelling in the vicinity of the Cape and occasionally some at Scott's hut only 200 yards away, but none of them ever came to visit us. In a moment of inspiration, and hoping to attract some of the Americans who were still officially restricted from visiting us, Tim made a four- by six-foot sign which we placed about 500 yards away at the tip of the Cape. Like a highway tourist sign, it bore the traditional hospitality symbols for food, accommodation and gas. As well, it proclaimed that ahead was the CAPE EVANS REST AREA. On the other side was printed in bold letters: THIS SIGN ERECTED BY PRIVATE ENTERPRISE. When the sign failed to produce the desired reaction, Tim had the brilliant idea of replacing CAPE EVANS REST AREA with CAPE EVANS LEPER COLONY. It worked! From then on, visits increased and we often saw guests stop to have their picture taken by the sign.

Although I too was feeling lazy, the return of the sun offered a mild incentive to do some outside chores. We had no concrete evacuation plan so I was reluctant to do much packing, but in anticipation I oiled the bander and strapped the first box anyway. Our weather was still unpredictable, with winds exceeding Force 5. Summer was some way off.

Steve and Tim, two of the "lepers" of Cape Evans. (PHOTO BY GARETH WOOD)

CHAPTER SEVENTEEN

DEPARTURE

THROUGHOUT SEPTEMBER WE were blessed with the return of daylight visitors, all anxious to examine Scott's hut but equally curious about us. Whenever officials accompanied them, however, relations were cordial but strained. On September 10 we received a visit from a U.S. navy captain whom we found rather amusing. He had driven out in a tracked vehicle with three other navy personnel to see Scott's hut. They had not been in the Antarctic long and we assumed that they had only arrived in late August. Nevertheless, they had heard of us and seemed genuinely interested in what we were all about. While Steve and Tim entertained the others in the hut over hot chocolate, I took the captain outside to give him the big picture. I spent 20 minutes walking him around our hut and then, stopping to show him our sledges, pointed up to Mount Erebus and described in detail our traverse of Ross Island, the winter journey to Cape Crozier and finally, our manhaul to the South Pole. He looked at me frequently, nodded his head occasionally and muttered "uh huh" in the right places.

"Well, that's about it," I said. "We haven't done much this year, just the usual back and forth to McMurdo."

The captain turned and once again surveyed the whole base.

"Man, that's fantastic," he finally said, "but I don't see any vehicles around here."

"That's just what I've been saying, we don't have any vehicles," I emphasized, not sure of his meaning.

"Well," he asked, looking at me, "how'd you guys do all these trips?"

Throughout the month I kept in radio contact with Scott Base and on September 15 was advised that there was a considerable pile of mail for us. On the 17th we left late for the post office, planning to spend the first night at the Glacier Tongue hut.

Blowing snow and 30-knot winds prevented an early departure from the hut the following morning, but by 10:00 a.m. the grey mantle lifted to reveal a gorgeous day. Halfway to Hut Point we spotted a van crossing the sea-ice on the flagged route to McMurdo. It changed direction and drew up alongside. I was surprised to see Rachko, the McMurdo commander, step out. Inside were Dr. Dalton and three others.

"If you're headed to Scott Base for mail, I've got it here. Two bags," he said, nodding toward the van. "We can give you a lift back to your base if you want. Unless you've got other business at McMurdo."

"No, we don't. Thanks very much," I replied, grateful for the offer.

Rachko, turning to me in the van, said, "By the way, we didn't bring the mail and this lift never happened. Right?"

"Right," I nodded in agreement, astonished that the paranoia that infected the lower ranks claimed the boss as well. We completed the journey in awkward silence.

At Evans I invited them in for tea but they declined and after a quick tour of Scott's hut they departed for McMurdo. Although I sensed hesitation before they rejected our offer, if they had accepted they would have felt obliged to return the favour. Despite the volumes of mail they delivered, a call to Scott Base four days later revealed that there was still more, most of it registered parcels for Tim. Three days later Tim and I left for the post office, arriving on September 26.

Rankin appeared happy to see us and immediately offered us an evening meal and a room for the night. He was over-solicitous, even asking if we'd like some fresh vegetables, fruit, meat and fuel. I insisted that we had ample supplies.

Later that evening he approached me while I was talking to Clayton, the mechanic.

"When're you heading back to Evans?" he asked.

"Tomorrow," I replied.

"We've got a party going out that way next Monday or Tuesday. Maybe we could move it up and give you fellows a lift back," he said.

"That would be great if it's not out of your way, but we can easily ski back," I replied cautiously.

"No problem," he said. Turning to Clayton, he asked, "Do you think you can move the trip up to tomorrow?"

"Sure. I've just installed a new engine in the Snowmaster. It needs a good run," he answered.

"That's fine then. Once you're past Hut Point, whatever happens I don't want to know about," Rankin said.

"Hold on a minute," Clayton said. "You mean this trip isn't sanctioned?"

"No, you know we're not allowed to go to Evans," Rankin replied.

"Well, I'm not comfortable with it then," Clayton said.

I was in total agreement and to his relief refused the offer. The New Zealanders appeared so intent on placating us that I wondered what they were up to. Later, Rankin approached Tim and me again.

"There's something you should know," he said. "In August, I met with Rachko, Wilkniss, Shrite and Thompson, and one of them, I won't say who, but one of them said, and I quote, 'Things may have changed and they may be forcibly removed from the continent.'"

"I don't understand," I said, shocked. "London's organizing our evacuation right now. I don't see what the damned hurry is. What else do you know?"

"Sorry, I don't know anything more. I'm not even sure where the idea came from, but I think it might have originated in Washington during a meeting with Heap," he replied.

"Oh," I said. "Thanks for telling us."

I was very confused, and London's failure to communicate with us did little to ease my discomfort. As well, the rumours about our future, which we began to hear almost daily, only added to our sense of insecurity. In a telephone call to one of the *Southern Quest* crew in Australia, Tim was told that we were not to count on 90° South as they were in trouble. We also heard that Greenpeace was not coming to the Antarctic that year. There was a distinct possibility that we might be spending a third winter at Cape Evans. The thought did not fill me with joy.

At 10:30 the following morning we left to ski back to Evans. Three hours later, with a 25-knot wind at our backs, we reached the Glacier Tongue hut. After preparing a meal and having a short nap, we packed up and departed for base in good visibility.

The next day, three Kiwis — Steve the cook, Steve the postmaster and Steve the scientist — showed up.

"I've got a message for you boys," Steve the scientist said.

"What's that?" I asked.

"Dr. Wilkniss passed a message to Rachko who passed it to Rankin that he's due in any day and he wants to make an appointment with you as soon as possible."

"An appointment!" I said, laughing. "Where does he think we're going? We're stuck out here at Cape Evans, for god's sake. Do you know what it's about?"

"Sorry, I don't," Steve responded, shrugging his shoulders.

I was curious and a little worried. Could he really forcibly remove us from the Antarctic? Did he have the legal authority? I suspected that our presence in the Antarctic was dividing loyalties at Scott and McMurdo where some employees were sympathetic to our plight, and I also thought that this might be causing some concern for the New Zealand and U.S. authorities.

I had a revealing discussion with Steve the postmaster, who was the one man at Scott Base not under the Department of Scientific and Industrial Research's direct control. When they asked him for copies of the telex messages we had sent and received, he refused to provide them and when the department appealed to New Zealand's Postmaster General, Steve's actions were supported. I had to chuckle that it took the post office to put the lofty DSIR in its place.

At noon on October 5, Peter Wilkniss, Stewart Guy, the incoming Scott Base commander, Jim Rankin, Dave Geddes, Dave Breznahan and Captain Perrigan, the new McMurdo commander, arrived at Cape Evans. Although we knew they were coming, we were unsure of the exact time. Steve spotted them first.

"Christ, there's a tracked vehicle on the ice and six guys are piling out," Steve shouted excitedly in his thick Glasgow accent.

Tim looked out the window. "Well, at least they're not carrying violin cases," he joked.

We were galvanized into action. I wanted to record the conversation so that there would be no later misunderstanding. As I scrambled up the ladder to set the microphone up in one of the ceiling vents, I yelled down, "It must be important for all these heavies to show up."

I joined the others just as Tim opened the door to Peter Wilkniss.

"Hi. We were in the neighbourhood and thought we'd come in for a friendly visit to see how things are going," Wilkniss said, extending his hand to each of us as he entered our tiny quarters. His stern features of our last meeting were now creased with a cautiously friendly smile. He was followed closely by his five companions, their heavy boots clumping noisily on the plywood floor.

"No problem until now," I said cheekily, "but do sit down."

"How's your food and fuel?" Wilkniss asked almost immediately, leaning forward on his elbows in anticipation of my reply.

"We have plenty," I said quickly. "Even for another year." I wondered if he was building up to advising us that we were to be forcibly evacuated from the continent.

"There're too many better things for you guys to be doing than wasting another year down here," Wilkniss replied. "I just wanted to come by personally to let you know that we've renewed our offer of last year. To fly you and whatever you can carry out."

"Aren't you concerned that you're setting some kind of precedent?" I asked.

"No, the way I look at it is that you missed your airplane and we're just replacing the ride you've already paid for," he replied, referring to the $29,000 the expedition had sent the National Science Foundation for the evacuation flight.

"I don't want to appear cocky, but my obligations go beyond myself. I'm responsible to sponsors — a lot of this equipment's on loan and I feel committed to getting it out," I said.

"I understand," Wilkniss replied, "but I just want you to be aware that we're friends and if you want to take us up on our offer just say when. We understand that you have some options, but Mr. Swan isn't telling us anything," he concluded.

"I'm afraid that I'm not prepared to divulge any of our plans without consulting with the expedition in London, so I won't confirm or deny anything," I said.

"Sure, I understand," Wilkniss responded.

"That, Gareth, puts me in a little bit of a dilemma," Stewart Guy said.

"I'm not quite sure what you mean," I replied.

"Simply put, the minute you tell us your plans we can continue to offer you access to the public post office and telephone facilities at Scott Base," he said. "Otherwise, we will bar you entirely from the base including the post office. Our foreign office has advised us that we do have that authority. You will appreciate that I'm caught in a difficult position here administering government policy. If I help you I'll be shot to pieces, but if I don't help I'll also be shot."

"I'll relay your message to London. I'm sure my thoughts won't go unnoticed," I said. "I've been involved with the expedition from the beginning and I've spent an extra year here which I didn't think I'd have to."

"I know, you did more than any of them," Wilkniss interrupted, leaning back in his chair and staring absently at the ceiling.

My heart skipped a beat as I followed his upward gaze. The microphone was dangling a couple of inches below the vent. I glanced furtively toward Steve and Tim, whose eyes met mine with barely concealed anxiety. Wilkniss' face remained impassive as he waited for me to continue my response to Guy.

"I'll do what I can to get the plans released," I said noncommittally, wanting to know them as well. London either had no concrete plans or our people there were keeping us in the dark on purpose. I had no idea which.

Sensing that the meeting was now coming to a close, I asked if there was any mail at Scott Base for us.

"Yes, we've brought two bags of mail for you. It's just outside the door," Jim Rankin replied.

"And, they've broken every rule in the book bringing it to you," Wilkniss joked.

The tension of the last 40 minutes immediately evaporated and everyone broke into laughter. As Wilkniss got up to leave he turned to me and asked again if we had enough food. I explained that press reports of our having limited rations had prompted clandestine gifts of food from both bases. I asked him to ensure the word got out that we were fine and, while we appreciated people's concern, we would prefer the practice stopped.

On October 11, Steve and I went to Scott Base to try to sort out the truth of our plans. As we passed through McMurdo, we noticed that the station was littered with garbage, and blown against the *Discovery* hut was a huge discarded cardboard box with Frigidaire printed across the top. The roads were dusty and the air reeked of diesel fumes. Summer was not McMurdo's most glamorous season.

Upon arriving at Scott Base I headed directly for the post office to book a call to London and was handed an urgent telex message from Richard Down, our expedition coordinator. I made my first call to him.

"Peter Wilkniss held a press conference in New Zealand two days ago," he said, "and he's claiming three main things: one, that your morale is low; two, that you're running low on food and are on emergency rations; three, they believe there are problems with the generator. They're saying that they've offered to fly you out at no cost to the expedition and that it's becoming imperative. Over."

"I just had a meeting with Wilkniss at Cape Evans together with some DSIR reps," I said, "and if that's what he said, I'm disappointed. It's the opposite of what we discussed. We've got 18 months' full rations and 18 months' fuel. With respect to the generator, we don't need it. We have the wind generator. As for our morale, it's definitely not low. Over."

"That's excellent," Richard said. "That's just what Robert and I said in a press conference yesterday. Over."

"With respect to our coming out," I said, "the gist of it is that DSIR have amended their policy and when I explained about our previous problems with Thompson they said that Thompson doesn't make DSIR policy and that the matter was recently addressed by the Prime Minister. Scott Base is now prepared to offer us ice reports and weather in exchange for us revealing our evacuation plans. The American situation hasn't changed but Wilkniss was very courteous during our talk. I'm surprised and annoyed at his comments to the press though. Over."

"As far as the New Zealand situation goes," Richard said, "it certainly appears that they're changing and if you're asked, I think you should say that, 'Yes, the expedition will release its plans through John Heap of the Foreign Office.' As far as the U.S. position, though, it couldn't be more negative. They even included a doctor's opinion that you are under great strain psychologically. Over."

"That contradicts a newspaper article I've got here. It quotes Wilkniss as saying that we're fit and in good spirits," I said. "I don't know what else I can tell you, Richard, except that I'm not looking to take advantage of their offer of a flight out. If it really came to the crunch we could spend another winter here but we're hoping that you'll do something to get us out before then. Over."

"Of course, we're definitely going to get you out this year," Richard said. "I'm sure you realize that we're proceeding with a complete plan to withdraw you, the hut and the equipment. I'm sorry we haven't communicated recently, but I'm sure you understand we're behind you. Over."

"Yes. Over," I said, uncertainly.

"I'll brief Robert. Get back to us in about a week, okay? Over," he concluded.

"Right. Over," I said, wondering if he realized that we had to travel 34 miles, there and back, to use the phone.

A few days later I returned to Scott Base by myself to call Richard. I made it to Hut Point in a record four hours and 40 minutes and walked to the post office to book the call to London.

Contact was made the following morning. Richard confirmed that the British Foreign Office had already notified the New Zealand Government of the expedition's intentions that either the Norwegians of 90° South would take us out by ship or that Giles would pick us up by air from South America. Both plans meant that the hut and equipment would be secured on the beach for retrieval at a later date. As I did not know the exact details of either plan and as both still appeared to be somewhat unsettled, I sent a telex to Peter Malcolm in Australia, asking him to keep me informed. (Although we had contact with Peter via the ham radio, at that time poor reception prevented reliable communication.)

On November 1, I recorded in my diary, "Another month gone. Have no motivation to do anything. Wish there was some pressure. Can't plan anything while we wait for word from expedition. Just reading and looking out window these days. Still no reply to telex sent to Peter. Communication is terrible and don't understand why — can't see that there can be any excuse. Can't wait till all over."

Four days later we returned to Scott Base to call London. Richard finally confirmed that we would be coming out with Giles, although I was not holding my breath — the plan could change at a moment's notice. If worst came to worst, however, there was still the Norwegians' *Aurora* to fall back on, and if that failed we would have to either prepare for another winter or accept Wilkniss' offer. We also received a telex from the 90° South people requesting that we build a runway on the ice in front of the hut for their plane which would be arriving in a few days from New Zealand.

Returning to base, we laid out a runway with plastic bags and flags atop bamboo poles, and immediately began to monitor the ham radio for word of their arrival. I slept on the floor beside it so as not to miss their communication. Early on November 14 I heard them request weather prior to taking off from a large ice floe eight hours north where they had been refuelled by the *Aurora*. A few hours later I called McMurdo.

"Mac Centre, Mac Centre, Cape Evans, do you read? Over."

"Cape Evans, Mac Centre, read you loud and clear. Over."

"Mac Centre, would you please relay a message to Oscar Yanky Papa Oscar Foxtrot that the runway is complete and smoke ready. Over."

Before Mac Centre could answer, the *Aurora*'s aircraft replied loud and clear.

"Cape Evans, Papa Oscar Foxtrot, copy. We're now at 66 south, ETA Evans 9:20. Over."

At 8:30 a.m. they notified Mac Centre that they had Ross Island in sight and would be landing shortly. They had made better time than expected. Tim ran out to light the orange flare and almost immediately spotted the plane, a Twin Otter, which touched down minutes later. It pulled up to the working crack in front of the hut and two pilots and a mechanic, Sven-Olof Ahlquist, Jan Friden and Allen Laugensen, spilled tiredly out onto the ice. The aircraft would be used to lay 90° South's depots, but until the *Aurora* reached the Bay of Whales, the expedition's starting point, the pilots and mechanic would remain with us. The ship was still at 65° south and would take three weeks to reach her destination.

That night I contacted Sydney by ham radio to get an update on Giles' plans and to seek permission to provide Monica's aircrew with three drums of fuel as a backup for their long flight from Cape Evans to the Bay of Whales. We had 41 drums, almost enough to cover Giles' flight twice. Anticipating a problem, I told Sydney that we had 38 drums — I was planning to give Monica's pilot three anyway.

On November 26 the radio crackled at our prearranged sked. Although the connection was staticky and broken, Peter told me that we were not to support 90° South with fuel. HQ was placing me in an awkward position and I was damned if I was going to play politics; I was at the front while they were safe in Sydney and London. Neil, from 90° South, had been informed by Footsteps in London that the party could expect two or three drums. In an October 19 taped message, Robert had said that Giles would need only 22 drums but to save 30 in case of an emergency. Richard was now saying that we needed it all. I was frustrated and wondered if anyone knew what was happening.

The next day we had a visit from four American geologists. Over coffee they told us that two carpenters had died on November 23 in a crevasse fall near McMurdo. While walking back to base from Castle Rock they decided to take a shortcut away from the flagged route. To the shock of their companion, they plummeted into a crevasse, jamming 65 feet down where the ice narrowed to ten inches. It seemed especially tragic, considering that they were so close to McMurdo. Since I had arrived in the Antarctic, a U.S. Hercules aircraft had fallen into a crevasse on take off, causing significant damage to its undercarriage and engines, and a U.S. helicopter had crashed in the Trans-Antarctic Mountains. And, over the previous few years, several support ships had been trapped in the ice and one, its hull crushed, had sunk. Luckily, no lives were lost in these accidents. A year later, a tiny headline in the newspapers would report another blow to the U.S. scientific effort. A C-130 Hercules crashed, killing three people on board, while involved in the recovery of yet another Hercules that had crashed ten years earlier. All this served to emphasize that in the Antarctic, danger is always lurking, even for government-sponsored expeditions.

On December 1, blowing snow and poor visibility greeted us for most of the day. Sven tried to talk with the *Aurora* at 8:30 p.m., but the ship was having trouble with her radio. At 10:00 p.m. I made poor contact with Sydney. Eventually I elected to relay through Sojo, an employee with the Australian National Antarctic Research Expedition Station on Macquarie Island. London was still arguing about the fuel. Peter, in Australia, advised that Neil had been told in London that he could have backup fuel only after Giles had used what he needed, not before. That was ridiculous — they needed the fuel long before Giles would even reach Cape Evans.

Two days later, the temperature rose to close to 0°C, making sleep impossible in the heat. I felt like moving to the box tent, hoping for a cool breeze. Before I lived in the Antarctic, if anyone had ever told me that one day I would consider 0°C hot, I would have questioned his or her sanity.

At 10:00 p.m. I made good contact with Sydney. London finally agreed to release four drums of fuel to 90° South. Giles would need a maximum of 22. Peter expressed some reservation about Giles even being able to make the trip. Was the plan unravelling? According to Peter it was now only 80% assured.

On December 5, I made the 10:00 p.m. sked with Sydney and although Peter was absent, I was advised that I would be flown to Canada after leaving the Antarctic. I wondered why Canada? I wanted to see my family, but there was still unresolved business in London.

Although the 90° South plane was to leave in the morning — the *Aurora* was in position at the Bay of Whales — Jan said that if Giles failed to make it, and if Monica agreed, they would be able to return for us.

The following day, at 9:00 a.m., the Twin Otter departed. We maintained radio contact every half-hour until the crew landed several hours later. Communication was excellent the whole way.

We spent the rest of the day dismantling the interior of the hut and packing equipment we would not need before we left. Steve was busy at his corner, breaking apart the shelving that had absorbed his hands and mind for so many hours during the winter.

I heard Christmas carols on the BBC for the first time, but instead of enjoying them, I found they deepened my anxiety. During the sked with the *Aurora* I asked Neil to confirm that they would take us out as a backup to Giles. He said they would get back to me.

By December 8, the upstairs of the hut was completely gutted and the roof prepared for dismantling. My sked with Neil revealed that

90° South would take us out either by ship or by aircraft should Giles' plan fail. I was praying that Giles' success or failure would be known before 90° South's departure for New Zealand. They were within four or five days of completing their depots, and time was becoming very critical.

The next day we dismantled the roof in blissful heat. The temperature was a rare +7°C. Relaxing on the upper floor, we basked in the sun.

On December 10, I contacted Sydney and spoke to Peter who confirmed that Giles was still on and would be leaving Punta Arenas, Chile, on the 13th. He also told me why I was to go to Canada. As we spoke, Robert and Richard were in Banff, Alberta, negotiating the rights to my story with a daily newspaper. My sked with the *Aurora* revealed that they would be on our doorstep in about three days should Giles fail to leave Chile. Either way, our evacuation was looking more positive. I was beginning to get excited.

As we sat in the hut drinking tea, I glanced around me. The floor was littered with packing boxes; outside, the great ridges of snow the wind had sculpted during the long polar night were melting and were now poor reminders of winter's tempest. I was glad that we were planning to pull everything out, but wondered when the hut and equipment would be evacuated. I wanted the beach to be swept clean once more, restored to the condition it was in before our arrival.

On December 14 during the evening sked, Peter told me that Giles had left Punta Arenas at 10:30 p.m. on the 13th. I stayed up, listening every three hours to two frequencies, hoping to catch word of him. At 6:00 the following morning I made contact on frequency 8945. Giles, in *Xray Bravo*, was about 800 miles southeast of Cape Evans and was expected at 11:30 a.m. I listened as he called in for weather every hour and was surprised that McMurdo responded. I assumed they were confusing his aircraft with one of their own whose abbreviated call sign, *Xray Delta*, was similar.

The day was bright, with no wind and just a thin cover of high cloud. Near the anticipated time, Tim spotted the plane away in the distance. Within minutes it was over the hut, circling to investigate the crude runway we had marked out with fuel drums, black plastic garbage bags and streamers atop bamboo poles. We watched it float over the far end of the runway, heat boiling from its twin engines as it gently touched down. We all breathed a collective sigh of relief. We were going home!

Giles taxied close to the beach below the hut. For the first time I read "ADVENTURE NETWORK INTERNATIONAL" on the side

The Twin Otter arriving to evacuate Steve, Tim and Gareth. (PHOTO BY
GARETH WOOD)

of the plane, a red-and-white Twin Otter that I later learned was
from Calgary, Alberta. The engines shut down one at a time and as
the whisper of the props died away in the still, warm air, I walked
under the cockpit and smiled up at Giles. He extended his hand
through the pilot's window and I could just barely shake it by
standing on the tips of my toes.

"You made it," was all I could say.

"Yes," Giles said laughing, "we did."

He then introduced me to Ron Kerr, his co-pilot and mechanic,
sitting next to him.

I was just about to say hello when the rear door of the plane burst
open and a yellow-suited figure jumped down onto the ice. It was
Robert.

"Ta daa!" he said, his eyes wide, grinning like a vaudeville actor.

"Robert," I said, moving toward him with my hand awkwardly
extended, not quite in charge of my emotions. "What're you
doing here?"

"Just came down to get you out," he said.

"Oh," was all I could muster. Then I smiled. I should have known
that Robert would have to be seen to be rescuing his men. It was this
same enthusiasm, this same showmanship and ability to excite others
that had got us here, and was now taking us home.

Within minutes of deplaning, Giles, exhausted after the long flight, asked me where he could sleep for a few hours. I directed him toward the Kiwi caravan. Ron was concerned that the sea-ice might break up while they slept so he remained with the plane. Now that Giles had arrived, the hut walls had to be dismantled and stacked in an orderly fashion on the beach and loose items of equipment boxed and banded for whoever would be sent to retrieve it. I scoured the area for garbage and boxed that as well. We had promised to leave the site as clean as when we came.

Robert, after a short rest, requested the radio to call McMurdo in hopes of arranging a meeting with their OIC. They refused but he then called Scott Base and managed to set up a meeting with the OIC there. Giles and Robert immediately flew off to Scott Base while we finished packing and organizing the equipment. Then the three of us spread our Thermorest mattresses on the gravel amid our boxed possessions and slept at the Cape for the last time.

When we awoke we were ready to travel. With our snowsuits, down jackets, salopettes, full mountaineering boots, goggles, gloves etc. on, we were fully prepared to survive should the plane be forced down in a remote location.

We then squeezed into the Twin Otter beside two large, cigar-shaped fuel tanks, taking our places in a single row of six window seats facing forward. Giles did his run-up, the Twin Otter gently rocking as great streams of snow blasted out behind each roaring engine. Soon we were moving across the ice, the plane jostling over the uneven surface as it picked up speed and began a long slow climb to the north before turning back on the Cape. As it banked I looked down on my home for the past two years, the dismantled hut reduced to tiny squares on the black-ash beach. Little to show for two years' effort, I thought, but the memories were big.

Scott's hut, some yards away, looked as if it had always been there. As I gazed down upon this familiar scene, I knew in my heart that I might never see it again, and thought that although we had come away unscathed, it was perhaps due to chance as much as to good planning. The Antarctic had been kind to us.

Soon we were over the frozen expanse of the Ross Sea, far above the wind that had dogged our every step a year earlier. I dozed off, the steady drone of the engines lulling me to sleep. Every hour I woke briefly to hear Giles asking South Pole station for a weather update: we were flying into deteriorating conditions. I had the utmost respect for Giles. He had flown over 250 hours in the past seven weeks and was still alert after making the marathon flight from Chile only hours before.

Our flight proceeded in stages. Weeks ago, Giles had deposited fuel at various bases on the main body of the continent and along the Antarctic Peninsula. Our first stop was in the Ellsworth Mountains where Adventure Network International maintained a camp for its expeditions to the continent. We landed beside an impressive backdrop of rugged crags and pulled up to a small tent camp. The Chilean watchman, Alejo, was still in his sleeping bag when we jumped down onto the snow. The temperature in the mountains was considerably lower than at the coast, lending a sense of urgency to our business which included helping to strike the camp, burying the tents and equipment in the snow, flagging them for retrieval next year and refuelling the aircraft. Within two hours we were on our way to the Chilean base, Carvajal, on Adelaide Island at the base of the Antarctic Peninsula.

Giles told us that even at this late stage, the Americans, still angry over our refusal to leave on the scheduled flight a year earlier, appeared to be trying to block us. He had heard that the vessel *Polar Duke*, under contract to the National Science Foundation, was being pressured not to deliver fuel to the Chileans unless they provided a written guarantee that it would not be used by us. Fortunately, we had enough of our own.

At Carvajal we refuelled the aircraft from the prelaid stock of fuel and as Giles was impatient to resume the journey, took off soon afterward. Three and a half hours later we set down at another Chilean base, Teniente Marsh, on King George Island. There we sat in a lounge of sorts, dozing in our chairs while the plane was again refuelled for the last hop to Chile. We were asked to delay our departure in order to speak to a General Lopotegi, who had yet to arrive. No reason was given but we had a suspicion that it had something to do with the Americans. We decided not to wait.

Giles did not want to risk the weather and we were aboard and about to leave when we were asked to stand down for an American Hercules that had passed its point of no return on a flight from the Ellsworth Mountains. A few cups of coffee later we were given permission to depart. Crossing Drake Passage we were harried by furious tail winds which accelerated our ground speed to 145 knots. Low cloud prevented much of a view but as we approached the continent of South America the sky cleared.

Close to Punta Arenas we flew through a thick layer of low cloud. Rain and mist beaded the windows as the air currents jostled us about on our descent. Carpeting the ground beneath us was a bright green forest, startling after two years of ice and snow. The plane touched down a few minutes later with a gentle thump and squeak of rubber. It was noon on December 16 and our 22-hour flight was over.

Giles taxied the aircraft to one side of the runway.

"Are we supposed to stop here?" I asked.

"Yes, this is okay," he said, as he eased himself stiffly from the cockpit. "We'll walk from here. Grab your stuff and follow me."

I stepped down onto the tarmac in full Antarctic gear. The temperature, about 20°C, was stifling, but the rain, which I had not felt for two years, was a refreshing novelty. I turned my face upward to catch a few cool drops before following Giles through the side door of a nearby building. I felt conspicuous and wondered if we would be hassled for avoiding customs. It seemed very irregular. We passed several uniformed men who glanced at us suspiciously before turning away.

"Giles," I asked, "are you sure this's all right?"

All around us were baggage carts, some empty and some stacked with baggage ready to be pulled out to waiting aircraft.

"Yes," he said, "don't worry. I know the airport manager."

Moments later we crawled along a conveyor belt, ducked through an opening and entered the departure lounge through a baggage carousel. From there we made our way up to a restaurant where we met the airport manager who seemed pleased to see Giles. Nothing was mentioned about our unconventional entrance so I began to relax. We were all tired and dirty and I wanted nothing more than a wash and bed.

I got them a couple of hours later when we were taken to the Adventure Network International Headquarters, a house in Punta Arenas. There, while we waited for our connecting flights home, Giles filled us in on the mechanics of the evacuation. He had spent the southern summer flying for Adventure Network in the Antarctic and at the end of the season realized that he could fly across the continent to retrieve us. Dick Smith, publisher of *Australian Geographic*, had financially supported a portion of the flight and Giles had carefully laid a path of fuel to ensure our independence. It took good planning and incredible stamina to pull it off, both of which Giles had in abundance.

Three days later, after Giles had left, I flew to Santiago, Chile, on a local flying service. There, my surreptitious entry into the country caught up with me. I reported for my international flight only to be turned away because I had no entry stamp in my passport. "How did you get into the country?" I was asked. I began by explaining that I was a member of a British expedition to the Antarctic and that after sailing into the Antarctic and staying there for nine months, three of us had skied 900 miles to the South Pole. At this point they looked at each other and rolled their eyes. I continued to tell them about our ship sinking, my additional year at Cape Evans and our flight out, complete with the crawl along the baggage carousel. By this time a fair number of airport employees, including two Chilean policemen with submachine guns hanging across their chests, had gathered to hear my tale. I don't think they believed a word I said and refused to let me on the plane. The next day I visited the Canadian and British embassies and sat through an interview with Chilean immigration police before finally obtaining the necessary rubber stamp in my passport and being granted permission to leave.

My flight took me to Miami, Chicago and eventually Vancouver. I was exhausted, having spent 30 hours in the air, and just as I was getting out of my seat at Vancouver International, the loudspeaker squawked, "Would passenger Mr. Gareth Wood please remain seated until all passengers have departed."

I was annoyed at being detained. I just wanted to get home. After all the passengers had left, the stewardess walked toward me, followed closely by a man who introduced himself as a representative of Adventure Network International.

"We've got a press conference organized for you," he said.

"Okay," I said, tiredly, as I walked with him out of the plane toward a wall of waiting reporters. Bill Reid, B.C.'s Minister of Tourism, fastened a provincial pin to my lapel before expressing how proud British Columbians were of my adventure. I was then dragged away to another press conference before I was allowed to continue my journey to Victoria. There, I met another media crowd who followed me to my parents' home. It was December 24. I had made it in time for Christmas.

As I stepped through the door, the house decorated brightly for the next day's celebration, it suddenly dawned on me that my long journey was over. I had come full circle. Physically, I had met the Antarctic on its own terms and survived, but the greater reward was discovering in myself the resources for that success. The glory I would leave with those Antarctic heroes who had really earned it: those who had shown us the way.

EPILOGUE

I LEARNED, SOON after my arrival in Canada, that the story of my
evacuation from the Antarctic had been featured on the front
pages of many Canadian newspapers for days preceding my home-
coming. From total obscurity I was suddenly thrust into the
limelight. At first it was dizzying and I often wondered who this
person was that everybody was talking and writing about. It was a
golden time and I basked in it with a mixture of delight and awe.

Within weeks I boarded a plane for England to meet with Roger
and Robert and help wrap up the expedition's affairs. Once there, I
discovered that our finances were in a shambles and, as more than a
year had passed since Roger's and Robert's return, it was difficult to
pull people together to sort out this and other unfinished business.
The expedition was old news and our team had moved on to other
pursuits. One large chore required immediate attention. I set to
work organizing the evacuation of our hut and equipment from
Cape Evans. After several weeks of negotiation with the Greenpeace
Antarctic Expedition, I returned to Canada, having finally arranged
that they would bring out our equipment in exchange for the hut
and various other items. Flying back to London in May, I was disappointed to find that not all of the gear had arrived. Greenpeace
informed me that due to severe ice conditions that summer they had
been forced to depart Cape Evans earlier than expected. We
returned any loaned equipment to our sponsors and sold some
things to cover shipping costs.

Since there was nothing more I could do in London, I flew home to Victoria. Greenpeace agreed to try to remove the rest of our equipment from Cape Evans the following year. I then made an effort to catch up on the many reports I had to write and submit to sponsors on the performance of their equipment. It was a busy but largely uneventful time.

On December 6, 1988, however, the excitement of the expedition was renewed in a big way. On that day, Roger, Robert and I were summoned to London to be presented with the Polar Medal by Queen Elizabeth II at an investiture in Buckingham Palace. I had learned of the award in February of that year in a letter from the U.K. Polar Medal Assessment Committee which said, "I have great pleasure in advising you that Her Majesty the Queen has been graciously pleased to award you the Polar Medal in recognition of your outstanding achievement as a member of the 'In the Footsteps of Scott Expedition.' " After we had a short chat with the Queen, she shook our hands which was our signal to step back five paces, turn right and leave.

About that time, *Outside Magazine* profiled our expedition as one of the ten greatest feats of the decade along with Reinhold Messner's first ascent of Mount Everest without oxygen, Dodge Morgan's record-setting, non-stop, solo circumnavigation of the globe aboard the sloop *American Promise* and Naomi Uemura's solo dog-sled journey to the North Pole. Although I was too close to the expedition to judge its importance, ours was certainly an amazing journey. That we had defied all challenges the Antarctic had thrown us was remarkable. That we had survived each other was an even greater feat.

The animosity that plagued our organization was not unusual in expeditions but it was not until we were presented with our greatest challenge, the failure of the sledge runners, that I began to understand the root of our struggles. The lowest point of our morale, it was, ironically, this crisis that was the catalyst for my re-evaluation of our relationships and a personal journey of learning.

As a result of this fiasco, we were forced to reconsider the benefits of working together and, in the process, I recognized that we were the right team after all for the journey to the Pole. Sadly, it wasn't until late in our adventure that we began to discover the team within our trio. Still, it wasn't smooth sailing. While our discussions on the Beardmore and the Polar Plateau indicated that we had begun to recognize and appreciate our individual contributions, we still each expected the others to reflect our strengths as well. Robert, thanking me on one hand for the careful planning and organization of our base, accused me of being slow to move into action and of being overly meticulous in my preparations. In response, I accused Robert of moving forward too quickly and with little advance planning, while on the other hand recognizing that we wouldn't have been there if it weren't for his courage to dream. Under stress, we each retreated into what we knew and could do best, and measured everyone else against our own special talents.

I am continually fascinated by people, and by seeing how much conflict in our lives is attributable to our perceptions of others' different approaches to learning and problem solving. This caused a great deal of conflict between Roger, Robert, Mike and me. Is not 90% of the stress we deal with in our lives related to people?

I admire my companions and value their contributions. I realize, after all these years, that my real education has finally begun. I have learned to balance my caution with working closer to the edge, for in the process of meeting new challenges and reaching for our own South Poles, we must push perceived limits. I enjoy working with the Roger Mears and the Robert Swans of the world. We all enable people to grow through the challenges we present to each other.

Robert, too, has grown. We speak with each other regularly, and in one of our recent conversations, he told me that as much as my meticulousness annoyed him, he now places great value on the Gareth Woods of the world in moving his dreams to reality. He has even learned now to temper his haste with upfront planning and attention to detail.

Our success was a tribute to our individual courage and determination, but most of all it was the result of our combined efforts as a team. We are different people today for the experience. We are friends. I am convinced that the secret to any success is people, and I truly believe that in Robert, Roger, Mike, John and me, we had the best.

Gareth Wood

APPENDIX

PERSONAL STRENGTHS AND TENDENCIES OF THE EXPEDITION MEMBERS AND THEIR EFFECT ON TEAM BUILDING

by Rick Matishak, President, The Matishak Group Inc.

THE MATISHAK GROUP is a training and organizational development company. We have worked with a number of organizations which had previously experienced a great deal of pain in attempting to build a team, as did the South Pole expedition.

Central to all effective teams there must be a shared, common goal. In Gareth's story this was clear from the beginning — an unaided trek to the South Pole. However, those who have developed successful teams know that the underlying theme is the members' ability to understand, respect and value each other's strengths and tendencies (their way or style of doing things). A lack of respect and understanding for individual style differences consistently has a negative effect on cooperation and trust within a group. Here, I believe, is the fundamental reason for the personality struggles experienced by Gareth and his team members.

In the following analysis I have used the *Thomas Concept*®, the work of management psychologists Jay and Tommy Thomas, to assess and evaluate the team dynamics of the Footsteps of Scott Expedition members. Basic to the *Thomas Concept*® is an understanding that growth and creativity in every personality come from the interaction of three pairings of opposite strengths. These

213

strengths are found within all human beings, and are the tools for understanding human behaviour.

The strength pairings are:

Thinking *vs* Risking

Practical thinking *vs* Theoretical thinking

Dependent risking *vs* Independent risking

The thinking *vs* risking pairing gives us insights into the speed and process with which we move into action. The thinking strength provides the thought, reason, planning, structure and analysis from which actions can grow. The risking strength speaks to emotion, action, doing and planning as you go — often moving in a spontaneous, intuitive and dynamic fashion.

The practical *vs* theoretical pairing identifies opposite approaches to thinking. A practical strength is grounded in reality, builds on facts and past experiences, sees the way things are and is pragmatic in moving towards results. A theoretical strength looks at the possibilities, building on ideas, and is driven to create new realities. The theoretical strength sees many ways, and is often committed more to the process of moving towards a goal than to the goal itself.

The dependent *vs* independent pairing establishes how we work together as we strive towards a goal. The dependent strength has a strong relational focus and tends to be trusting of others. Caring, compassion, support and personal approval are central to its needs. The independent strength demonstrates self reliance, inner confidence and the determination and courage to move forward, even if no one else agrees.

Every person has all the above strengths but is naturally out of balance, and tends to lead with one of each pair. This personal combination of strengths remains the same throughout our lives, and is the foundation of our personal style or way of doing things. However, though we remain the same through life, we can change, in that with an awareness of our lead strengths, we can develop our supporting strengths, and recognize when it is appropriate to "flex" to them. Growing and maturing are about striving for balance.

People get into difficulty with their environment or find themselves in conflict with others when they don't bend or flex from their lead strengths. We say people become "polarized" (no pun intended!) on their strengths and, due to stress or other pressures, retreat into what is naturally comfortable. Certainly, with the stresses of organizing a multi-million-dollar project, polarization contributed to interpersonal conflict on the South Pole expedition. The members were not flexing to their supporting strengths.

Each member, and five other people who know the member well, completed the *Thomas Concept® Inventory of Core Strengths* and the results were averaged.

Robert Swan	Lead Strengths:	Risking	Theoretical	Independent
Roger Mear	Lead Strengths:	Risking	Practical	Independent
Gareth Wood	Lead Strengths:	Thinking	Practical	Independent
Mike Stroud	Lead Strengths:	Risking	Theoretical	Independent
John Tolson	Lead Strengths:	Thinking	Practical	Independent

With the strengths inherent in the five expedition members, the team could not have been more effectively chosen. As described so eloquently in Gareth's story, Robert provided the charismatic leadership, the vision and the drive to sell a dream. Roger had a strong drive to accomplish, was forceful and impatient to get into action. He demonstrated the tenacity and dogged determination to plan, practise and then work for that dream. Gareth was characterized by his stability and common sense, and the discipline to work through all the logistical details associated with building the dream.

Mike had strengths similar to Robert's. He favoured action and doing, dealt with ideas and overall concepts and followed his own convictions. John shared strengths with Gareth, and leaned towards stability, structure and caution in moving forward.

With seemingly the right stuff up front, why the disharmony and pain? They utilized their individual strengths effectively in the start-up of the expedition. Robert was skilful in building a network of patrons and supporters, and in profiling the expedition in the media. Roger brought practicality to Robert's dream, and Gareth, with focussed determination and meticulousness, gradually checked off the massive list of details for their base. As the expedition evolved, the roles and environment required a more creative utilization of each member's skills. The very strengths that had brought the team to their base camp also set the tone for the mistrust and disrespect which developed.

Once the expedition was in the Antarctic with the dream in place, Robert's strengths played a lesser role to Roger's strong technical background in preparing the logistics of the actual South Pole trek. The theoretical strength now had to make way for the practical, which was reinforced by Gareth's orientation towards detail and organization. This shift in leadership contributed to the stress and conflict.

Since all the members of the expedition led with an independent strength, the team was lacking a focus on harmony that a dependent strength member might have provided. With power and control needs being pivotal to an independent strength, not to mention the needs for personal space and freedom, the closeness of space and spirit definitely had a wearing effect on the team's ability to work together. To add further fuel to the fire, independent people tend to solve their own problems and keep their own counsel, hence the conflict and hostility grew and the team members moved more into themselves. People leading with a dependent strength tend to talk about their emotions while those with independent strength, although carrying just as much feeling or emotion, do not. This resulted in very volatile situations, as the differences grew and individuals were pushed to confrontation.

One of Gareth's strongest qualities was his ability to analyze a problem, generate possible solutions and move towards the result required. Though this was valued during the early planning stages of the project, those members with a risking strength grew to appreciate it less and less as the expedition carried on. He was seen as too focussed on the here-and-now, and as slowing the team down. Asking Gareth to leave the stability of solid plans moved him into an uncomfortable state of vulnerability — impulsively moving forward. The inherent disrespect for his natural tendencies reinforced the evolving mistrust.

I said earlier that the team could not have been more effectively chosen in terms of strengths required to move the project forward. Each member played a significant role in realizing the expedition's goal. At the same time, though, I am not surprised at the conflict that arose, considering the pressure, adverse conditions and strong independent personalities. They lacked both understanding of their own preferred strengths and basic "people working with people" skills.

One of the key events was the realization that the sledge runners had been placed incorrectly on two of the sledges. Here Gareth hints that the human spirit seemed to rise above the confusion, animosity and pain. Within these three personalities was the desire to be valued and respected — found in all humans. Again, Gareth hints that in their conversations, as they moved up the Beardmore Glacier, a slow respect grew from the ashes of discord to a new understanding of each member's contribution to reaching the goal.

People may think that the journey ended when the Pole was reached but Gareth, by recapping his experiences ten years later, demonstrates that the journey still continues.

GLOSSARY

Arete - a sharp snow or rock feature rather like the outside corner of a building. Also a steep mountain ridge.

Bivy - from bivouac. A night spent in the open during a climb.

Calve - the breakup of a glacial ice front.

Cine - short for cinematograph (movie camera). Hence cine-film and cine-camera.

Cirque or Cwm - bowl-like feature or amphitheatre carved out of a mountain by glacial action.

Col - a gap in a ridge between two peaks or at the head of a valley. Also known as a pass or a saddle.

Cornice - a lip of snow or ice protruding from the crest of a ridge, and formed by snow being deposited by the wind. Large cornices may overhang the slope beneath the crest by many yards.

Crampon - a spiked metal frame for attachment to a climbing boot to permit walking or climbing on ice.

Crevasse - a crack in the surface of a glacier, sometimes concealed by snow.

Dead reckoning - best estimate of position using compass bearing and distance marched that day (distance recorded by the sledgewheel counter). On the Polar Plateau, a sextant was used to calculate latitude, and as we had elected not to take the bulky calculation tables with us, we had to approximate longitude. The resulting position was then compared to our dead reckoning position.

Depth hoar - angular snow crystals enlarged with water vapour that not only make an unstable base for additional accumulations of snow, but also make for difficult skiing conditions because the skier breaks through the surface.

Erratics - boulders carried by glacial action from source to an atypical location.

Fumarole - a hole in the earth's surface through which steam and gases (volcanic) are vented. On Mount Erebus, the steam freezes into tall ice sculptures.

Gore-Tex - laminated fabric which is waterproof but allows water vapour to pass through.

Ground drift - ice crystals picked up by the wind from the ground and blown across the surface.

Hoosh - a heavy soup with a pemmican base.

Lenticular cloud - a lens-shaped cloud appearing over a mountain.

Manhauling - hauling a sledge with manpower only.

Met - meteorological.

Névé - hard-packed snow that eventually compacts into glacial ice.

Parhelion/Sundog - a bright image (mock sun) appearing on a solar halo. Occurs when ice crystals or water droplets in high cirrus clouds act as miniature prisms, breaking sunlight into its component colours.

Pulk - a sledge.

Rudder pintle - the posts on which a rudder turns. The lower one is located on the stern post while the upper one is attached to the rudder.

Salopettes - bibbed pants supported by shoulder straps.

Sastrugi - ridge of snow formed by the wind much as sand on a beach is ridged by moving water.

Scree - a slope of loose boulders and small stones on a mountain.

Serac - a tower or pinnacle of ice formed when a glacier breaks up or fractures over a slope. Usually evident in an ice fall or an ice cliff.

Sledgewheel - a wheel attached to the rear of a sledge for measuring the distance travelled.

Vapour barrier - clothing or boots with insulation between waterproof layers.

Windproofs - lightweight, wind-protective clothing.

Wind - calibration of the Beaufort Wind Scale established by Admiral Beaufort (1771-1857). Wind gradients are recorded in Forces from calm (0) to hurricane (12) as follows:

Force	Description	Wind Velocity
0	Calm	0 mph
1	Light air	1 mph
2	Light breeze	4 mph
3	Gentle breeze	9 mph
4	Moderate breeze	14 mph
5	Fresh breeze	20 mph
6	Strong breeze	26 mph
7	Moderate gale	33 mph
8	Fresh gale	42 mph
9	Strong gale	51 mph
10	Whole gale	62 mph
11	Storm	75 mph
12	Hurricane	92 mph

In the text, temperatures are shown in the Fahrenheit scale for historic references and Celsius for our own. For distances, we have used a combination of nautical and statute miles for historic references, depending upon the source, and statute miles for our journey. Shackleton used nautical miles while Scott used both. We have identified only the nautical miles, other mile references being statute. One nautical mile is equivalent to 1.15 statute mile.

ACKNOWLEDGEMENTS

P REPARING AN ACCOUNT of my Antarctic exploit has been a lengthy project, one that I could not have accomplished without the tireless energy of Eric Jamieson who interpreted my diaries, sat through many confusing interviews and finally put words to my thoughts. And, in direct contrast to the personal conflicts I experienced on the expedition, we had no disagreements. Eric would like to thank his wife Joan, his daughter Amanda, and his son Ian for the many sacrifices they made for this book.

I would like to thank Roger Mear, Mike Stroud, Steve Broni and Tim Lovejoy for allowing Eric and me unrestricted access to their diaries. I thank Robert Swan for being the visionary he is and for allowing me the use of many taped interviews and written statements of expedition members. I thank Roger for allowing me to photocopy our original maps and charts, for a copy of our taped conversation with the American authorities after our arrival at the Pole and, especially, for inviting me along on what turned out to be an incredible adventure. The South Pole is unarguably one of the most inhospitable regions on earth. Captain Robert Falcon Scott was indeed a worthy mentor, as was Ernest Shackleton who paved the way. I also want to thank all the expedition members and many friends who assisted with the preparations that got us to the Pole, especially Mrs. Emma Drake for her invaluable contributions and continued kind thoughts after all these years.

To the many personnel, too numerous to mention individually, at the United States of America's McMurdo and Amundsen-Scott stations, and New Zealand's Scott Base, I thank you for your friendship and concern. I would also like to thank the 700 individuals, organizations and companies without whose support the expedition would not have gone ahead. In particular, for facilitating my eventual removal from Antarctica in December 1986, I am indebted to the Australian entrepreneur Dick Smith and to Vancouver-based Adventure Network International.

I must also thank the many publishers from whose published works we quoted. Their names appear in the endnotes and the bibliography.

For the use of their photographs, I am grateful to Roger Mear, Robert Swan and Steve Broni and, for historical photographs, the Royal Geographical Society.

For his valuable assistance and contribution toward the production of the maps, I would like to thank Brian Stauffer.

I am greatly appreciative of the contribution of Tommy Thomas, Ph.D., and the Institute of Foundational Training and Development in Austin, Texas. Their *Thomas Concept® Inventory of Core Strengths* was completed by each of the expedition members and interpreted by the IFTD. I am indebted to Rick Matishak of the Alberta-based Matishak Group Inc. for agreeing to provide an appendix to this text, linking the *Thomas Concept®* inventories to the personality struggles we experienced during the expedition, as seen from a management training perspective.

A special thanks to Fred Wooding, author, for his interest and introduction to a publisher. And my thanks to the publishers, Marlyn Horsdal and Michael Schubart, for making it happen.

Finally, to my loving wife, Linda Owen, who has been looking forward to the day we cease speaking of the Antarctic at the dinner table: thank you for your unqualified support throughout this project.

Gareth Wood

ENDNOTES

CHAPTER ONE

1. Roger Mear & Robert Swan, *In the Footsteps of Scott*, Page 30.
2. Mear & Swan, Page 33.
3. Captain R. F. Scott, *Scott's Last Expedition*, Volume One, Page 544.
4. Scott, Page 607.
5. Apsley Cherry-Garrard, *The Worst Journey in the World*, Page 541.

CHAPTER TWO

1. J. C. Beaglehole, *The Life of Captain James Cook*, Page 431.

CHAPTER FOUR

1. Cherry-Garrard, Page 282.
2. Scott, Page 334.
3. Cherry-Garrard, Page 329.
4. Cherry-Garrard, Page 330-331.
5. Cherry-Garrard, Page 335.
6. Cherry-Garrard, Page 314.
7. Cherry-Garrard, Page 314.
8. Cherry-Garrard, Page 347.
9. Cherry-Garrard, Page 350.

10. Scott, Page 366-367.
11. Cherry-Garrard, Page 356.

CHAPTER SIX

1. Linda Dodge, *The Star Newspaper*, Christchurch, New Zealand, November 8, 1985.
2. Edward Wilson, *Diary of the Terra Nova Expedition to the Antarctic 1910-1912*, Page 105.
3. Scott, Page 452.

CHAPTER SEVEN

1. Scott, Page 456-457.
2. Scott, Page 461.
3. Scott, Page 595.
4. Scott, Page 599.
5. Scott, Page 592.
6. Christopher Ralling, *Shackleton*, Page 89.
7. Ralling, Page 91.
8. Ralling, Page 91.

CHAPTER EIGHT

1. Ralling, Page 93-95.
2. Scott, Page 487.
3. Scott, Page 489.
4. Ralling, Page 97.
5. Scott, Page 571.
6. Scott, Page 572-573.

CHAPTER NINE

1. Ralling, Page 97.
2. Ralling, Page 98.
3. Roland Huntford, *Scott and Amundsen*, Page 455.
4. Scott, Page 505.
5. Ralling, Page 109.
6. Ralling, Page 110.
7. Ralling, Page 110.
8. Scott, Page 511.
9. Ralling, Page 110.

CHAPTER TEN

1. T. E. Lawrence, *The Seven Pillars of Wisdom: A Triumph*, Page 27.
2. Ralling, Page 111.
3. Ralling, Page 113-114.
4. Scott, Page 520-521.
5. Ralling, Page 111.
6. Ralling, Page 112.
7. Ralling, Page 115.
8. Ralling, Page 116.

CHAPTER ELEVEN

1. Scott, Page 541-542.
2. Scott, Page 543.
3. Scott, Page 543.

CHAPTER TWELVE

1. Steve Broni, *Part 4, School Journal, Number 2*, 1990, Page 17.

CHAPTER FIFTEEN

1. Ralling, Page 54.
2. Reader's Digest, *Antarctica, Great Stories From the Frozen Continent*, Page 229.
3. Ralling, Page 65.
4. Reader's Digest, *Antarctica*, Page 45.
5. Alfred Lansing, *Endurance*, Page 102.

BIBLIOGRAPHY

The following books have either been quoted from or used as reference in preparation of this book.

Beaglehole, J.C., *The Life of Captain James Cook*, A & C Black (Publishers) Limited, London, 1974

Broni, Steve, *Southern Quest, Part II, Shipwrecked in the Pack-Ice, Part 4, School Journal, Number 2, 1990*, Learning Media, Ministry of Education, New Zealand, 1990

Browning, Robert, *Selected Poetry*, Holt, Rinehart and Winston, New York, 1967

Cherry-Garrard, Apsley, *The Worst Journey in the World*, Angela Mathias, 1922, 1965, and Chatto & Windus, London, 1965

Eliot, T.S., *Collected Poems 1909-1962*, Faber and Faber Limited, London, 1989

Huntford, Roland, *Shackleton*, Hodder & Stoughton Ltd., London, 1985

Huntford, Roland, *Scott and Amundsen*, Hodder & Stoughton Ltd., London, 1979, and A.P. Watt Ltd. on behalf of Roland Huntford

Lansing, Alfred, *Endurance, Shackleton's Incredible Voyage*, Granada Publishing Limited, London, 1984

Lawrence, T.E., *The Seven Pillars of Wisdom: A Triumph*, Penguin Books in association with Jonathan Cape, 1962

Limb, Sue, and Cordingley, Patrick, *Captain Oates, Soldier and Explorer*, B.T. Batsford Ltd., London, 1982

Mear, Roger, & Swan, Robert, *In The Footsteps Of Scott*, Jonathan Cape, London, 1987

Ralling, Christopher, *Shackleton*, "Extracts reproduced from 'Shackleton, His Antarctic Writing' selected and introduced by Christopher Ralling published by BBC Books," London, 1983

Reader's Digest, *Antarctica*, "Reproduced with permission from Reader's Digest (Aust) Pty Ltd from the book Antarctica", New South Wales, 1985

Scott, Captain R.F., R.N., C.V.O., *Scott's Last Expedition*, Smith, Elder & Co., London, 1913

Wilson, Edward, *Diary of the Terra Nova Expedition to the Antarctic 1910-1912*, Humanities Press, New York, 1972